The Ethics of Sex

NEW DIMENSIONS TO RELIGIOUS ETHICS

Series Editors: Frank G. Kirkpatrick and Susan Frank Parsons
Trinity College, Hartford, US, and Margaret Beaufort Institute of Theology, Cambridge, UK

The aim of this series is to offer high quality materials for use in the study of ethics at the undergraduate or seminary level, by means of engagement in the interdisciplinary debate about significant moral questions with a distinctive theological voice. Each volume investigates a dimension of religious ethics that has become problematic, not least due to the wider climate of reappraisal of Enlightenment thought. More especially, it is understood that these are dimensions which run through a number of contemporary moral dilemmas that trouble the postmodern world. It is hoped that an analysis of basic assumptions will provide students with a good grounding in ethical thought, and will open windows onto new features of the moral landscape that require further attention. The series thus looks forward to a most challenging renewal of thinking in religious ethics and to the serious engagement of theologians in what are most poignant questions of our time.

Published

1. *The Ethics of Community*
   Frank G. Kirkpatrick

2. *The Ethics of Gender*
   Susan Frank Parsons

3. *The Ethics of Sex*
   Mark D. Jordan

4. *The Ethics of Nature*
   Celia Deane Drummond

Forthcoming

The Ethics of Race
Shawn Copeland

The Ethics of Sex

Mark D. Jordan

Blackwell
Publishing

BLACKWELL PUBLISHING
350 Main Street, Malden, MA 02148-5020, USA
108 Cowley Road, Oxford OX4 1JF, UK
550 Swanston Street, Carlton, Victoria 3053, Australia

The right of Mark D. Jordan to be identified as the Author of this Work has
been asserted in accordance with the UK Copyright, Designs, and
Patents Act 1988.

First published 2002 by Blackwell Publishing Ltd
Reprinted 2003, 2004

Library of Congress Cataloging-in-Publication Data

Jordan, Mark D.
    The ethics of sex / Mark D. Jordan.
        p. cm. — (New dimensions to religious ethics)
    Includes bibliographical references and index.
    ISBN 0-631-21817-3 (alk. paper) — ISBN 0-631-21818-1 (pbk. : alk. paper)
    1. Sex—Religious aspects—Christianity.   2. Christian ethics.   3. Sexual ethics.
I. Title.   II. Series.
BT708 .J67 2002
241'.66—dc21

                                                                                2001001609

A catalogue record for this title is available from the British Library.

Set in 10.5 on 12.5 pt M. Bembo
by Graphicraft Ltd, Hong Kong
Printed and bound in the United Kingdom
by MPG Books Ltd, Bodmin, Cornwall

The publisher's policy is to use permanent paper from mills that operate a sustainable
forestry policy, and which has been manufactured from pulp processed using acid-free and
elementary chlorine-free practices. Furthermore, the publisher ensures that the text paper
and cover board used have met acceptable environmental accreditation standards.

For further information on
Blackwell Publishing, visit our website:
http://www.blackwellpublishing.com

Contents

Acknowledgments

Two sorts of thanks are needed. The first thanks go to friends, colleagues, and a patient partner, all of whom endured me during the unsettling work of drafting this little book. The second thanks go to those who have read the manuscript at one stage or another. I am particularly grateful to Ted Smith for reviewing the whole of it with such charitable thoroughness. His questions and objections moved me to rewrite all of the book's entrances and exits – so that I could understand them.

M. D. J.

Prologue: Candid Advice to the Reader

The beginning of any speech about Christian ethics is risky for both hearer and speaker. The hearer risks being misled about important things. Accepting bad religious counsel in ethical matters can lead to diminished life or, in the extreme case, to destruction. Even listening for long to some supposedly "Christian" discourses about sex can confuse clear thinking and dull moral sensibility. So hearers have good reason to be suspicious at the start of a speech about Christian ethics. They should exercise suspicion not by making violent accusations or rejections, but by attending deliberately to the motives and effects of the speeches aimed at them.

Speakers ought to be suspicious too – and not only of themselves. Certainly speakers should scrutinize their own motives, characters, and prejudices. Theological ethicists always suffer the temptation to pretend that they stand outside of their particular interests, genders, races, classes, or nationalities and can speak directly and universally of human experience. They often seem to confuse speaking about God's law with laying down the law on God's behalf. The temptation is acute in sexual ethics, where the hidden economy of one's desires or the secret wounds of one's past are all too conveniently overlooked. But speakers cannot stop with suspicion of themselves. They need to remember that they were hearers before they began speaking and that much of what they now say will be repetition.

Every new speech about Christian sexual ethics comes out of a library of older speeches. Before you speak Christian theology, you have already heard it. You have attended to the words of some scripture, of a local community, of authoritative individuals, of a denominational position or tradition. These words will repeat themselves in what you try to say. Indeed, many Christian speakers claim to do nothing more than repeat exactly what they have been taught (a claim that merits another exercise of suspicion). Others unwittingly repeat as their own clips of older speech.

Christian speeches about sex are full up with terms, images, arguments, and rules recorded from older speeches. These clips are remixed to produce new speech, which is sometimes music, sometimes cacophony. So speakers must be suspicious about how they are repeating what they have heard.

By describing the suspicions that should surround Christian speeches about sexual matters, I don't mean to suggest that the speeches cannot be uttered responsibly. On the contrary, the risks they run are risks worth running. Christians should keep talking about sex so that they can learn to speak about it more adequately, that is, more theologically. Christians can do this best by talking first with other Christians, within and without their immediate communities. In talking across community boundaries, there are a dozen more risks of misunderstanding and offense. Let me admit them, but then set down three counter-assumptions about why it must be possible to engage in this kind of conversation. The assumptions seem to me connected to important Christian convictions about the possibility of revelation.

My first assumption is that human beings can listen to speeches about sex across divisions of gender and sexual orientation. This assumption doesn't authorize us to speak "for" the members of another group, much less to explain them to themselves. We should be suspicious of men who tell women how to be women or of "heterosexuals" who prescribe the real essence of "homosexuality" to lesbians or gay men. But we shouldn't let this suspicion deny our capacity for learning, for entering some way into the language of another human community. If we did not have the capacity for learning something of a radically different language, then we also could not receive the revelation of a God who lives beyond the limits of sex, of body, and who offers us a share in divine life.

The second assumption is that Christians can listen to theological speeches across sectarian lines. This doesn't mean that a Christian can stand outside of all denominations or enter equally well into every one of them. Each of us has a small number of "mother tongues," of first forms of Christianity in which we were raised or to which we converted. These remain with us in the way that our first languages do. But we also have the capacity to learn second languages. We can enter into the speeches of at least some other Christian groups well enough to engage their texts. If we could not, then we also could not receive a divine revelation mediated through a text, because a revealed text always comes to us from outside even if in our mother tongue; it always speaks to us as a foreigner.

The third assumption is that a Christian can listen to theological speeches across history, that is, over lengths of time. The assumption means that we can learn the languages of some older texts well enough to hear human voices in them. Engaging these voices is much more important theologically than constructing classifications for them or telling narratives about them. We need historical access, not historical explanation or systematization. Gaining access to the older voices through texts means hearing enough of them so that we can recognize rhetorical purposes and then respond. If we cannot carry out this kind of engagement with older human texts, then we also could not inherit a revealed text.

With these assumptions, I mean not only to secure a beginning for the speech that follows, but also to foreshadow its procedure. This book assumes that it is possible to introduce the main topics of Christian sexual ethics by engaging a variety of particular texts. The texts come from different churches and different times; they speak in diverse voices in order to give contradictory counsel. Certainly you will hear my own voice, with its prejudices and secrets and repetitions, but hopefully not just my voice.

One thing that you will not hear often in what follows is comparison with the teachings on sex in other religious traditions. I pass over them not because I think that they are unimportant, but because engaging them well presupposes deep conversation among Christians. In my experience, inter-religious "dialogue" often tends to reduce the complexity of the participating traditions. So an insistence on the variety and contradiction of Christian teachings about sex seems to me a prerequisite to serious engagement with other traditions. Once you have finished reading, I encourage you to go further than I do by bringing voices from other religious traditions into conversations with the Christian voices sampled here – and to do so with a vivid awareness of how difficult interreligious comparison really is.

Whether you are inside the discourses of the Christian churches or outside them, you should be suspicious of all the voices you hear. You should listen to each with careful attention – with the same compassionate skepticism you should apply to your own interpretations.

Chapter 1

The Vices of Christian Ethics

Much of what Christians say about sex is confession. In the confessional "box" or the pastor's study, in public declarations of repentance or in murmurings of private prayer, Christians accuse themselves of being impure, unchaste, weak, luxurious, lustful. They are tempted by "the flesh," and they wrestle with a Satan who is master over it. Indeed, Christians can seem to have lavished too much attention on the language of sexual self-accusation. To take only the best-known example: Some of Augustine's most carefully contrived images in the *Confessions* are descriptions of disordered desires for sexual pleasure. Aged 18, he hears about him the clanging of the "cauldron of shameful loves."[1] Much later, as a grown man, and in the moment of that we call his conversion, Augustine will hear softer sounds – but the same shameful music. His "old friends," "vanities of vanities," tug at his flesh and whisper, "'Are you going to send us away? . . . From this moment forward we will never, ever be with you again.'" "Violent habit" speaks as well: "'Do you really think that you can get along without them?'"[2]

When Christians are not confessing sexual acts, they can seem to be preaching about them – or, rather, against them. The language of self-accusation

---

[1] Augustine, *Confessions*, 3.1.1, ed. M. Skutella, rev. L. Verheijen, Corpus Christianorum Series Latina, vol. 27 (Turnhout: Brepols, 1981), line 26. Throughout this book, I translate afresh from the sources whenever I can, because theological writing about sexual matters has suffered particularly from thorough mistranslation, both voluntary and involuntary. Where there is a recommendable and readily available English translation for a text I discuss at length, I will also include citations to it. For this passage in the *Confessions*, see the translation by Henry Chadwick (Oxford: Oxford University Press, 1992), p. 35.

[2] Augustine, *Confessions*, 8.11.26 (ed. Skutella, rev. Verheijen, lines 20–1, 30; trans. Chadwick, p. 151).

turns quickly enough into the language of rebuke. Certainly it does so in the *Confessions*, the punning title of which means at once (and at least) declaration, admission, and accusation. For example, Augustine mocks his teachers for speaking according to the Ciceronian rules, "copiously and ornately," whenever they speak about their lusts.[3] He quotes lines from Terence: A "worthless young man" points to a wall-painting of Jupiter's seduction of Danae in order to justify his own fornications.[4] With these examples, we find ourselves swept along in the great river of human desire, we are drowned in pandering fictions, we sink blindly under the weight of the divine judgments on illegal desires.[5]

Preaching against sex may be the most familiar Christian speech of all in our pluralistic, secular societies. People who know nothing of Christian creeds or scriptures can recite the most notorious Christian sexual prohibitions. They will be deeply confused about Trinity and Incarnation, but they will rightly report that this or that Christian group condemns artificial contraception, or masturbation, or second marriages, or genital pleasures between persons of the same sex. In the public imagination, Christianity can figure as nothing more than a code of sexual conduct, a code that likes especially to elaborate prohibitions.

Christians often reply to these stereotypes by shifting the blame to cultural conditions – say, the sensationalism of news reports about religion or a (contemporary?) tendency to reduce everything in human life to sex. These replies may have merit, but we Christians would do better not to excuse ourselves so quickly. The stereotypes about our hypocrisy over sex or our hatred of it are reactions to the ways we have chosen to talk about sex – and especially to the ways in which we have tried to stigmatize it so as to regulate it. If sexual acts can carry many motives, so can speech about sex. The speech of Christian sexual ethics seems often to have been moved by unchristian fears and fantasies. It has served to sanction old designs rather than to announce good news. Instead of confessing yet more sexual sins, or preaching yet again against them, we might want to confess the sins we have committed in presuming to teach about sex as we have. We might want to consider our bad habits, our vices, when it comes to setting forth a Christian ethics of sex.

---

[3] Augustine, *Confessions,* 1.18.28 (ed. Skutella, rev. Verheijen, lines 24–5; trans. Chadwick, p. 20).

[4] Augustine, *Confessions*, 1.16.26 (ed. Skutella, rev. Verheijen lines 3–4; trans. Chadwick, pp. 18–19).

[5] Here I combine the master images of Augustine, *Confessions*, 1.16.25–1.18.28.

Vices Seen and Unseen

Vices spread through the genres of Christian speech. Many can't be assigned to the "popular" as against the "academic." Indeed, in Christian speeches about sexual topics, it is impossible to draw a clear line dividing the "academic" from the "popular." Some of the most technical theologians have not so much written about sex as thundered against it. They share with street preachers the highly charged rhetorics of ridicule or intimidation, meaning to harm opponents instead of addressing them. In these and other ways, some theological discussions of sexual topics resemble what is now called "hate speech," that is, speech that uses irrational caricature as an incitement to violence.

Other theologians share with "popular" ministries the devices of enforced silence. They simply refuse to discuss something so filthy or spiritually dangerous as carnal copulation. They surround it instead with a zone of silence – into the middle of which they project indescribable horrors. The canonical letter "to the Ephesians" traditionally attributed to the apostle Paul admonishes that "fornication [so the most common translation] or uncleanness of any kind and greed must not even be named among you" (5:3).[6] Generations of Christian theologians have read the remark as an allusion to a whole class of "nameless" sexual sins, sins too horrible to deserve a name.

Whether as horrified silence or as thundering condemnation, theological speech about sex displays the vices of the most widely broadcast Christian languages. But its failures are not only in these shared features. Theologians who have tried to create a separate language or method for treating sexual topics have fallen into bad habits on their own. These vices abound in the plodding, pedantic, all-too methodical texts of the most "academic" Christian writers on ethics. Some of them are obvious, others not.

The obvious vices in theology range from false precision and premature codification to the multiplication of disconnected cases or problems. Too many volumes of Christian ethics have wanted to be precise or rigorous after the model of some other discipline – of some version of mathematics, say, or of one or another of the natural sciences. They have sought to

---

[6] We will consider the translation of *porneia* more carefully in chapter 2. Note now that I routinely pass over complicated theories about scriptural authorship, interpolation, and redaction because they are not necessary for our purposes. For reasons I will explain at the end of chapter 2, Christian ethics must often deal, not with philological hypotheses about scriptural texts, but with the histories of their reception, that is, with their traditional authority.

perfect a list of sexual sins, each unambiguously defined and carefully graded. They have set forth axioms and proceeded with sequences of demonstrations. Other volumes have tried to model Christian moral theology after some system of civil or criminal law. They have wanted to codify comprehensive principles for directing sexual behavior in order then to tabulate and adjudicate every important case of sexual sin. Indeed, models taken from the other sciences have been projected onto the Christian scriptures themselves, so that they are read as an exhaustive legal code or a completed encyclopedia of human behavior. But the obvious vices, however common and however powerful, are not the most dangerous.

The most dangerous vices in theological treatments of sex are not obvious. They are hidden habits of thought. Particularly important are two vices of tacit expectation or assumption. The first I call the Vice of the Obligatory Answer. It is the bad habit of assuming as obvious that Christian ethics is obliged to solve any moral puzzle that we pose it. Sometimes we indulge the vice by assuming that there must be a rule or principle that responds to whatever general questions we can formulate about sex. Is adultery a serious sin? Is masturbation right or wrong? We formulate general questions. We demand general answers. We ought rather to ask ourselves why we assume that there are Christian "principles" to cover such general questions, a system of "rules" for deciphering every moral abstraction. The same vice shows itself in what seems the opposite direction – as the expectation that properly described individual cases must be decidable one way or another. Is it a sin for this particular woman to have sexual intercourse with this particular man in such and such circumstances? We suppose that it is the business of Christian ethics to settle the question. Is it really? We ought rather to ask: What warrant do we find in Christian revelation for expecting that ethics, like elementary algebra, will be able to solve word problems? In making this assumption about cases or the related assumption about general principles, we tacitly assume that Christian ethics should be like the aggressive versions of regulatory law or behavioral management that now dominate our lives.

It might be objected that the "Vice of the Obligatory Answer" is not a vice at all. It is a cynical name for the breadth of Christian faith. If God is Lord of all creation, then we should expect God's direction in every sphere or moment of our lives. Indeed, we must expect to answer for our every action to God, who wills something particular of us from action to action. Christian ethics is the study of what God wills for our actions. This objection is serious, but perhaps also misleading. It supposes that Christian ethics can be in fact a complete expression of God's will. I don't believe that it can. Even if you expect to find the divine will completely in books, there are much more helpful kinds of books – the Scriptures, clearly, but also lives of saints, liturgies, hymns, novels. Since I have a limited view of the role of books of ethics in Christian discernment, I regard the assumption that Christian ethics is obliged to have answers for every kind of moral question as a vice and not a virtue.

The second hidden vice of theologians I call the Vice of Timeless Science. It is the habit of conducting Christian ethics as if its categories and conclusions had no history, as if it could think entirely in the present tense. This denial of history is encouraged by powerful motives, both institutional and personal. Christian institutions often tie their claims for authority to assertions that they are merely repeating or applying an unchanging truth. What God wrote on the tablets of stone, what the Lord Jesus spoke to the disciples, that very same thing the institution now hands down as moral truth. Such a claim to authority is often coded into the words "biblical" or "scriptural," as in the phrase "biblical standards for sexual conduct." Again, the claim for institutional authority over morals can be an appeal to an alleged Christian unanimity: The institution promises to teach only what Christians have always and everywhere believed. The difficulty with these institutional claims is that Christians have understood Mosaic law or Gospel instructions very differently over centuries. Even in a single time, they have disagreed sharply over important ethical questions. These embarrassing facts are often concealed by Christian institutions precisely in order to maintain authority. That is one reason why there are fewer histories of Christian sexual ethics than handbooks of it. If theological ethics is cut off from a dialectical engagement with its own history, it loses not only much of its evidence, but also its most elusive meanings.

Indeed, the subtlest version of the Vice of the Timeless Science occurs as a distinction between historical theology and constructive theology. The distinction asserts that it is possible to do history without construction and construction without history. But no theologian can read her or his predecessors deeply without constructing along with them, without cooperating in their constructions. No theologian can construct a recognizably Christian ethics without using terms, topics, and starting-points from the historical texts of Christianity. History without construction is at best a kind of parroting; construction without history is private reverie.

We want a Christian ethics of sex. We come to the traditions of Christian theology in search of one. But we need to be sure that our search is something more than an occasion for repeating their bad habits – or ours. We should not want to encourage theologians in the belief that they can provide an algebra for Christian behavior that will calculate an answer to every general question or particular case. Nor should we foster the belief that the point of Christian ethics is to find a science that escapes history, either by solving its perennial debates once for all or by presiding over them.

We want a Christian ethics of sex. We come with certain expectations and write them into our questions. How must I behave sexually if I am to be saved? How can I act sexually in order to avoid hurting others or myself? Should I marry or not? How can I marry so as to be happiest? These questions and the many others like them have already been instructed by traditions inside and outside of the churches. We have already been taught to have certain expectations about what Christian ethics or moral theology might be. It should be a science or a law code or a perfect therapy. As so often in theology, the "should" becomes an "is." Because we assume that there is already a Christian ethics of sex conforming to these patterns, then we accept as true teaching speeches that conform to our unexamined expectations. Whatever kind of moral theology we have been taught to expect, there are speakers eager to provide it. Christendom has no lack of loud moralizers.

We want a Christian ethics of sex – but unless we are particularly careful, that may be too much already. The terms of our request may already mislead us. Both "ethics" and "sex" not only risk asking for more than can be decently given, they can lead us to conceal complicated and disconcerting histories.

Behind the Vices: Terms and Topics

There is no need now to recite complicated histories behind the Christian appropriations of older terms such as "ethics." We need only notice that Christians still use different words to describe their teaching about sexual desires and acts. For some it is a part of "Christian ethics," for others it is "moral theology." This is rather more than a difference between a Greek etymology (*ethikê*) and a Latin one (*theologia moralis*). It is even more than a trace of different epochs in the history of theology, with Protestants favoring "ethics" and Catholics "moral theology" (at least until recently). The difference between the two names recalls different projects for dividing up Christian theology and for relating it to (Christian?) philosophy.

Let me illustrate this point with some overly simple contrasts. When Peter Abelard boldly entitled a work *Ethics or Know Yourself* (in the late 1130s), he was deliberately importing a word from the ancient schools of philosophy – as well as yielding to a literary fad in Greek titles. Part of his boldness consisted in using what was evidently a philosophic word for a discussion that crossed and recrossed the border between philosophy and theology. After all, medieval encyclopedias regularly gave the name "ethics (*ethica*)" to one of the three parts of philosophy. But Abelard seemed to use it for a teaching that was both philosophical and theological – or at least a teaching that a Christian theologian needed to have.

Despite Abelard's boldness, "ethics" remained a philosophic term for most medieval theologians and their modern Catholic followers. Thomas Aquinas, for example, wrote a detailed exposition of Aristotle's *Nicomachean Ethics* around 1270, but did not apply the Aristotelian term "ethics" to Christian theology or any of its parts – as he never applied the term "philosopher" to a Christian. For Thomas and the Thomists after him, Christian moral teaching was "moral theology," understood either as the moral moment of an integral theology or as a separable specialty. But the terminology began to shift after the Protestant Reformation, and the Greek philosophers' term gained currency among theologians. Many Protestant authors were better classicists than the medievals, but they also envisaged a more complete conquest of philosophy by Christianity – that is, a more thorough despoiling of it for Christian purposes. To say "Christian ethics" was both to record that philosophy had been taken captive and led back to Christ and to suggest new conceptions of the relations between civic life and faith, between external duties and inward spirit.

To take a single example: Philip Melanchthon was, like Aquinas, famous as an expositor of Aristotle's *Nicomachean Ethics*. But it is Melanchthon, and not Aquinas, who deploys the term "ethics" within a comprehensive Christian teaching. Indeed, from 1550 on Melanchthon published in one volume his own "elements of ethical doctrine" and epitomes of sections from the *Nicomachean Ethics*. At the beginning of his elements, "ethics" names a doctrine that includes both teaching on the virtues and a consideration of the "norms for human life in external actions."[7] The whole of the doctrine testifies to God's justice as the source of moral law. Ethics or moral law is distinguished from the Gospel, which is the preaching of sin and the promise of redemption. Nonetheless, ethics as the study of the divinely disposed natural law is very useful to the Christian for the discipline of actions in this world. Melanchthon repeats the definition more succinctly at the opening of his paraphrase of Aristotle: "ethical doctrine is the part of divine law about civil actions," "ethics is part of the law of nature" that God instituted and intends us to understand.[8]

---

[7]   Philip Melanchthon, *Ethicae doctrinae elementa*, 1, opening paragraph and "Quid est philosophia moralis?," in his *Opera quae supersunt omnia*, vol. 16, ed. K. G. Bretschneider and H. E. Bindseil, Corpus Reformatorum, vol. 16 (Halle, 1850; repr. New York: Johnson Reprint, and Frankfurt am Main: Minerva, 1963), cols. 167–8.

[8]   Melanchthon, *Enarrationes aliquot librorum ethicorum Aristotelis*, as in his *Opera*, vol. 16, ed. Brentschneider and Bindseil, cols. 277–9.

Faced with such complications (and there are many more), we need some sort of convention to continue speaking. In this book, I will use "ethics" and "moral theology" interchangeably, because I use both suspiciously. After all, my point is not to supply the Obligatory Answer or to unveil a Timeless Science. I am eager for those vices to be questioned and then corrected. Nor am I going to propose a novel "solution" to the problem of the relations of theology to philosophy or of Christian faith to public life – as if those were single problems admitting of single solutions. My point is not to complete a Christian teaching about sexual actions, but to begin thinking anew about that teaching – by describing some of the terms, topics, and rhetorics that appear when Christian theologians talk about sex.

I should add immediately that my use of "Christian" will also be very broad. It will include major and minor Christian groups that are claimed as predecessors by denominations still existing, but it will also reach out to groups that no one now claims, that have disappeared after being excluded from Christian "orthodoxy." Used in this way, "Christian" is not so much a term of theological judgment as it is of rough designation or description. We will be reading widely across speeches on sex by authors who counted themselves Christians and who stood in various relations of continuity with the sources, methods, and conclusions of other, self-described Christians. Any stricter use of the term "Christian" would require untangling the oldest knots of Christian history – namely, the occasions and causes of Christian division.

Equally tangled histories lie concealed behind that word "sex," though it may be hard to see at first that its history might hold any surprises. After all, our societies are supposed to be saturated with sex. It surrounds us in tabloid headlines, academic jargon, novelistic obsessions, and in the most powerful and seductive images – from the glossiest upscale advertisements to the sleaziest pornographic videos hawked over the Internet. Sex is everywhere, right? For that very reason, we are not likely to have thought about its construction as a category.

Some theologians try to get at the category by conducting a survey of ordinary English uses of the word "sex" or of terms that often appear alongside it – say, the terms "gender" and "sexuality." This kind of survey often just repeats the concealment of familiarity. As native speakers of English, we can easily produce samples of "sex" in ordinary speech. But it may be that our linguistic habits were constructed to conceal certain controversies, as it may be that there is no ordinary language about "sex." Our "ordinary" uses of "sex" and its related terms may be points of tension and willed forgetfulness. They may be points of sharp controversy. Certainly they have been in recent decades.

When American speakers of English think of controversies over sex in language, they tend to focus on the quarrels over "gendered" language (say, the use of the pronoun "he" for all human beings). There have been other struggles. For example, one of the most urgent tasks for contemporary feminist thinking was to block a direct inference from genital configuration to social and political subordination. Feminists had to show that being a woman physically did not mean being a "woman" socially, that is, someone who should be denied the right to own property or to vote, who should be excluded from education and the professions, who should always remain the ward of some man (father, husband, bishop, pastor). In order to distinguish these two senses of "woman," theorists and activists alike began to insist on the difference between (physically determined) sex and (culturally constructed) gender. Sex was the kind of body you were born with. Gender was the way you were taught to use that sexed body within a certain sociopolitical regime. Sex was nature, gender was nurture. Between "sex" and "gender" so contrasted, there came "sexuality," which seemed to some (or sometimes) physiologically based and cross-cultural; to others (or at other times), culturally specific and always under construction. This ambivalence is familiar enough in the compound "homo-sexuality," which appears alternately as a fate, a biological fact, a choice, and a lifestyle. It appears, in short, sometimes at the pole of sex–nature, sometimes at the pole of gender–nurture.

Of course, the trichotomy sex/sexuality/gender was never particularly stable, and not only because of the instability built into the conception of sexuality.[9] It was never clear, for example, what was to be included in "gender" and what not. Some feminists objected that general discussions of "woman" or "the feminine" were hopelessly confused attempts to universalize culturally-specific gender roles. The discussions, they thought, took features of gender and tried to make them features of sex. Others pointed out that the idea of physical sex was itself hardly clear. To begin with, modern medicine finds cases where there is contradictory evidence of sex at different physical levels. External genital anatomy is hardly the only marker of physical sex, though it may be the most decisive socially. What is more important, the duality of "male" and "female" bodies is figured quite variously across cultures. The scientific notions of sex that prevail among educated Europeans and Americans are conditioned by culturally-produced systems of gender. So far as our medical descriptions

[9] I here skim over a complicated and interesting series of critiques. One of the best of them can be found in Judith Butler, *Gender Trouble: Feminism and the Subversion of Identity* (New York and London: Routledge, 1990), esp. pp. 1–34.

of female bodies are in important senses still masculine descriptions, for example, they falsely impose gendered categories as if they were neutral, universal, natural categories of sex. Feminists too have to combat the vices of the Obligatory Answer and the Timeless Science.

The situation is perhaps more confused with regard to "sexuality," which has a quite specific pedigree in European law and medicine of the nineteenth century. It goes along with classifications of perversions and with the strict dualism, heterosexuality/homosexuality. It also privileges sexual desires or appetites in constructing personal identities. The importance of this historical origin is hotly debated, especially in relation to the notions of heterosexuality and homosexuality. No debate among contemporary writers on same-sex desire has been more long-lived or more rancorous than the debate about the very application of the term "homosexuality" before the nineteenth century – or in cultures that do not participate in the medico-legal project of European "sexuality."

So far as the category "sexuality" enacts a historically particular set of relations to criminal law, medicine, and the natural sciences, it shows another complication in the histories behind the terms. "Sex," "sexuality," and "gender" are not just terms in Christian theology, they are terms in law, medicine, and what we now call the "social sciences." When Christian ethics uses them, it places itself inside a long competition between theology and other sciences or technologies concerned with the human body or soul. The meanings of the terms cannot be settled or stipulated by theologians in complete disregard of their other uses. Nor can the theological teaching about sex proceed as if no one else were talking about it.

Theology risks crude ignorance if it refuses to learn new legal and medical theories about sexed human bodies. It risks silliness if it simply adopts those theories without examining their origins, purposes, and consequences. If theology is no longer Queen of the Sciences, it shouldn't become just their gullible sidekick. This is especially important in sexual matters, which are so vulnerable to abuse by scientific, medical, and legal structures of power. But it is no easy thing to negotiate the conflicting claims of theology and modern medicine or science. Indeed, much argument would be required just to claim that religious and medical or scientific discourses overlap enough to produce negotiable conflicts. On some views, theology and science or medicine must talk past each other because they never talk about the same things, even when they use the same words. On other views, they do talk to each other, but with one or the other in an assumed position of superiority. For example, some theologians hold that Christian revelation cannot in principle be corrected by science or medicine, since it has higher standing so far as it derives from revelation.

In this book, I don't intend to argue for a general view of the relation of theology to medicine and the life sciences. I want also to avoid revolutionary proposals for new languages. I consider instead important Christian discourses about holy and unholy uses of human genital organs. Those organs are also called "sex" organs or "sexual" organs, and so I will call the Christian discourses I consider teachings about "sex." But I mean this term vaguely and inclusively. It will certainly include what many people call "sexuality" and "gender," as it will include other things. I will not be obeying the contrast between "sex" as nature and "gender" as nurture because I will treat both terms as ambiguously physical and cultural, determined and determinable. In short, I am using the term "sex" with a definite center and a vague or absent circumference.

The center consists of what Christian ethics has said or might say about genital acts. The circumference runs through many other topics that Christian writers have talked about in teaching about genital acts. Of course, the term "genital acts" is also notoriously ambiguous. It does not mean just any acts or events by or in the vicinity of reproductive organs. It names acts that are or that resemble the copulations that result in human reproduction – or else acts that produce the kind of pleasure associated with copulation – or else acts . . . . Christian authors disagree when they define "genitals" and "genital acts." It will be our business to follow them as they do their defining – and not to preempt them by offering a falsely clear definition at the start.

I want to insist that my speaking of "acts" as the center of concern is only for the sake of having a central point from which to start. Moral definitions of "genital acts" invoke various elements. For example, different circumstances have been considered pertinent in judging their morality. In a justly influential essay, Gayle Rubin sketches axes along which we distinguish "good, normal, natural, blessed sexuality" from "bad, abnormal, unnatural, damned sexuality."[10] The axes include the partners' genders and legal/religious status, their number and ages, together with such issues as whether their relations are exclusive or commercial, whether the act is accompanied by pornography or simulated violence, and so on. Most Christian theologians have considered such circumstances morally significant. Some of them have also counted as morally decisive certain circumstances that contemporary theologians tend to ignore – for example, whether the sexual act was performed on liturgically prohibited days, in the vicinity of a church or other

---

[10] Gayle Rubin, "Thinking Sex," in *The Lesbian and Gay Studies Reader*, ed. Henry Abelove, Michèle Aina Barale, and David M. Halperin (New York and London: Routledge, 1993), pp. 13–14.

consecrated space, while uncovering more of the body than absolutely necessary, and so on. We should remind ourselves of the variety of circumstances
that have been counted into theological analyses of "genital acts."

And not only circumstances. One of the most remarkable things about
Christian discourses on sex is that they are always reading acts up into other
contexts, other explanatory schemes. Sexual acts cause or express a sexual
state (purity, pollution) or a sexual status (virgin, wife). The state or status
is often connected in turn to what might be called an identity. Christianity
has manufactured and distributed a number of sexual identities – the Virgin
Martyr, the Pure Priest, the Witch, the Sodomite. These are theological
roles for which the scripts contain much sexual matter – which is to say,
much presumed reference to sexual acts and their refusal.[11] Indeed, "Fallen
Humankind" is itself an indispensable sexual identity for many Christian theologies, so far as the sin of Adam and Eve was conjectured to have something
to do with sex and certainly to have resulted in shame at naked, sexed bodies.

A study of the Christian ethics of sex can start with "genital acts," but it
can hardly stop with them. It must consider how these acts figure in states,
statuses, identities. Different ethical models or conclusions will invoke
different elements of this assortment. Condemnations of sexual "sin" sometimes aim at acts, but often enough at states, statuses, or identities. In fact,
the arguments offered in support of particular condemnations often resist
analysis because they shift from one object to another without notice. The
assortment of elements discussed by Christian sexual ethics makes for its
richness, but also for its tendency to flirt with sophistry.

Not all of this can be blamed just on Christian theology, of course.
Sexual acts are notoriously open to use by a variety of motives. This is true
both personally and socially. One person can copulate with another for
any number of motives: to express passionate love, to console, to repay
past or future gifts, to escape daily consciousness, to hurt, to subjugate.
Societies can read sexual acts as raising or lowering social standing, as
fitting rewards for military service, as punishable manifestations of criminal
intent. Moral theology of sex cannot ignore the extraordinary availability
of sexual acts for so many personal or social uses.

---

[11]   I am using the term "role" on rather naïve analogy to what happens in rituals or
liturgies. There are of course well-developed theories of sex- or gender-linked roles in
sociology and psychotherapy. There are even well-developed theologies of Christian
roles in community, liturgy, or salvation history, for a magisterial analysis of which see
Hans Urs von Balthasar, *Theo-Drama: Theological Dramatic Theory*, vol. 1: *Prolegomena*,
trans. Graham Harrison (San Francisco: Ignatius Press, 1988). I don't mean to endorse
any of those accounts at present.

It might be objected that the choice to concentrate on sexual acts or states, statuses, and identities misses the most important way of conceiving sex ethically – as the expression of a relation of reciprocal love. I reply that conceiving sex as relational from the start would restrict our inquiry unhelpfully. First, it would restrict us historically. Most of the Christian discourses we need to examine argue that human sex is usually not about reciprocal love; it is about selfish gratification. If we look only to speeches about intimacy, we will miss most of what Christianity has said about sex. Second, a definition in terms of relationships would restrict us conceptually. It would prejudge central ethical issues. To say that sex is an expression of loving relations is not to offer a definition. It is to make a normative judgment. We will hear that normative judgment in a number of discourses, especially recent ones. We will need to consider it carefully when we reach it. We cannot now begin with it.

Can "genital acts," their circumstances or larger contexts (however exactly defined), or their consequent states, statuses, and identities, or even their roles in loving relationships, be made a principal topic for Christian ethics just by themselves? They have long functioned as a principal topic (or set of topics), not least in Christian authors who divided them from other ethical topics. Long before modern law, medicine, and social science began to talk endlessly about sex, sexuality, and gender; long before what some regard as our present obsession with sexual matters, Christian theologians treated genital acts and their consequences as particularly important – uniquely fearful, powerful, disruptive. A rhetorical emphasis on sexual matters has been shared across differences of theological method. It goes without saying that distinct Christian traditions have conceived an ethics of sex differently. For example, Catholic moral theology in the modern period has tended to separate itself from dogmatic theology in order to constitute itself as a more or less autonomous theological specialty. Many Protestant theologians, by contrast, have wanted to resist the methodological segregation of moral topics, including sexual ones. Still Catholic and Protestant writers have shared an anxious emphasis on sex as a topic.

There are conceptual dangers in taking "the ethics of sex" as a reasonably coherent field of inquiry. I will try to show throughout the book how often Christian discussions of sexual topics run into other theological topics or other historical contexts. I will be particularly concerned to suggest how discourses about sex lead and echo discourses about gender, that is, about what it is to be a woman or a man. But we should avoid simply equating an ethics of sex with an ethics of gender. Sex is not something that happens only "between the sexes." Nor are sexual states, statuses, and identities simply reducible to the prevailing gender scheme in a society.

Indeed, it may be very important to analyze some theological discourses precisely by thinking about sex without or against gender so far as that can be done. There is a coherence to the Christian discourses about sex that is not just the coherence of Christian teachings on gender – however much the two discourses unroll through, over, against one another.

We will be studying Christian discourses about "sex" as discourses centered around "genital acts," but only so that we can learn how widely these discourses then range through circumstances, states, statuses, identities; how regularly they disagree over topics and methods; how inevitably they merge with adjacent discourses, especially the discourses about gender.

From Vices to Questions

To read in the libraries of Christian speeches on sex is to reanimate their rhetorics – to offer ourselves as readers (students, novices, earnest inquirers) in whom their rhetorical effects can be played out once again. Exactly the same rhetorical effects are not reproduced infallibly. Readers are not identical compact disks into which the same track is cut again and again. Good theological writers not only recognize the diversity of readers, they work assiduously to craft texts that take account of that diversity. The best theological writers produce texts that entice, chastise, persuade, teach, sanctify – all in deliberate order, all in different relations to readers at different spiritual stages. If such texts cannot be reduced to narrative history or classified system, they also cannot be reduced to exhaustive analysis. This book is not a series of finished interpretations of texts. It is a series of incomplete engagements with their theological rhetorics, that is, with their effectual patterns for teaching Christian ethics.

Here it might well be objected that in emphasizing the rhetoric of texts, I am overlooking the complex institutionalization of Christian moral judgments. The objector could rightly point out that the Christian teaching about sex has been shaped by innumerable political, social, and economic forces – and has expressed itself in countless institutional arrangements, both clerical and lay, monastic and secular, pastoral and legal. Indeed, much of the history of marriage or the family in Western Europe, not to speak of the history of criminal law, seems a chapter in the history of Christian sexual ethics.

I make two replies to this important objection. The first is that institutional evidence for the meaning of texts is indeed helpful, but also risky. What we can know of old institutions is often much hazier than what we know about old texts (which is hazy enough). One reason for this is that we know those institutions by combining texts, each of which requires reading.

Institutional contexts are not more certain than theological texts. They are usually less certain, because they require the hypothetical combination of multiple textual interpretations. So I offer rhetorical reading of Christian speeches on sex not as a replacement for institutional analysis, but as a prelude to it. Indeed, in early chapters I will be looking at how institutions register in speech – for example, in bureaucratic regulation of sexual sins or in community sanction of marriage. In later chapters, I will consider the deep changes in the social and political standing of Christian teaching and the challenges they pose for persuasive moral theology.

The second answer to the objection is rather different. What we today call Christian ethics is the remnant of the much larger project of "Christendom" – that is, of the project of aligning God's law, church law, and civil law in order to make a truly Christian society. Many of the old texts and practices only make sense within that larger project, and no narrative history of Christian teaching on sex could refuse to include legal and institutional histories of the most diverse kinds. But Christian ethics does not often proceed now under the assumption that it is building Christendom. When it does proceed in that way, it may be suspected of suffering from delusions of grandeur. It seems better to concede that Christian ethics has suffered a sharp decline in its overt influence on increasingly secularized or religiously plural societies. Not many people expect professors of moral theology to serve as legislators. We ought to concede this, and we ought to be glad of it. Freedom from the old demands to build Christendom may permit us to be virtuously clear about the limits of what we are doing – and about the dangers of what has been done. We begin to claim this freedom by asking what applications of Christian speeches about sex could be made apart from their enactments in older institutions. So I will not be concerned with what Christians were doing or with what they accused one another of doing, but with what they said they should be doing, because thinking about those idealized Christian speeches seems to me to offer most hope for thinking forward.

What are the best questions to put to two millennia of idealized speeches about sex? Many critical readers of these speeches ask questions about coherence or distinctiveness. Do Christian texts, taken singly or collectively, have anything *coherent* to say about our sexual acts or identities or relationships? If so, can it be repeated in ways that do not invoke either violent ideas (such as misogyny) or violent institutions (such as church bureaucracies for policing morals)? Again, do the Christian texts have anything *distinctive* to say about sex? If not, is this an objection against Christian theology – or is it rather an objection against our expectations of how Christianity ought to teach about sex?

Questions about coherence or distinctiveness are useful, but perhaps not the most useful. More useful questions concern the rhetorical power of those idealized speeches – over the old readers, over us. "Power" in rhetoric means both (and at least) the power to persuade and the power that comes in having persuaded. Christian moral theology has long used the most powerful rhetorics in both senses, but a doubly powerful rhetoric is not only morally effective, it is morally dangerous. It is dangerous because it is effective. More useful questions should ask how Christian moral theology can teach, inside the churches or outside of them, without becoming immorally dangerous – without becoming, for example, an ideology in the service of some structure of human power. How can Christian ethics be persuasive and even authoritative without becoming abusive and even tyrannical? These questions about power are related to the questions about coherence and distinctiveness in several ways. On the one hand, you cannot ask about the coherence or distinctiveness of the teaching in a persuasive text unless you ask about its power, since the teaching may only have its sense in and through the exercise of that power. On the other hand, you may condemn a persuasive teaching precisely because its coherence and distinctiveness seem to come only from an abuse of power. Again, most importantly, it may be that one of the things that distinguishes Christian sexual ethics is the way it mobilizes power around sex.

All of these questions will run through the book, but they have to be applied first of all to the texts that are taken to be the source of theological authority – the books, that is, of the Christian Bible. The most urgent task for a Christian ethics of sexuality is to learn how to speak convincingly without repeating old vices and without offering itself as the instrument of one or another earthly power. Theological speech ought to be powerful enough to describe human sex persuasively without becoming simply the propaganda for some all-too-human tyranny. Christian ethics can begin to find such language by being scrupulous in the examination of the languages it already has. It needs to read its own texts with particular attention to their rhetorical programs, which means with particular concern for their claims to teaching authority. The first and great text for Christian morals has been the Christian Bible.

Chapter 2

Scriptural Authorities

Nothing is more controversial among Christians than bible reading. The controversies are as old as Christianity itself, and so they are embittered and repetitive in the way that old fights tend to be. Indeed, controversies over scriptural interpretation have long been institutionalized as divisions among denominations and among parties within denominations. The question, How do I read the Christian Bible and for what purposes?, is now inseparable from the question, What decisions do I take about joining one or another Christian community? No one can begin to read the Bible alone. A reader can only begin by depending on others – certainly those who have provided the text and the ability to read its languages, but also those who have motivated the reading. Any attempt to invoke the "authority of the Scriptures" calls up prior questions about personal allegiance and group identity.

Someone who begins a sentence with the words, "The Bible says . . . ," should be asked to pause for a set of prior questions. How do you decide what the Bible says? Do you consult what you accept as denominational tradition, what you account as natural reason, what you accredit as mystical vision? Do you think it enough to read the Bible just in English translation, or do you try to read it in some collated edition of the ancient manuscripts in their original languages? Do you think it possible to interpret a snippet of biblical text just by itself, or do you subordinate snippets to some reading of the whole book – or to the whole collection of books? And what procedures does your interpretive community follow when you've gone through all the prescribed steps and you still disagree with each other about what the Bible says? There is no way to divide Christians into groups more quickly than by looking at how they read the Bible. Someone who wants to tell you "what the Bible says" is not making a statement about interpretation so much as a declaration of denomination.

Of course, to call it a decision or declaration is already to mislead. The motives for denominational allegiance or group membership are mixed, and many of them cannot be easily articulated. Moreover, the principles of interpretation set forth by a denomination or still smaller group of Christians may have little relation to the members' actual practices of reading. It is not enough to ask questions about the principles for interpretation. One also has to try to get candid answers about deeper motives for it – so far as these can be articulated. A person may claim to be reading a scriptural verse under the direct inspiration of the Holy Spirit when in fact the main influence is the charismatic leader of a local study group. A person may justify a specific interpretation by appeal to Christian tradition, but in fact the "tradition" is no more than the latest communiqué from a denominational agency. There are significant psychological issues here, and I do not want to reduce them. I do mean to suggest that the stated principles for biblical interpretation are often not the real or effective principles behind a particular practice of reading. In reading the Christian Bible, as in so much of church life, lengthy discussions of principle often fail to touch the original causes of disagreement. What is needed is not so much a statement of principles as a humble dissection of motives.

When moral matters are at stake, even more motives (over-)determine biblical reading, as they conspire to conceal its actual sources. New questions multiply. How does a particular group of Christian readers understand the relation of biblical narration to biblical legislation, of example to injunction? Are there ethical examples or injunctions in the Bible that were "true then," but not "true now"? Are there parts or aspects of biblical law that are "symbolic" rather than "literal," "ideal" rather than "obligatory"? Presenting a collection of biblical verses does not address these questions. Neither will a collection resolve concrete disputes, which often depend on motives or choices that precede and determine the collection. All sorts of contradictory moral positions have justified themselves, quite sincerely, by gathering biblical verses.

In moral matters, again, there are so many incitements to religious hypocrisy or self-deception. One needn't be "postmodern" to realize that moral questions invite answers from unsavory motives. The stories about Jesus that we have in the canonical gospels are full of sharp critiques of various abuses of religious authority over morals. "You are like whitewashed tombs, outside splendid to the eye, but inside full of the bones of the dead and every uncleanness." This is quoted, not from Nietzsche or Foucault, but from a report of Jesus' condemnation of certain moral teachers (Matthew 23:27). Christians have hurled equally strong accusations against each other. Indeed, however violent the secular polemics against Christian moral hypocrisy have been, they were preceded and in some ways invited by a long history of moral polemic within Christianity.

The challenge for Christians is not to disagree over biblical interpretation, but to find ways of talking with each other given the well-defended disagreements. For this reason, Christians now appeal to scholarly readings as a discourse beyond partisanship. There is something to be gained in this appeal, but it also makes for new difficulties. Scholarship has its own assumptions about the origin, transmission, and moral claims of the biblical texts. These assumptions are by no means self-evident, nor can they assert some special privilege in settling ethical controversies. Indeed, in bureaucratic societies managed by experts, scholarly claims of authority can often be abused more easily and more subtly than religious claims. What is just as important, some biblical scholarship that wants to claim the authority of secular expertise is in fact not secular. It is denominational theology barely or badly disguised. The old moral teaching of a particular group dresses up in the supposedly universal costume of Reason. Some of what passes for biblical social history or philology is fully denominational in origin and intended effect.

So "secular" scholarship is no sure way to step beyond denominational disagreements. It may offer some hope, nonetheless, for helping us to talk across denominational lines. "Secular" scholarship can offer this hope to the extent that it professes to rely on standards of evidence and reasoning that are shared across denominational lines or that divide the speakers differently than do denominational allegiances. These scholarly standards are not universal, of course. Universal reason is a fantasy – and a dangerous one. Still, scholarly standards are often more or at least differently inclusive than denominational standards. They increase the chances that we will be able to begin and sustain new conversations beyond our denominational circles. If we approach the biblical texts in roughly the same ways that we approach other historical texts, we may both reduce the number of our prior assumptions and increase the number of people we can persuade to share those assumptions, at least for a time (though these two effects need not be connected).

Of course, in reducing our interpretive assumptions, we also run the risk of reduction in the pejorative sense, that is, of missing what is distinctive in the Christian scriptures. When we approach these texts with the philological, archeological, literary, and historical techniques we use with other ancient religious texts, we may prevent ourselves from engaging their claims to be unique texts that cannot be read well so long as they are read just like other texts. Yet the risk of secular reduction has to be run in order to begin conversation about the Christian Bible outside of ever-shrinking conventicles of true believers. It is a risk that we must run now in order not only to talk with one another, but to learn some of the more startling results of scholarship as applied to scriptural teaching on sex.

Secular scholarship has alerted readers to many problems in biblical passages that are regularly invoked as deciding sexual questions, beginning with the problem of knowing which texts might actually be concerned with those questions. Where do you look in the Christian Bible for Christian precepts about sexual behavior? No matter what modern English translations might suggest, for example, terms like "sodomy" and "homo-sexuality" do not appear in either the Old or New Testaments. Much blander English translations, such as "fornication" or "adultery," conceal as much as they reveal. The corresponding Hebrew and Greek terms are quite difficult to parse, either because they are rare or because they reflect unfamiliar social arrangements. There is the further difficulty of knowing whether particular passages in the Christian Bible record specifically Chris-tian moral precepts. The familiar sexual prohibitions of Leviticus 18 and 21 form part of a system of purity taboos that Christians have not observed with any consistency in more than nineteen centuries. Or, again, many of the Pauline sexual condemnations come within "sin lists" borrowed in part from pagan philosophers. They might not seem to be distinctively Christian at all, and so we might want to ask whether or on what terms they form part of the revelation in Christ.[1] There are, in short, no self-evident lists of biblical passages about sexual matters. The pertinence of any particular passage to contemporary sexual ethics has to be established case by case, often at considerable length.

We cannot here review or even adequately sample secular scholarship on all the scriptural verses that have been or might be cited in Christian teachings about sex. What we can do is to try to classify interpretive issues

---

[1] I do not mean to prejudge the question, whether a moral teaching must be distinct-ively Christian in order to be binding as revelation on all Christians. Certainly a number of Christian theologians have held that God reveals different kinds of truths, some of which can be discovered rationally apart from revelation. In contemporary theology, there have been attempts both to stress or disprove the distinctiveness of Christian sexual ethics and to discover their sources or parallels outside of Christianity. For recent attempts to complicate these debates differently, see John Milbank, "Can Morality Be Christian?," in *The Word Made Strange: Theology, Language, Culture* (Oxford: Blackwell, 1997), pp. 219–32, and Stanley Hauerwas, "On Doctrine and Ethics," in *Sanctify Them in the Truth: Holiness Exemplified* (Nashville: Abingdon Press, 1998), pp. 19–36; for an exemplary genealogy of Christian sexual teaching, see Wayne A. Meeks, *The Origins of Christian Morality: The First Two Centuries* (New Haven, CT: Yale University Press, 1983).

that typically arise in citing such verses, and then to look at some of the
most notorious examples under each kind. The very rough classification I
propose is as follows: what a passage says, why the passage says it, how the
passage is traditionally assigned to a topic, and whether the passage is
normative for contemporary Christians. The same classification could be
described more concisely as issues about textual terms, textual purposes,
textual topics, and textual norms. The classification is very rough indeed,
and any good interpreter could show its deficiencies in a few minutes. I
offer it not as an enduring Table of Categories, but as a useful division of
issues that would otherwise remain uselessly confused.

Textual Terms

To know "what the Bible says" requires, first, an agreement on which
texts belong to the Christian Bible. It is common enough to ask what
authority is to be accorded to the books we call the "Apocrypha." There
are much more basic questions. After all, which books from the early
Christian communities are to be regarded as canonical? Many gospels were
rejected by those who compiled the New Testament and others were
simply unknown to them. Some of those writings represent issues of sex
or gender rather differently than the canonical writings do.[2] The "letter"
of our scriptural texts records a long series of decisions, most especially
decisions about which texts are scriptural.

Knowing what a text says requires, second, an agreed version of it. The
work of settling the text is too often done offstage so far as Christian ethics
is concerned. Theologians, ordinary believers, and even some kinds of
biblical exegetes take the words of the original text as given and proceed
to construe them. Yet the words are not simply given – or rather they are
given in multiple copies from diverse times and places that do not agree
with one another. The construction of a single version out of those multiple
copies requires innumerable decisions, some of which have important
theological implications – and so invite the projection of powerful theological motives. There are significant textual uncertainties in the New
Testament. For example, it matters for Christian sexual ethics whether you
accept as genuine a letter attributed to Clement of Alexandria which
suggests that there were public and private versions of the Gospel of Mark,

---

[2] For a well-known and controversial account, see Elaine H. Pagels, *The Gnostic
Gospels* (New York: Random House, 1979).

the private version containing passages with homoerotic overtones.[3] Again, and more familiarly, the story of the woman taken in adultery known to centuries of readers as the beginning of John 8 is now considered a later addition or interpolation. Christians have to choose not only which works will be canonical, but which versions of them will be regarded as standard. We should remember the fact of those decisions even when we cannot enter into their details. For what follows, I must pass beyond these editorial questions in the way that Christian ethicists typically do. I must restrict our attention to the most widely agreed canonical texts in their presently received versions.

New troubles appear. The texts are written in ancient forms of languages that are not first languages for most of us. We learn the scriptural languages not as "native" children in daily exchanges, but as adult "foreigners" in classroom study. When we have questions about these ancient languages, we resort not to the complex habits of a "native" speaker, but to the often misleading information in reference books. When we want to know what Paul means by *porneia*, for example, we consult one or another dictionary of New Testament Greek, and there we find that it means "illicit sexual intercourse in general," "prostitution, unchastity, fornication," "fornication" and "licentiousness," or "sexual immorality of any kind, often with the implication of prostitution."[4] These "definitions" are hardly either consistent or precise. If they were both, they could still mislead us.

A definition begins to mislead us as soon as we forget that the dictionary we are consulting was itself composed by people who are in our situation rather than Paul's. The dictionaries were composed, that is, by modern

---

[3] See Morton Smith, *Clement of Alexandria and the Secret Gospel of Mark* (Cambridge, MA: Harvard University Press, 1973), for the arguments in favor of the authenticity of this text. The arguments have been very controversial. Let me also repeat here what my first chapter ought to have made clear. Because this book is an introduction to rhetorical topics in Christian discourses on sex, and neither a history nor a reference guide, I have trimmed my footnotes to the minimum. In no case do I pretend to give a bibliography of the most famous or infamous works of scholarship on the topics I am discussing. I intend only to give enough bibliographical information so that the reader can find the texts to which I refer.

[4] Respectively Henry Joseph Thayer, *A Greek-English Lexicon of the New Testament*, corr. ed. (New York and London: Harper & Bros., 1899), pp. 531–2; William F. Arndt and F. Wilbur Gingrich, eds., *A Greek-English Lexicon of the New Testament and Other Early Christian Literature* (Chicago: University of Chicago Press, 1957), p. 699; Gerhard Friedrich, *Theological Dictionary of the New Testament*, trans. Geoffrey W. Bromiley (Grand Rapids: W. B. Eerdmans, 1968), 6:593–4; Johannes P. Louw and Eugene A. Nida, *Greek-English Lexicon of the New Testament Based on Semantic Domains*, 2nd ed. (New York: United Bible Societies, 1989), 1:771, entry no. 88.271.

readers for whom New Testament Greek was a foreign and rather circum-
scribed artifact. At least two consequences follow. First, dictionary entries
are subject not only to the choices that limit any dictionary, but to the fact
that the quantity of early Christian writing is rather small and the quantity
of canonical writings much smaller. Sometimes the only passage illustrating
a particular dictionary meaning will be just the passage we are asking the
dictionary to interpret for us. New Testament dictionaries can also lead us
to forget, second, that they often suffer in severe form the problem of
prejudiced reading. By "prejudiced reading," I mean reading that already
knows in advance and in detail what the words in a given text *must* mean.
The meanings in New Testament dictionaries are overdetermined by centuries of Christian interpretation, especially in regard to moral matters. Because
so many Christian lexicographers and exegetes "know" already what particular New Testament texts prohibit or endorse, they are entirely too
ready to fix meanings for uncertain or ambiguous terms.

    That Pauline word *porneia* serves as a telling example.[5] It stands at the
center of a number of passages that are read as prohibiting many or most
sexual practices. In recent English versions, the term has been translated as
"lust" (NEB), "immorality" (NAB, REB), and "fornication" (JB, NRSV).
These translations neither agree among themselves nor represent the ambi-
guities of the Greek. The New Testament term *porneia* descends from older
Greek terms that were most specifically applied to prostitutes and prostitution. Paul himself recalls this connection in 1 Corinthians 6:12–18. "The
body is not for *porneia*," he says (6:13), adding a few lines later that the
Christian's body, as "members" of Christ's body, should not be made into
the members of a prostitute (*pornê*, 6:15). Given the play on words, we
might want to understand *porneia* here as copulating with prostitutes (while
noting that the perspective is strictly masculine).

    We might then be tempted to extend this reading to 1 Thessalonians 4,
where Paul urges his readers to "keep away from *porneia*" by each learning
"to possess his own vessel in holiness and honor" (4:3–4). In view of our
earlier reading, we might understand this as saying, "Don't resort to prostitutes. Have sex with your own wife" (who may be conceived, perhaps in
dependence on some ancient medical theories, as a purely receptive "vessel"). Or the verse might mean, on a different reading of "vessel," "Don't
resort to prostitutes. Learn to control your own body." But Paul then adds
that none of his readers, unlike the idolatrous Greeks, should "outreach his
brother in the matter and be greedy" (4:5–6). This seems like a counsel

---

[5]   I repeat that I am using "Paul" to refer to the author(s) of the 14 New Testament
letters traditionally ascribed to the Apostle Paul.

against adultery conceived as a violation of male property rights within the group. If Paul is still talking about *porneia* here, then *porneia* would seem sometimes to be translatable as use of prostitutes, sometimes as adultery (or, at least, adultery with the wife of another member of the Christian community). Back in 1 Corinthians 5:1, Paul had also applied *porneia* to the case of a man who "had his father's wife" (presumably not his birth-mother). So that *porneia* would now seem to refer in different places to the use of prostitutes, adultery (within the community?), and (statutory?) "incest" – unless the last case is rather to be counted a species of adultery.

It is tempting to reconcile these different meanings by dissolving them back into a single, more general one. We might be tempted, in short, to assume that the particular cases are only instances of a more general moral category or principle that somehow entails all of them. The temptation is encouraged by other Pauline passages that include *porneia* within long and broad lists of sins. In Galatians 5:19–21, for example, *porneia* stands at the beginning of a list of "deeds of the flesh" that includes two other sins that might have to do with sex ("uncleanness" [*akatharsia*], "self-indulgence" [*aselgeia*]), but that then goes on to idolatry, sorcery, and a longer series of sins against community unity or good order. In Colossians 3:5–6, we read the injunction, "Put to death, then, the members that are on earth, *porneia*, uncleanness, passion, evil desire, and the greed that is idolatry." In Ephesians 5:3 and 5:5, the term appears in the triplet, *porneia*, uncleanness, and greed. In all of these lists, Christian readers have wanted to see *porneia* as a comprehensive and radical sexual sin.

To generalize the term in this way is, I said, a temptation. It ought to be resisted. In fact, it is not clear why exactly Paul arranges these lists as he does or how he understands their terms to be connected (if we are even dealing with the same author in all cases).[6] Two points stand out. The first is that such lists give us very little evidence about the exact meanings of the terms in them. They do not refer to specific acts or cases, as they do not present an evident set of internal distinctions. The second point is that these lists need not be speaking literally at all. The juxtapositions of *porneia* and idolatry or uncleanness or greed remind us that terms for sexual acts are often used – in the Jewish scriptures, in ancient philosophy – as metaphors for other moral conditions. When the Old Testament prophets speak of Israel's prostitution, they are not referring to genital behavior. They refer to spiritual unfaithfulness, to idolatries and ritual impurities. So, too, the

---

[6] See, for example, the alternate analyses in L. William Countryman, *Dirt, Greed, and Sex: Sexual Ethics in the New Testament and Their Implications for Today* (Philadelphia: Fortress Press, 1988), pp. 104–9.

Pauline texts may be using *porneia* metaphorically or symbolically, not intend-
ing to refer to specific sexual acts at all. Just as the term need not mean the
same thing wherever it occurs, so it need not mean in the same way –
need not mean everywhere literally.

Fiercer controversy has swirled around another Pauline sexual term –
indeed, one that occurs in lists together with a term related to *porneia*. In 1
Corinthians 6:9, we read condemnations of several classes of sinners, including *pornoi* (those who commit *porneia*), *malakoi* (the "soft" or "effeminate"),
and *arsenokoitai*. Again, in 1 Timothy 1:10, a list that begins with patricides,
matricides, and homicides goes on immediately to *pornoi* and *arsenokoitai*.
Who are the *arsenokoitai*? Etymologically the term would seem to refer to
men who copulate with other men. Any more precise meaning is a guess.
John Boswell pointed to the absence of the term in pagan authors and its
great rarity even in Christian authors after Paul. He contrasted it with the
large and nuanced vocabulary for male–male relations in ancient Greek,
which Paul could have borrowed if he had wanted to condemn such
relations precisely – and to which Christian expounders of Paul returned
when they wanted to make such condemnations. Boswell concluded that
Paul coined *arsenokoitai* by grammatical analogy in order to name something
quite particular, namely, "male sexual agents, i.e., active male prostitutes, who
were common throughout the Hellenistic world in the time of Paul."[7]

One implication of Boswell's analysis is worth stating more clearly than
Boswell himself does. Paul's most specific terms are not terms for acts or
sins, but for agents or sinners. The arts for stigmatizing classes of persons
by pejorative naming are rather better developed than the rhetoric for
stigmatizing classes of acts. They can achieve meanings by imaginative
projection rather more quickly than moral or legal definitions might. But
pejorative naming also demands a different kind of reading – one that
allows for a certain looseness or "play" in the boundaries of the class.
Sexual conduct is seen as creating a status, like the status of the criminal or
those ritually unclean. A status can afford to be vague in many ways about
the particular acts attached to it.

Boswell's argument about the meaning of *arsenokoitai*, published in 1980,
has not been widely accepted. It certainly has not influenced biblical translators, who continue to translate the term tendentiously. The New RSV
(1989) renders it as "sodomites" – an unhistorical, unclear, and deceptive

---

[7]   John Boswell, *Christianity, Social Tolerance, and Homosexuality: Gay People in Western
Europe from the Beginning of the Christian Era to the Fourteenth Century* (Chicago and London: University of Chicago Press, 1980), p. 344, with the whole argument pp. 341–53.

translation. Certainly Paul knew the story of Sodom from Genesis 18–19; if he had wanted to allude to it in condemning certain sexual practices, he could have. (We will come to that story from Genesis in a moment.) Boswell's argument has also not convinced many scholars, who have offered alternate guesses as to the meaning of *arsenokoitai*. One of the most interesting concedes Boswell's point about the lack of evidence for the term before Paul, but then hypothesizes that it had been coined in Greek-speaking Jewish circles to translate the rabbinical term for male–male copulation, *miškav zakur*, "lying with a male."[8] Perhaps so, but this would only push our question about the term's meaning back one stage so far as scriptural exegesis goes. The Old Testament passages most often cited by Christians in condemnation of same-sex relations pose their own problems of terminology.

The passages are a pair of verses from the middle of the "Holiness Code" in Leviticus. The code contains purity regulations or taboos meant to ensure that the Israelites will be kept apart from their enemies, the Canaanites, who have defiled the land. The code designates as "unclean" in one degree or another blood in animals, human corpses, menstruating women, some foods, and particular diseases or physical defects. The code further and specifically prohibits mixing some substances that are neutral in themselves. So, in Leviticus 19:19, we are told that there are to be no interbred cattle, no mixed plantings of crops, and no mixed fibers in cloth. In a moment I will raise questions about the pertinence of the entire Holiness Code to Christian ethics, but now I underscore just a terminological problem. In the middle of this Code, we find these two verses:

> And with a male you shall not lie the lying down of a woman (*miškebê 'iššâ*); it is *tô'ebâ*. [18:22]
>   And as for the man who lies with a male the lying down of a woman, they – the two of them – have committed a *tô'ebâ*; they shall certainly be put to death; their blood is upon them. [20:13][9]

There are two difficult phrases here. One is the phrase translated as "lying down of a woman." This phrase occurs only in the Holiness Code, that is, only in these two verses. Every other sexual regulation in Leviticus is

[8]   Robin Scroggs, *The New Testament and Homosexuality: Contextual Background for Contemporary Debate* (Philadelphia: Fortress Press, 1983), pp. 107–8.
[9]   I follow here the translations proposed by Saul Olyan, " 'And with a Male You shall Not Lie the Lying Down of a Woman': Meaning and Significance of Leviticus 18:22 and 20:13," *Journal of the History of Sexuality* 5 (1994): 179–206, at p. 180.

repeated somewhere else in the Hebrew scriptures. This one is not, so we cannot compare alternate scriptural renderings of the same law. Arguing by analogy to other phrases, some scholars think that the first verse refers to anal intercourse between men and that it is addressed to the "active" or insertive partner. If so, the prohibition has nothing to do with women and – in 18:22 at least – nothing to do with the "passive" or receptive partner. It would also not prohibit same-sex erotic activities other than anal intercourse: the phrase does not include oral sex, or mutual masturbation, or a number of other practices.

The second difficult term in these verses is *tô'ebâ*, which has traditionally been rendered as "abomination." The term is used in Leviticus and other parts of the Hebrew scriptures for a wide variety of offenses that seem to be linked only in being violations of socially significant boundaries. The death penalty prescribed here for this offense is also not unique. It is given to a number of other sins, including cursing one's father or mother (20:9) and adultery (20:9–10). By contrast, exile is prescribed for having sexual intercourse during menstruation, while the daughter of a priest who turns to prostitution is sentenced to burning. So the meaning of the *tô'ebâ* is hardly captured by "abomination" – or indeed, by any other single term or phrase in modern English. English does not now have a category that would cover what is covered by the Hebrew term, since we do not share a current, well-articulated terminology for ritual transgressions. We can stipulate that "abomination" is such a term (since it is now rarely used elsewhere), but then we must add a footnote explaining what it does and does not mean. What we cannot do is present "abomination" without comment as a self-evident translation.

Faced with these kinds of difficulties in texts outside of the Christian scriptures, secular scholars often adopt an agnosticism about the exact meaning of obscure terms and a skepticism about the possibility of accurate translation. Pushed to render an obscure term into English, they will often adopt a cumbersome paraphrase or just transliterate the original term. A few Christian theologians have been equally willing to admit the vagueness of Pauline terms. John Chrysostom, for example, claims that Paul left sexual terms deliberately vague in order not to offend against propriety – and because those who knew about them could fill in the vagueness well enough.[10] Rabbinic commentators have boasted that Hebrew contains no precise words for sexual relations because it is so pure.

---

[10]   John Chrysostom, *In epistulam I ad Thessalonicenses homiliae* (*Homilies on I Thessalonians*), 5.1, on verse 4.3, as in Jacques-Paul Migne, ed., *Patrologiae cursus completus . . . Series Graeca* (Paris: Migne, 1857–66) [cited hereafter as "Migne PG"] 62:424.

Most Christian moralists have generally not been agnostic about the meaning or rhetorical properties of sexual terms in their Bible, nor have they hesitated to translate them fluently and precisely. They have been so confident because they have assumed that they already knew which acts the terms named. They have been obligated to know, because they have understood how high the stakes in translation were. Christian moral theology has not been willing to let the biblical texts express precepts equivocally or unclearly. It has required that the texts be clear and certain. In order to ensure this, it has regularly imposed meanings on uncertain terms and projected general principles to reconcile conflicts among them. There may be reasons for doing these things, but they are not reasons within the scriptural texts.

While illustrating these points, I have deliberately reproduced one of the worst vices of the Christian use of scripture. I have jumped from verse to verse across documents of different genre and structure. I have treated the biblical verses as if they were free-floating atoms. They are not really atoms. They are small and often arbitrary segments cut from a much larger discourse. Hunting for the meanings of individual biblical words is barely the beginning of careful reading. Indeed, it can be something less than a beginning so far as it misleads us into thinking that words have meaning completely apart from their contexts. The meaning of words is determined by the uses to which they are being put. In texts, these uses are understood as rhetorical purposes – as the ends for which the text is written.

Textual Purposes

In its generational oscillations, the Christian reading of scripture has recently turned back toward larger units of meaning – to narratives and rhetorical patterns and sociohistorical contexts. News of the turn has been slow in spreading to the parts of Christian theology that claim to depend on scriptural exegesis. Christian ethicists still cite biblical verses as discrete sections of a universal moral code. Official denominational documents are particularly liable to quote the New Testament as if it too were an official denominational document – that is, a string of numbered rulings with independent force. This is a very crude misreading of the varied and sophisticated moral rhetorics deployed in the New Testament. Failure to attend to the moral rhetoric of scriptural passages results, I think, in the loud misreadings of one of the best-known of Pauline passages, the first chapter of Romans. The passage has had a particularly important role to play in Christian sexual ethics, because it is the only passage that speaks of same-sex desire in both men and women, as it is the only one that speaks of both same-sex desire and same-sex activity. It has provoked – and certainly needs – the kind of attention to terms we have already practiced on other scriptural passages. But this passage requires even more urgently a rhetorical reading of its structure – a correlation of its structural features with persuasive motives.

Romans 1 is not principally about sex. It is principally about the consequences of idolatry, that is, the consequences of gentile refusal to acknowledge the one God, whose hand is evident even in the natural order. Paul's argument is that God delivered the gentiles over to various kinds of sin because they should have known better than to be idolaters. (In this he is following traditional Jewish depictions of idolatry, such as Wisdom 12:23–16:4.) After alluding to two kinds of sins in desire, Paul goes on to list some 21 other consequences of not knowing God (Romans 1:29–31), including greed, gossip, pride, disobedience to parents, and lack of mercy. This long list is part of Paul's grand accusation in Romans 1 through 3: all human beings, gentiles and Jews alike, are without excuse before God.

For sexual ethics, the crucial verses from Romans 1 have been the following:

> Claiming to be wise, they [the gentiles] became fools [1:22]; and they exchanged the glory of the immortal God for images resembling a mortal human being or birds or four-footed animals or snakes. [1:23]
>
> Therefore God gave them up in the desires (*epithumiai*) of their hearts to the impurity of dishonoring their bodies among themselves [1:24], because they exchanged the truth about God for a lie and worshipped and served the creature rather than the Creator, who is blessed forever. Amen! [1:25]
>
> On account of this God gave them up to dishonorable passions (*pathê*). Their women exchanged the natural use for one against [*or* beyond] nature [1:26], and in the same way also the men, giving up natural use of women, were consumed with willing (*horexei*) for one another: men committed what is shameful in men and received in themselves the fitting penalty for their error. [1:27]

You can hear the strict parallelism of these verses, which are laying out a disastrous history: Because the gentiles exchanged God's glory for idols, because they exchanged the truth of God for a lie, therefore God abandoned them to the "desires of their hearts," and so gentile women exchanged the natural "use" – of organs? partners? positions? – for "use" against nature. The men did the same, by a more or less strict analogy. Same-sex practices between gentile women or gentile men are here explained as the continuation or consequence of idolatry. Does this analysis imply that all same-sex love is a form or consequence of idolatry? No. Paul seems rather to be telling a particular historical narrative in which God's anger permits same-sex desire among the ancient gentiles as a punishment for their idolatry. That is a connection that we have seen already in the Pauline sin-lists, where idolatry, sexual sin, and greed are closely linked.

For what is the "natural use" exchanged? Obviously for one somehow distinct from nature: pagan women "exchanged the natural use for one beyond [or against] nature (*para phusin*)" (1:26). If Paul does mean to speak of sexual acts, he doesn't specify which ones are *para phusin*. Scholars debate whether the phrase refers to oral or anal sex between husband and wife, to bestiality, or to any kind of genital contact between members of the same sex. Other scholars think that it doesn't refer to specific sexual acts at all, but rather to a more general disruption of the social order caused when women, who are supposed to be subordinate to men, abandon their subordinate role in order to enter into equal relations with other women. What is beyond the natural use, on this reading, is for two women to be equal – or for any man to assume a submissive, "womanly" role.

Scholars are forced to debate these meanings because the phrase "beyond [or against] nature" is not elsewhere explained in the Christian Bible. If it was not scriptural, the concept of natural use was in Paul's time a technical notion for some schools of ancient philosophy, as it was in ancient medicine. Paul may have encountered the notion in popular philosophic teaching – indeed, he may have been competing against versions of the teaching in his own preaching. In the moral rhetoric of pagan Stoicism, the concept "*para phusin*" has wide rhetorical force. It is applied to anything excessive, anything beyond the reasonable course. So, for example, the early Stoics are reported as allowing that even a wise man will suffer impulses or melancholies that are against nature. At the same time, they are said not to have considered it unnatural to share their wives in order to put an end to jealousies arising from adultery.[11] According to another author, the great moralist Plutarch, any disease or fever is *para phusin*.[12] So are eating meat,

[11]   Diogenes Laertius, *Vitae philosophorum* (*Lives of the Philosophers*), 7.118, 131, in the life of Zeno of Citium. Greek and English versions can be found in Diogenes Laertius, *Lives of Eminent Philosophers*, trans. R. D. Hicks, Loeb Classical Library (Cambridge, MA: Harvard University Press, 1925). For a meticulous analysis of these and other possible parallels for Paul in Romans 1, see Bernadette J. Brooten, *Love between Women: Early Christian Responses to Female Homoeroticism* (Chicago and London: University of Chicago Press, 1996), pp. 241–53.

[12]   Plutarch, *Quaestiones conviviales* (*Table-Talk*), 731E, as in Plutarch, *Moralia*, trans. Frank Cole Babbitt, Loeb Classical Library (Cambridge, MA: Harvard University Press, 1927–). The Loeb volumes provide texts and translations for all of the passages from Plutarch mentioned here.

the use of an emetic or cathartic, and courage in women.[13] Perhaps Paul
has one of these gentile rhetorics in mind. Or perhaps he is thinking of a
second group of texts, ones in which Jewish writers borrowed the category
para phusin for their own rhetorical uses. Philo of Alexandria, for example,
uses the category *para phusin* to condemn sexual relations between a man
and a boy, but he also condemns as against nature the couplings of one
kind of animal with another, of a man with a menstruating woman, and of
a man with a woman known to be sterile.[14]

Hunting sources is uncertain business. Even if we had a much larger
sample of the texts Paul knew, even if we could convince ourselves by
verbal resemblances that we had in our hands the exact text(s) from which
Paul learned the phrase "natural use," there would be no reason to assume
that Paul understood that source text as we do – or that he meant to copy
its argument or other rhetorical patterns instead of revising them in some
fundamental way. Even if we became quite convinced that certain gentile
or Jewish parallels were pertinent to our reading Paul, we would have to
realize that our interpretive work had then only begun. We would have
still to understand how the argumentative or persuasive purposes in the
parallel texts might be related to the purposes in Paul's text.

Consider, for example, the fragments of the teaching of Musonius Rufus
(before 30 CE to before 101 CE). These fragments are often juxtaposed
with Paul's teaching on sexual matters to show the rhetorical contexts on
which Paul might have drawn. Among the surviving bits of Musonius's
teaching, there is a fragment "on the things of Aphrodite," that is, on
something like what we call sexual acts. The fragment begins by asserting
that sexual pleasures are no small part of voluptuousness. Voluptuaries
desire a variety of sexual partners "both according to the law and beyond
the law, not only women but also men," moving promiscuously from one
to another in search of rarified pleasures. "Those who are not voluptuaries
or evil should count as just only those sexual pleasures that are within

---

[13]   Plutarch, *De esu carnium* (*On Eating Meat*), 993E-F, 995B, 995D, 996B: for humans
to eat meat is *para phusin*; *De tuenda sanitate praecepta* (*Counsels on Caring for Health*),
134B: using emetics or cathartics is acting *para phusin*; *Amatorius* (*Dialogue about Love*),
761E: love can lead women to courageous acts *para phusin*.

[14]   Philo of Alexandria, *De spec. leg.* (*On the Special Laws*), 3.6.32: respect "law of nature" by not having sex with a menstruating woman; 3.6.36: only "enemies of nature"
marry women known to be sterile; 3.7.39: the pleasure of pederasty is *para phusin*; 3.8.47:
mixing animal species is against the "pronouncement of nature." The Greek text and
an English translation can be found in Philo of Alexandria, *Works*, trans. F. H. Colson
and G. H. Whitaker, Loeb Classical Library (Cambridge, MA: Harvard University Press,
1929–62).

marriage and directed to begetting children."[15] The most unlawful copulations are adulterous ones and those between men. Male–male intercourse
Musonius calls "an audacity contrary to nature" (86:10). All sexual intercourse outside of marriage dishonors a man, shows him to be susceptible
to shameful pleasures, makes him like a pig.

Now this passage from Musonius is not an argument in any ordinary
sense. It is an appeal to one's ideal of manly self-control, of superiority in
resistance to pleasure. It presumes that the hearer does not want to be a
voluptuary, and then it identifies a number of sexual acts as voluptuous.
The terms used to stigmatize these prohibited acts are "unlawful" (*paranomos*),
"ugly" or "shameful" (*aschêmôn*), and "unjust" (*adikos*). The one who does
the last of the prohibited acts is called "dishonorable" (*atimoteros*). The
only argument that Musonius offers comes in support of his most unusual
claim, namely, that a man shouldn't have sex with his female slaves. The
argument is a refusal of a double standard: You wouldn't want your wife
to do it, so don't do it yourself. This argument fails to apply, of course,
both to the unmarried and to those men who are indeed willing to let
their wives do it.

Shame also figures prominently in Paul's narrative of idolatry. Indeed,
terms for shame cluster particularly around the verses that describe same-
sex desires and acts, though they also appear elsewhere in the chapter. The
terms of shame seem to function in Paul as in Musonius, though not to the
same end. Musonius wants to reactivate feelings of shame in order to control
sexual behavior. Paul wants to reactivate them in order, immediately, to
link them to a long series of other sins, but more generally to argue that all
human beings, gentiles and Jews, have failed to respond rightly to God.
Romans 1 invokes strong feelings about some sexual desire or activity,
feelings of hot shame, within a narrative of idolatry that supports one half
of a general condemnation of human claims to righteousness apart from God.

Invoking Romans 1 as a prohibition against same-sex acts mistreats the
text in various ways. First, it overlooks difficulties about the meaning of its
central terms or the clarity of its central categories (especially the category
para phusin). Second, more importantly, it ignores the text's main purposes.
I myself believe that Paul viewed same-sex activity among the gentile
idolaters with queasy disdain and that he judged it a consequence of their

---

[15] Musonius frag. 12, as in Cora E. Lutz, "Musonius Rufus 'The Roman Socrates,'"
in *Yale Classical Studies*, vol. 10, ed. Alfred R. Bellinger (New Haven, CT: Yale
University Press, 1947), p. 86, lines 4–7. The same edition provides an English translation on facing pages. I will refer to the Greek text parenthetically in the discussion
that follows.

idolatry. He was willing to invoke the terms of pagan philosophy to condemn that activity, thus condemning the gentiles out on their own testimony, as it were. I further believe that the rhetorical force of Romans 1 depends on the presumption that his intended readers will share – or will profess to share – in his disdain for same-sex desires or acts. None of this makes Romans 1 a suitable source for a general Christian account of same-sex desire. Paul's rhetorical purpose in the passage is not to teach sexual ethics, but to refute all human claims to righteousness.

The interesting exegetical question about Romans 1 is not, What are its general arguments against same-sex relations? It offers no arguments of that kind, and it needs none for its purposes. The interesting question is, How did this passage get to be used as a proof-text in Christian moral teaching? This question points to a more general problem in our reading of scripture, which is the problem of always receiving scripture already categorized under some scheme of moral topics. We already know which verses are supposed to answer which moral questions.

Textual Topics

Texts do not interpret themselves. They also don't apply themselves to moral problems. Even detailed legal codes require judicial application, because there is a conflict of rules, or a dispute over interpretation, or a set of facts that do not fit neatly within any of those the code provides. The diverse scriptural texts require greater feats of interpretation before they can be applied to the moral difficulties of daily life. A Christian community's tradition has as one of its major tasks deciding which parts of scripture ought to be cited for which kinds of situations. Each interpretive tradition assembles a kind of index for connecting cases to scriptural authorities. It must then immediately change the index. New cases appear; old texts are reinterpreted. The changing index carries on its work of connecting cases to texts – that is, of labeling certain passages for moral purposes. Once the assignment is made, it can be quite difficult for Christian readers to see through the assignment to earlier meanings or purposes in a text. Scriptural verses disappear under their ethical interpretations. This is illustrated nowhere more clearly than in the reception of the story of the destruction of Sodom and Gomorrah in Genesis 18–19.

The story is fairly odd for modern readers, no matter how it is applied to moral cases. It can seem easier to understand as a piece of ancient folklore than as a moral teaching. In anthropological perspective, for example, the story contains a number of recognizable elements: divine messengers or manifestations who save hospitable humans from general destruction, as in the Greek myth of Baucis and Philemon; or perilous escapes from the kingdom of death, as in the myth of Orpheus and Eurydice; or ancient catastrophes that explain natural phenomena, like the pillars of salt. If we want to understand what the story is about in scriptural context, we can turn to the closely parallel Hebrew story in Judges 19–20. That story is about the lethal rape of a travelling Levite's concubine, an outrage that leads the other tribes of Israel to slaughter the offenders. What the two stories share is not the motif of same-sex desire, but the motif of violence against strangers. It is according to this motif that the sin of Sodom is interpreted in the Hebrew scriptures themselves.[16] We read in Ezekiel 16:49 (NRSV): "This was the iniquity of your sister Sodom: she and her daughters had pride, overabundance of bread, abundance, and leisure, but they did not extend their hand to the poor." Isn't that exactly what Lot himself says to the threatening crowd? He doesn't say, You men can't have sex with another man – or, rather, an angel masquerading as a man. He says, "Do nothing to these men, for they have come under the shelter of my roof."

How then did Christian readers come to think of the sin of Sodom as a sexual sin? That is a good question, to which there is a long historical answer. I will only point to the beginning of the answer now. The association of Sodom with strange sexual practices happens under the influence of what are now extra-canonical Jewish writings from the period between the two Testaments (as Christians call them).[17] The change is reflected in some of the minor writings of the second Testament. In what we know as the letter of Jude, we read:

> Just as Sodom and Gomorrah and the nearby cities, committing *porneia* and going after other flesh in the same way [as the fallen angels] – just as they were made an example, suffering the punishment of eternal fire, so too will it be for those who stain the flesh and spurn authority and blaspheme against majesties. [vv. 7–8]

"Other flesh" – a strange phrase. It seems to remind us that the objects of attack in Sodom were angels, not men. It may also allude to a desire for

[16] When it is not used generally as a figure of desolation, or of divine judgment, or of a poisonous land (desolation: Deuteronomy 29:23, Isaiah 13:19, Jeremiah 49:18 and 50:40, Zephaniah 2:9; judgment, Lamentations 4:6, Amos 4:11; poisonous: Deuteronomy 32:32; general sin: Isaiah 3:9, Jeremiah 23:14).

[17] This argument is now an old one. It was already put forcefully in Derrick Sherwin Bailey, *Homosexuality in the Western Christian Tradition* (London, New York, and Toronto: Longmans, Green, 1955), pp. 9–28.

sex with celestial beings (as in Genesis 6:1–4, where the sons of God mate
with the daughters of humans and produce a race of giants). In short, the
story of Sodom is associated with sexual sin rather late in the history of
Judaism and as part of a system of unusual ideas – to put it mildly. The
association works because of the ambiguity of the Sodomites' request.
"Where are the men who came to you tonight? Bring them out to us, so
that we may know them" (Genesis 19:5, NRSV). Sometimes the verb "to
know" is a euphemism in Hebrew for copulation, and Lot seems to take
it that way in the next verse. Of course, most often "to know" means to
know, and so reading it sexually here is a conjecture. Lot may have misunderstood the request, after all. He may have wanted to misunderstand
it. If the Sodomites are speaking sexually, the sexual act they intend would
not be male–male intercourse so much as rape.

On no reading of Lot's answer can he understand them to be men who
only want sex with men. Lot says to them, "Look, I have two daughters
who have not known a man; let me bring them out to you, and do to
them as you please" (19:8 NRSV). This is an appalling offer. The best that
can be made of it is that Lot is emphasizing the seriousness of the crime of
violence to guests. Lot seems to be saying, "Better that you should do
violence to my own virgin daughters than to these strangers." Whatever
Lot is thinking, he cannot be thinking that he is dealing with a crowd of
"homosexuals" in the modern sense. What sense would it make for Lot,
surrounded by violent male homosexuals, to try pacifying them by sending
out women as a sexual offering? It is a horrible offer, but also a silly one if
he knows the men outside desire only other men.

Only a long-received tradition of interpretation could lead readers to
keep using this story in contemporary discussions of homosexuality. When
we stand by such interpretations, we say more about the force of reception, about the persistence of systems of theological topics, than we do about
the biblical text. Similar traditions also tacitly determine our relation to the
normativity of biblical texts. After all, why would a modern Christian
theologian be looking to a *narrative* about the destruction of a quasi-
legendary city for a law about sexual behavior? Why, indeed, except that
centuries of tradition require that we should do so – both by connecting
that narrative to the moral topic of same-sex acts and by confusing ordinary
notions of where to find normative moral teaching.

Textual Norms

The first moral controversies in the Christian communities were disputes
over how much of Jewish law should apply to Christians. We find traces

of the controversies in the New Testament – in the Pauline letters, of course, but also and quite importantly in the historical narrative of Acts. The controversies were resolved for "mainstream" Christianity by a fairly dramatic rejection of ritual demands: no circumcision, no purity rules, no observance of Jewish holy days, no animal sacrifices, and so on. The Christian who now wants to cite Leviticus as law has to show why the original Christian rejection of Jewish law doesn't rule out such use. Of course, the problem about the normative value of Jewish law for Christians is part of a larger problem for Christian reading – indeed, part of the original problem. For decades before the elements of the New Testament were composed, and for centuries before they were canonized, Christians were faced with the Torah and the texts affiliated with it. The original Christian scriptures were the Jewish scriptures, interpreted or corrected by memories about Jesus and by apostolic teaching. So Christians had to become adept at explaining their relation to the provisions of Jewish law.

One typical explanation distinguishes ritual or ceremonial precepts from ethical or moral ones. Christians are bound by the moral commandments of the Old Covenant, but not by the religious observances built around them in Judaism. In medieval Christian authors, this dichotomy becomes a triplet: the laws of the Old Testament are divided into ceremonial, judicial, moral.[18] Ceremonial laws are the laws of Jewish ritual, intended by God to be observed only until the coming of Jesus. With the coming of Jesus, the ceremonial laws are supplanted by the ritual of the Christian community, and it is no longer permissible to observe them. The judicial laws comprise the various provisions for the government of Israel. These laws had been provided by God for the time of Israel's political independence. After the coming of Christ, they might be observed by Christian rulers, but there is certainly no moral obligation to do so. The last set of Old Testament laws, the moral laws, were given by God through the Jews for all time. They are as binding on Christians as on non-Christians.

This trichotomy has been described in varying detail by generations of Christian theologians. It is much easier to describe than actually to apply. The Hebrew Bible does not come with authoritative indications of which verses belong to which kinds of law. Christian theologians have been

---

[18]   See, for example, Thomas Aquinas, *Summa theologiae*, part 1–2, question 99, articles 2–4, as in the edition by the Institutum Studiorum Medievalium Ottaviensis (Ottawa: Studium Generalis Ordinis Praedicatorum, 1941–5). The most accessible contemporary translation of the *Summa* is probably the so-called "Blackfriars" version, *Summa theologiae: Latin Text and English Translation, Introductions, Notes, Appendices, and Glossaries* (London: Eyre & Spottiswoode, and New York: McGraw-Hill, 1964–73), in 60 vols.

required to impose the distinction on texts that resist it in many ways. So it is not surprising that Christian theologians have disagreed over which precepts were ceremonial and which moral. Even the most obvious candidate for an Old Testament moral text is not free from these disagreements – I mean, the "Ten Commandments."

The Commandments have seemed so central to biblical morality that they have been the staple of Christian moral instruction. They have been used both for the structure of large-scale theological treatises and for display in Sunday-school classrooms. Still, we must admit that the Commandments are not without their difficulties as moral law. Leaving aside issues about how to number them, there is the challenge presented by the presence of the Sabbath commandment. Is that a moral law or a ceremonial one, or some mixture of the two? Moreover, if the Commandments are indeed fundamental moral law, why are they so selective? They offer very little guidance to sexual morality, for example. The only sexual sin explicitly mentioned in them is adultery (Exodus 20:14 and parallels). There is also the commandment against desiring to possess "your neighbor's wife, or male or female slave, or ox, or donkey, or anything that belongs to your neighbor" (20:17 NRSV). It seems, at least on its face, principally a commandment about property rather than about sexual organs or their pleasures.

The Commandments do not speak explicitly about a whole host of other sexual practices. In order to include these sins within the prohibitions of the Decalogue, Christian theologians have labored to show that they were logically or symbolically included in the prohibition of adultery. They have been doing this at least since the time of the *Didache*, which interpolates "corruption of boys" and "whoring" or "fornication" (*porneia*) after adultery in its list of prohibited acts for catechumens.[19] Fifteen centuries later, the Jesuit casuists would be reading hundreds of pages of detailed sexual regulation under the heading of the sixth Commandment (following one system of numbering). In the "Outline of the Faith" appended to the Episcopal Church's current *Book of Common Prayer*, the Commandment is rendered as the injunction "To use all our bodily desires as God intended."[20] We may be accustomed to these additions to the Decalogue, but we should recognize them as additions.

---

[19] *Didache* 2.2, as in *Patres apostolici*, ed. F. X. Funk (Tübingen: Laup, 1901), vol. 1, pp. 6–8.
[20] *The Book of Common Prayer and Administration of the Sacraments and Other Rites and Ceremonies of the Church together with the Psalter of Psalms of David according to the Use of the Episcopal Church* (New York: Oxford University Press, 1990), p. 848.

So even in the exemplary case of the Commandments, there is considerable difficulty not only in marking off ceremonial or judicial law from moral law, but in making the moral law clear and comprehensive. Christian moral theology wants to take certain Old Testament passages as permanent moral precepts. How is it to recognize a moral law in the midst of ritual laws? Is there something in the form of a statement that distinguishes it as a moral law? Do we expect, for example, that moral laws will be fair, will apply equally to all acts or agents of a certain kind? Do we expect moral laws to privilege intention over unintended effect or to take account of mitigating circumstances like coercion and ignorance?

Many passages that Christians have wanted to read as moral laws about sex don't seem to meet such expectations. I have already mentioned terminological problems about male–male relations in Leviticus 18 and 20. A larger question would be whether these verses much resemble what we now call moral or ethical precepts. They do not seem to categorize human actions in the way we expect of moral precepts. For example, 18:22 addresses only the "active" partner in anal intercourse. The corresponding verse in 20:13 begins by addressing the "active" partner, then shifts awkwardly in the middle to consider both "active" and "passive." It seems as if the second verse has been edited after the fact to make the receptive partner also subject to punishment. Note moreover that neither verse mentions such morally significant considerations as the age of the parties or the presence of consent. On the strict reading of the second verse, a boy of 12 raped by a man would have to be put to death. This is certainly how one ancient Jewish interpreter understood the phrase.[21] If this really is a moral precept rather than a ceremonial or judicial one, it will require us to articulate and defend rather different notions of the sphere of the "moral."

Similar questions can be raised about sexual matters in the surrounding verses of Leviticus. For example, many of them are couched in terms of one person "uncovering the nakedness" of another. It is traditional to construe this simply as a euphemism for sexual activity of one kind or another, but that interpretation leaves a number of puzzles. If the prohibitions of incest within various degrees of blood relation or marital kinship seem understandable as moral laws (Leviticus 18:6–18), the prohibition of intercourse during menstruation that follows immediately after them might seem to modern readers more a ceremonial law (18:19).[22] We might then

---

[21]   Philo, *De spec. leg.*, 3.7.38–39, but cf. 1.60.325.

[22]   For an introduction to changes in Christian views of menstruation, see Dyan Elliott, *Fallen Bodies: Pollution, Sexuality, and Demonology in the Middle Ages* (Philadelphia: University of Pennsylvania Press, 1999), pp. 2–5.

think it unjust that the penalty prescribed for the latter offense is being cut off from the community (20:18). But the more urgent question is whether the phrase "uncover the nakedness" really is just a euphemism for unspecified sexual activity or whether it doesn't also invoke notions of pollution by sight. Might it be that the very category we take as a moral categorization of sexual acts is in fact ceremonial?

Traditional disagreements over dividing moral from ceremonial or judicial precepts are structurally similar to very contemporary difficulties posed by advances in scholarly study of ancient Judaism. As a historical record, the books of the Old Testament refer to a number of sexual practices or arrangements that Christian churches have wanted to condemn. The basic family or kinship structures of early or First Temple Israel were certainly not ones that Christian churches want now to adopt. The urgency of reproduction, of continuing the family line or kinship unit, authorized not only polygamy (for such exemplary figures as Abraham, Isaac, Jacob, and Moses), but also the use of surrogate childbearers (Genesis 16 and 21). The survival of the family was also judged to require a frightening degree of authority over female children, which, if not unusual in ancient societies, hardly seems a moral model for contemporary Christians. We have already noticed Lot's willingness to hand over his virgin daughters to a crowd of violent men (Genesis 19:8). We read elsewhere provisions for selling daughters into slavery as a "wife" in a polygamous household (Exodus 21:7–11) and of the (regretted) sacrifice of a virgin daughter as a thank-offering to God (Judges 11:29–40). The social history of ancient Judaism presents a number of disturbing features that make it difficult to think of using ancient Hebrew law *in toto* as a moral guide for Christian ethics.[23]

The Old Testament stories can also seem to authorize rather different ethical precepts. It is often argued that some of the most striking stories of commitment are between members of the same sex, as Ruth and Naomi or David and Jonathan. Other Old Testament stories about male–female marriage suggest that God cares little for the ordinary proprieties, as when the prophet Hosea is directed to marry the prostitute Gomer. Certainly the story is an allegory of God's relation to Israel, but it is an interesting allegory for what it suggests of human marriage.

---

[23] For some examples, see Joseph Blenkinsopp, "The Family in First Temple Israel," in *Families in Ancient Israel*, ed. Leo G. Perdue, Joseph Blenkinsopp, John J. Collins, and Carol Megers (Louisville, KY: Westminster/John Knox, 1997), pp. 48–103, here pp. 64, 67, 75; John J. Collins, "Marriage, Divorce, and Family in Second Temple Judaism," in *Families in Ancient Israel*, pp. 104–62, here pp. 147–9.

If the social history of ancient Israel is sometimes distressing for modern Christians, the theological core of Old Testament teaching might offer something more consistent and more helpful. But what is in that theological core? Some would say that it consists of certain core "values," such as creation or fidelity in covenant relations, illustrated most of all in God's relation to the world and especially to Israel. Others would say that the core values are found in Old Testament stories of personal commitment or long trust despite trials. Unfortunately, appeals to general principles of fecundity and fidelity or to exemplary stories only postpone ethical questions to another stage of interpretation. The principles and the stories are open in their turn to conflicting ethical interpretation – and to some doubts about their moral character. For example, "fecundity" as a principle might require that every human copulation be aimed toward conception and child rearing or it might require rather that every erotic relation be nurturing to those within it and around it. A principle of "fidelity" might imply a lifelong, mono-gamous commitment or it might only imply a steadfast respect for a partner's spiritual growth – precisely as that partner moves on to another relationship.

These are some difficulties in Christian appeals to the Old Testament as normative for sexual ethics. Do they also afflict appeals to the New Testa-ment, which might seem much more normative for Christian living? We will encounter pieces of this question in the chapters that follow, but it is worth noting here the most basic issues. First, it is notoriously true that the New Testament texts do not offer anything like an unambiguous and comprehensive code for daily behavior, including sexual behavior. They do not set out anything like the detailed codes found in parts of the Old Testament or in many other religious scriptures. Moreover, the different genres of the New Testament do not always agree about the moral points they do address. It is misleading to speak of "a biblical ethic" or "biblical morality" or even "a moral vision of the New Testament" unless one specifies how exactly these biblical texts are being reconciled.

I can illustrate some of the difficulties by juxtaposing (too simply) moral teaching in the genre of the Gospels with that in the genre of the Pauline letters. The Gospels that we have contain a number of radical injunctions that seem to require a complete rejection of sex and biological family. "Make yourselves eunuchs for the sake of the kingdom of God" is not a large foundation on which to build an ethic of sexual behavior. How exactly would one treat that as a norm – unless by allegorizing it or ignoring it in favor of a sexual ethic derived from elsewhere? The Pauline texts, by contrast, do seem to offer more particular counsels, some of them borrowed from Jewish or pagan sources. Yet these counsels are, in ways we have seen, unclear or abstract to the eyes of ordinary reading. If the

Old Testament seems to give too many norms about sexual matters too confusedly, the New Testament says too little about them and does so enigmatically or abstractly. Certainly there is no explicit discussion in the New Testament of a number of sexual practices that preoccupy modern moral theology. The Gospels and the other kinds of texts never provide anything like a classification of sexual behaviors, much less specific directives about them.

Many or most kinds of human sexual activity may have occurred in the societies that produced and first read the biblical texts. Indeed, we presume that people then were having sex in various combinations of genders (or species) and using various parts of their bodies. Still, we may also conclude that the scriptural texts were not much interested in analyzing or regulating that behavior in detail − except as it affected other urgent concerns, such as family survival, or community purity, or openness to the call of Christ. It may be that secular reading discovers in the Christian Bible, not so much a series of norms about sex, as a series of asides and a larger silence.

From Scholarly Reading to Faithful Interpretation

Secular reading of the Christian Bible is not the believer's reading. The four levels of textual engagement we have come through, from terms to norms, are not the limits of what faith sees or seeks in its Bible. Christian interpreters appeal to many interpretive principles other than scholarly ones in finding moral guidance within the scriptures. They invoke the Holy Spirit's private inspiration, a traditional rule of faith, the testimony of liturgical experience, or the authority of denominational declarations and agencies for interpreting them. These and other principles discover in the scriptural texts many levels of moral meaning beyond those available to secular scholarship. For example, they allow faithful readers to understand the erotic imagery in the Song of Songs not only as a norm for married life, but as a deep teaching about progress in prayer. They authorize moral theologians to discover under the brief text of the Ten Commandments a whole code of sexual prohibitions.

These are legitimate and even necessary ways of reading scripture within communities of faith. They are also necessarily divisive in the ways I suggested at the beginning of this chapter, since they exclude readers who are not within a particular community. What is more important, these ways of reading enact a very different relation to the text of the Christian Bible than the relation of secular reading. Faithful readings of scripture treat the text as an occasion for divine instruction. The text becomes an instrument through which moral truths are discovered, constructed, and handed down. The text no longer *contains* moral teaching so much as it *gives occasion* for moral teaching. Different communities have received contrary moral teachings on the occasion of a single text, not least because they have expanded or supplemented the text according to contrary practices of interpretation. If the Christian Bible is and must be the foundation of Christian ethics, it is a foundation that invites believers to construct very different buildings.

There is no neutral way to cut through the diversities of faithful reading – any more than there is to cut through the painful divisions among Christian groups. But I want to end our consideration of scriptural authorities for sexual teaching by pointing out that the differences among Christian uses of scripture are in some ways a faithful reflection of inescapable multiplicities in our present situation.

The oldest of these multiplicities are contained within the scriptures. The scriptural texts that Christians have typically cited when teaching about sex contain different systems of images or principles. These images and principles cut across each other as they pick out and dichotomize aspects of human sexual life. Some of the scriptural passages regard sexual desires, organs, or secretions as intrinsically shameful and impure substances. Contact with them contaminates. Others divide sexual acts into the permitted and prohibited according to various analyses of them precisely as acts. Performing certain kinds of illicit sexual acts brings judgment and punishment. Still other passages conceive types of persons distinguished by their devotion to certain sexual practices. These persons are to be avoided or excluded. Such different ways of thinking about the matter of sex not only divide it differently, they also fuel different sorts of preoccupations – which is to say, different sorts of rules, justifications, and exhortations.

We need to be faithful as well to other multiplicities in our present situation as readers of our Bible. The plain fact is that anyone who wants to be both a faithful reader in some Christian group and a student of modern biblical scholarship will find herself or himself having to be multilingual. The languages of faithful reading and of contemporary biblical scholarship are not the same. We have been living for two centuries now in a situation where the academic study of the Christian Bible has pulled so far away from the other parts of Christian theology as to seem a separate country. It is not only in ethics that theologians find it very difficult to be both "constructive" and "exegetical," to build a coherent theology on the formidable and yet foreign labors of biblical scholarship. The most we can hope for, I think, is to be able to speak the languages of both construction and exegesis with tolerable fluency.

Being faithful to the scriptural authorities means being faithfully multi-lingual. This is no new challenge for Christian thinkers. From its beginnings, Christian discourse about sex has had to contend with diversity in the readings of its most authoritative source. There has never been a monolithic Christian tradition from which dissidents or decadents have departed. There has only and always been a contradictory set of discourses accumulated over time in response to complex and perhaps contradictory authorities. Christian sexual ethics has always had a plurality of languages, and it has played them off against one another with different results. When modern ethicists play the languages off each other differently, they are not for that reason being unfaithful to the scriptures. They are doing what Christian readers have always done – which is to use new problems or cases to force a reconsideration and recombination of scriptural authorities.

The scriptural texts have authority because they function in Christian communities as perennial topics. In classical rhetoric, a topic is a pattern for generating new speech, for finding something to say about a given case or theme. The long history of Christian reading has made certain scriptural passages into topics within the discourse of sex. These scriptural texts have been authorities not only because of what they say about sex. They have been authorities because of how much they have enabled generations of Christians to say. We return to certain scriptural authorities again and again because we find them saying new things – which is to say, because they enable us to say new things.

Chapter 3

A New Life beyond Sex

The original Christian ideal for sex was of a new life beyond it – of a life in which there had never been sexual relations or in which sexual relations had been renounced. Early Christian communities, of course, welcomed couples who had been married according to Jewish or pagan law. Indeed, they welcomed married persons and couples into roles of leadership. We read in the New Testament letters advice and regulation for Christians who are or will be married. Still the original *ideal* presented in authoritative Christian texts was a life before marriage or beyond it. It was an ideal of celibacy or (better) virginity as a response to the Gospel and a premonition of the coming of the Kingdom.

The original ideal has been rediscovered by centuries of Christian readers. They thought that they found it as a scriptural topic in a number of New Testament passages.[1] They then implemented it in a variety of institutional arrangements. Between exegesis and legislation, hundreds of conceptions or justifications for the call to celibacy or virginity have been constructed. Tracing some of the constructions, we may be able to understand a little better both the attractions and the tensions in the textual ideal of a life beyond sex.

Hard Sayings

Some Christians seem to believe that ideals of celibacy or virginity were produced by decadence in the church, by falling away from the pristine message of the New Testament. They find this decadence especially in the "worst" periods of medieval Catholicism or in the "bizarre" customs of the Eastern

---

[1] For an extended argument that patristic writing exaggerated or distorted passages in the service of these topics, see Elizabeth A. Clark, *Reading Renunciation: Asceticism and Scripture in Early Christianity* (Princeton, NJ: Princeton University Press, 1999).

Churches. For these Christians, the New Testament teaches that most or all Christians should enter into something very much like a modern, bourgeois marriage. But this view seems incompatible with important passages in the canonical New Testament, not to speak of theological traditions or whole epochs of church history. The teachings of the different pieces of the New Testament on the unmarried state may not be unambiguous, but then much less are they a ringing endorsement of marriage. On the contrary, many of them have plausibly appeared to centuries of Christian readers rather the opposite.

In the synoptic Gospels, several of Jesus' more obscure sayings have been taken as calls to a new life without sex. The most famous is the curious saying about eunuchs. In a conversation with "some Pharisees," Jesus replaces Jewish law on divorce with a much stricter standard: "'whoever divorces his wife except for *porneia* and marries another commits adultery (*moicheia*)'" (Matthew 19:9).[2] The disciples interject: If that is the rule for marriage, it would be better not to marry. Jesus replies:

> Not everyone can accept this saying (*logos*), but those to whom it is given. For there are eunuchs who have been so from their mother's womb, and there are eunuchs who have been made eunuchs by others, and there are eunuchs who have made themselves eunuchs for the kingdom of heaven. Let this be accepted by the one who can accept it. (19:11–12)

Jesus' saying is indeed obscure. As some contemporary readers have noted, it is introduced here by a discussion of divorce, and so it may refer to conduct within marriage. To live in a marriage according to the severe standard announced by Jesus is to make oneself a eunuch for the sake of the Kingdom. But many older Christian traditions did not read the saying as an illustration of the rigors of marriage. They read it as an invitation to renounce marriage for the sake of the kingdom. To these readers the passage seemed a counsel of virginity or celibacy. (Indeed, some went further, taking it as a literal command: there are mentions of voluntary castration and praises for it in some important Christian authors.)[3] Unfortunately, the saying is not reported in the parallel discussions nor, for that matter, elsewhere in the canonical Gospels. Its meaning cannot be settled by appeal to another

---

[2] I will consider in chapter 5 the differences between this passage and its parallels as regards the possible grounds for Christian divorce.

[3] The most famous remarks are by Origen. See, for example, his comments on Matthew 19:12 at *Commentaria in Matthaeum* (*Commentary on Matthew*), 15.2–3, in *Origenes Werke*, vol. 10, ed. Erich Klostermann and Ernst Benz, Griechischen Christlichen Schriftsteller der ersten drei Jahrhunderte [cited hereafter as "GCS"], vol. 40 (Leipzig: J. C. Hinrichs, 1935), pp. 353–7 (Migne *PG* 13:1257–61). Compare Justin Martyr, *Apologia* ("*First Apology*"), 29 (Migne *PG* 6:374), for an approving mention of a Christian youth in Alexandria who sought permission to be castrated.

version. Still, those who wanted to read the saying as a call to a life beyond sex could draw on related Gospel passages.

There are, for example, moments in which Jesus denigrates the biological family in favor of the new, spiritual, sexless "family" of his followers. In Matthew 12:46–50, Jesus is told that "his mother and his brothers" are waiting outside to speak to him. " 'Who is my mother?,' " he responds, " 'and who are my brothers?' " Jesus points to his disciples. " 'Here are my mother and my brothers! For whoever does the will of my father in the heavens is my brother and sister and mother.' " The same story is told in Mark 3:31–5 and Luke 8:19–21. Elsewhere, Matthew's Jesus teaches that faithful discipleship requires or provokes the rending of biological families (e.g., 10:21, 34–7). In Luke, too, the call to discipleship cuts against family obligations. One man wants to bury his father before joining Jesus. " 'Let the dead bury their own dead; but as for you, go and proclaim the kingdom of God' " (Luke 9:60). Another man wants to say goodbye to his family before leaving. " 'No one who puts a hand to the plow and looks back is fit for the kingdom of God' " (9:62). These sayings remind us that the men who followed Jesus as "disciples" are represented as having left everything, including any wives or children that they might have had. " 'Leaving our own behind we followed you' " (Luke 18:28). So it is easy to understand that Christian readers would have taken the saying about eunuchs as a call to discipleship in a life beyond sex. They heard from the Lord himself that there is not marriage after resurrection; the end of Christian striving is to be "like angels in heaven," neither married nor given in marriage (Matthew 22:30).

Christians who favored this view could also point to a much more explicit passage, not from the Gospels, but from Paul. In 1 Corinthians 7, Paul takes up a set of sexual issues supposedly raised for him by the Corinthians. (How far Paul reframes or invents these issues for his own rhetorical purposes is another matter.) His response is, as always, rhetorically complicated and dialectically stressed. Certainly Paul means to reject both the libertine permission for Christians to do whatever they want with their genitals (compare 6:12) and the ascetical demand, " 'It is good for a man not to touch a woman' " (7:1). Paul will endorse marriage as a protection against lust, but he will also commend a life without marriage – especially in view of impending, eschatological tribulations.

Are you bound to a wife? Do not seek to be free. Are you free from a wife? Do not seek a wife. Still if you do marry, you do not sin, and if a virgin marries, she does not sin. Yet those [who marry] will have distress in the flesh, and I would spare you that. I say this, brothers: the appointed time is coming close; from now on, let even those who have wives be as though they had none. . . . The unmarried man is anxious about the things of the

Lord, how to please the Lord; but the married man is anxious about the things of the world, how to please his wife, and he is divided. And the unmarried woman and the virgin are anxious about the things of the Lord, so that they may be holy in body and spirit; but the married woman is anxious about the affairs of the world, how to please her husband. . . . A wife is bound as long as her husband lives. But if the husband dies, she is free to marry anyone she wishes, only in the Lord. But in my judgment she is more blessed if she remains as she is. And I think that I too have the spirit of God. (1 Corinthians 7:27–9, 32–4, 39–40)

If this passage authorizes Christian marriage, it also advocates that Christians stay unmarried so long as they decently can. The advocacy is performed not just in Paul's recommendations, but in the system of images he uses to contrast the married and unmarried states. The person who is married is bound (vv. 27, 39), but the unmarried is freed or free (vv. 27, 39; the latter in regard to the choice of whom or whether to marry). The unmarried woman seeks to be "holy in body and spirit"; the married woman seeks her husband's satisfaction. The unmarried attend to the Lord; the married, to "the world" (*kosmos*). The married life is, at least for the near future, a life particularly vulnerable to distress of the flesh and its preoccupations (v. 28, in contrast with v. 32, their opposite). The choices would not seem to be evenly balanced or neutrally described. The rhetorical coloring commends a life without marriage. More importantly, twice in this chapter Paul points to his own unmarried state as what is preferable (vv. 7, 8), and he reiterates at the end of the discussion his prediction that an unmarried woman will be more blessed (*makariôtera*) – justifying it with a gently ironic reference to his own inspiration (v. 40).

Now Paul is quite clear that he does not have any "precept of the Lord" with regard to Christian virgins (*epitagê kuriou*, 7.25). Still his appeal to his own celibacy reminds us that we see in the New Testament no detailed representation of a married believer. All of the central models for the faith are, when Christian readers encounter them, living the faith outside of marriage. Who is the exemplar for the married Christian? Not Paul. Not the Twelve, who, whatever their marital state, are shown following Jesus as unmarried men.[4] Not Mary, whose virgin motherhood figures in Luke

---

[4] In non-canonical writings, there are representations of the apostles as married, but these often reinforce the teaching against sex. In the "Acts of Peter," for example, the apostle is taunted with not curing his own daughter's paralysis. To show what God can do, Peter cures her for a brief time, then returns her to paralysis. After all, she had been paralyzed by God to prevent her from sexual defilement. See the translation in J. K. Elliott, *The Apocryphal New Testament: A Collection of Apocryphal Christian Literature in an English Translation* (Oxford: Clarendon Press, 1993), p. 397.

and preoccupies the later tradition. Not Jesus, about whose sexuality it has always seemed blasphemous to inquire. If conformity to Jesus Christ is the standard for Christian ethics, then it is hard to see what the standard for Christian marriage might be.

We should contrast this with the question of the "sex" of God. It is often remarked that the God of what Christians call the Old Testament is distinguished from neighboring gods in being single. Yahweh does not have a divine consort and does not beget the world by copulation. If Yahweh is gendered male, it is with the presumptive maleness of power, not that of physical procreation. In the canonical scriptures, if not in the popular religion of ancient Israel, the God of the Hebrews is the only God, which means that there can be no copulation among divinities. While the Christian God is somehow both triune and single, still that God is not overtly sexualized – though the issues are complicated, as I will later stress, by the incarnation. It could be interesting to speculate how far a monotheistic religion in which God is gendered male might always have difficulty not only with women, but with sexual relations. My point here is rather that these mythic or archetypal questions about how the monotheistic Hebrew or Christian God might or might not teach sexual relations are very different from questions about the models of Christian sexuality in the main figures of the New Testament. For orthodox readers of the Gospels, Jesus Christ may be fully divine, but he is also fully human. It becomes humanly significant, then, that he is pictured as a virginal male. Moreover, the other protagonists of the canonical Gospels or the Pauline letters are fully human without being divine. Their witness to celibacy is all the more convincing.

Marriage appears on the margin of Christian life as we read of it in the New Testament. We hear of Christians living within marriage, but we do not hear much about them. They do not speak to us in their own voices about marriage; their lives are not narrated in approving detail. Moral principles are laid down for the married by those living as unmarried – and chiefly by Paul, who is at pains in various passages to stress his celibacy. If marriage was or quickly became the statistical norm among the first generations of Christians, it was not for all that the ethical norm, the *ideal*. The Christian ideal was an ideal of discipleship beyond marriage, which means, beyond sex. Those who want to make marriage the ideal for modern Christians have to argue against many passages in the New Testament – and many more in the library of early Christian writings. Indeed, early apologists would make it a boast to pagans that Christians forego marriage in order to be closer to God.[5]

---

[5] For example, Athenagoras, *Supplicatio pro Christianis* (*Appeal on Behalf of Christians*), 33, in *Zwei griechische Apologeten*, ed. Johannes Geffcken (Leipzig and Berlin, Teubner, 1907; repr. Hildesheim and New York: Georg Olms, 1970), p. 152 (Migne *PG* 6:966A).

Sex and "the World"

Early Christian readers took some New Testament passages as criticisms of
the family – or, rather, as invidious comparisons between the biological family
and the "true," "higher," "spiritual" family of the Christian community.
These passages elicited commentary, and commentary quickly enough became
invective. Denigrations of married life constitute a regular genre of Christian
literature from the "patristic" period to the present century. Here I will
not prove that assertion by cataloging works, nor will I trace the differences in these critiques of "family values" from century to century. I want
to rehearse only some of the exemplary arguments in a few critiques as a
way of showing both their seriousness and their thoroughness.

One excellent example is the exhortation to virginity composed by
Gregory of Nyssa around 371. It was written at the request of his brother
Basil, recently consecrated bishop of Caesarea. As bishop, Basil would
have charge over the ascetical communities within his jurisdiction. But
Gregory does not provide him with a rulebook for monastic life. On the
contrary, he announces that his work is a persuasion to virginity as the best
way to virtue for both men and women.[6] Indeed, he borrows a number of
rhetorical devices from Greek persuasions in philosophy and civil rhetoric.
We should expect, then, that some of Gregory's arguments are exaggerated
and deliberately provocative. Greek diatribes or protreptics, as they are called,
frequently mean to startle. So we anticipate provocative reversals in Gregory's
exhortation to Christian virginity. We may still be surprised by how strong
his argument sometimes is.

We expect to find in Gregory appeals to Jesus and Mary as virginal
examples, as we expect to find him paraphrasing Paul from 1 Corinthians
7 at many crucial points. We might even have predicted that he would
extend Paul's judgment in favor of virginity to the claim that the virginal
life is a certain foretaste of heaven. We may still be surprised to read that
virginity brings about God-likeness, a participation in the purity and in-
corruptibility of God.[7] We may be even more surprised by Gregory's
depiction of marriage as a tragic mistake from which evils flow into human
life – not just adultery, divorce, and betrayal, but greed, envy, anger,

---

[6]   Gregory of Nyssa, De virginitate (On Virginity), prologue, as in his Traité de la vir-
ginité, ed. and trans. Michael Aubineau, Sources Chrétiennes, vol. 119 (Paris: Éditions du
Cerf, 1966), lines 1–10. For a summary of the dating and circumstances of this work,
see Aubineau, p. 235. The most vivid introduction to Gregory's treatise remains Peter
Brown, The Body and Society: Men, Women, and Sexual Renunciation in Early Christianity
(New York: Columbia University Press, 1988), pp. 285–304.

[7]   Gregory of Nyssa, De virginitate, 1 (trans. Aubineau, lines 20–4).

hatred, empty ambition, and so on.[8] "The wish to be above others, the intolerable passion of pride, which can be called (without sinning against likelihood) the seed or root of every shoot of sin, this same passion has its origin from a cause which is just marriage."[9] Marriage is the leader of the tragic chorus of human life, and the sufferings of married life can only be described in high tragic manner.[10]

The tribulations of marriage are the macroscopic effects of a microscopic "sequence of passions" or "of sinning" set in motion by sexual pleasure.[11] If marriage is permissible to Christians, it is nonetheless full of dangers to the soul. Even the moderate use of lawful sex brings the risk that the weak will be drawn down into the flesh and trapped by it – will lose contact with the God who requires separation from flesh. Better, especially for the weak, to seek refuge in the "secure citadel" of virginity.[12] Entering that citadel, they will leave the kingdom of death for the kingdom of life. Procreating children feeds the cycle of death. To choose virginity in place of marriage, to forego childbearing and child rearing, is to resist the advance of death. Christ, born of a virgin, brought resurrection in place of endless death. "In every soul that surpasses fleshly life by virginity, the power of death is somewhat broken or dissolved."[13] To marry is to acquiesce in the kingdom of death. Find a teacher, then, who can give not only counsel about how to avoid marriage, but a consoling example of life without marriage.

The sharpness of Gregory's critique of marriage is answered in Latin writers of the same period, who had to translate the ideals of Eastern monasticism into the different symbols and arrangements of the Roman heartlands. Jerome is perhaps fiercest in his critique. He attacks marriage in detail when defending the perpetual virginity of Mary against Helvidius.[14] He returns to the attack when he exhorts the virgin Eustochium to persevere in her virginity, even at the cost of family relations. She is not to associate

---

[8] Gregory of Nyssa, *De virginitate*, 4.1 (trans. Aubineau, lines 2–3, 15–17).

[9] Gregory of Nyssa, *De virginitate*, 4.2 (trans. Aubineau, lines 11–15).

[10] Gregory of Nyssa, *De virginitate*, 3.10 and 3.2 (trans. Aubineau, lines 23–5 and lines 1–2, respectively).

[11] Gregory of Nyssa, *De virginitate*, 4.6 and 12.2 (trans. Aubineau, lines 1–2 and line 46, respectively).

[12] Gregory of Nyssa, *De virginitate*, 9.2 (trans. Aubineau, lines 1–3).

[13] Gregory of Nyssa, *De virginitate*, 14.1 (trans. Aubineau, lines 28–30).

[14] Jerome, *Adversus Helvidium de Mariae virginitate perpetua* (*Against Helvidius on the Perpetual Virginity of Mary*), 20–1, in Jacques-Paul Migne, ed., *Patrologiae cursus completus . . . Series Latina* (Paris: Garnier Fratres editores et J.-P. Migne successores, 1844–91) [cited hereafter as "Migne *PL*"] 23:200–2. Compare the English version in *St. Jerome: Dogmatic and Polemical Works*, trans. John N. Hritzu, Fathers of the Church: A New Translation (Washington, DC: Catholic University of America Press, 1965), pp. 39–43.

either with married women or with widows, who often fall into sexual luxury after a husband's death.[15] If Jerome will admonish a virgin to obey her parents in general, he will insist that she disobey them when they try to marry her off rather than let her follow a call to virginity. "No one should prevent you [from dedicating yourself to virginity] – not your mother, sister, kinswoman, brother. The Lord has need of you. If they want to impede you, let them fear the plagues of Pharaoh, who, because he did not want to permit the people of God to go worship Him, suffered what the Scriptures tell."[16] Even in heaven, the virgin's biological family will be kept apart from the virgin's new, spiritual family: "Your mothers, of the flesh and of the spirit, will be there in different flocks. One will rejoice that she bore you, the other will exult that she taught you."[17]

There are hundreds of early, medieval, and modern texts that repeat the same attack on the biological family. Many of these texts are nowadays judged extreme. But something similar can be found even in more "moderate" texts that almost everyone would count as central. Indeed, you can find a critique of family and the call to continence in one famous book that seems to assert the role of the family in conversion. I mean the *Confessions*, where Augustine tells his conversion in part as a fulfillment of his mother Monica's ancient prayers, in part as full reunion with her in Christian community. What is left out of this familial reading of the *Confessions* is that Augustine's conversion is centrally a conversion to celibacy – and so a final repudiation of Monica's schemes for her son's marriage.

What we misleadingly call the "moment" of Augustine's conversion in that Milanese garden was the end of a long accomplishment of moral persuasion. This persuasion did not occur in a moment. It took more than twelve years, as he explicitly reminds his readers.[18] The persuasion did not concern matters of dogma, as we would call it. Augustine did not need to assent to articles of a creed. He required rather a persuasion to change his

---

[15] Jerome, *Epist.* 22, 16.1–3, in *Hieronymus: Epistularum pars 1, Epistulae I–LXX*, ed. Isidorus Hilberg, Corpus Scriptorum Ecclesiasticorum Latinorum, vol. 54 (Editio altera supplementis aucta, Vienna: Österreichischen Akademie der Wissenschaften, 1996), p. 163, line 10, to p. 164, line 15. There is an English version in *Letters of St. Jerome*, trans. Charles Christopher Mierow, Ancient Christian Writers, vol. 33 (Westminster, MD: Newman Press, 1963), p. 147.

[16] Jerome, *Epist.* 22, 24.3 (ed. Hilberg 177.9–13; trans. Mierow, p. 157). For the general admonition to obey parents, see 17.1.

[17] Jerome, *Epist.* 22, 41.3 (ed. Hilberg 210.3–5; trans. Mierow, pp. 178–9).

[18] Augustine, *Confessions*, 8.7.17 (ed. Skutella, rev. Verheijen, line 14; trans. Chadwick, p. 145).

actions – and most especially in regard to sex. Book 8 of the *Confessions*, the book that ends in that garden, is a set of persuasive stories about the moral effects of storytelling. The stories are narratives of conversion. There is the conversion of Marius Victorinus, the very man who had translated the Neoplatonic books so decisive for Augustine's philosophical education. Then there are the conversions of two imperial officials who stumble upon the story of Anthony the Great, credited then as now with sparking popular movements to Christian monasticism. Ponticianus tells the story to Augustine and his friend, Alypius: At a liturgy, Anthony heard a verse from the Gospel. It persuaded him to abandon his possessions and his way of life in order to pursue God into the desert as a celibate. Stories about Anthony draw many others into deserts – literal and symbolic, east and west.

These stories within stories prepare for Augustine's own conversion to a life beyond sex. Certainly the famous scene in the garden is described as a "controversy" of soliciting voices – indeed, as the "angry litigation" of Augustine against himself.[19] On one side, his "old friends," "vanities of vanities," and "violent habit".[20] On the other side, there appears "the chaste dignity of Continence herself, serene and cheerful without flirting, coaxing decently."[21] At first Continence seems to say nothing. She coaxes decently only by reaching out toward Augustine, as if to embrace him. He discovers that she holds in her hands, not his body, but "flocks of good examples."[22] Continence smiles in exhortation, and only then does Augustine imagine her to speak. " 'Can't you do what these boys do, what these girls do?' " Still Augustine hears the murmuring from behind. The decent coaxing of Continence; the seductive whisperings of his familiar pleasures.[23]

---

[19] Augustine, *Confessions*, 8.11.27 and 8.8.19 (ed. Skutella, rev. Verheijen, lines 48, 13–14; trans. Chadwick, pp. 151, 146).
[20] Augustine, *Confessions*, 8.11.26 (ed. Skutella, rev. Verheijen, lines 20–1, 30; trans. Chadwick, p. 150).
[21] Augustine, *Confessions*, 8.11.27 (ed. Skutella, rev. Verheijen, lines 32–4; trans. Chadwick, p. 151).
[22] Augustine, *Confessions*, 8.11.27 (ed. Skutella, rev. Verheijen, line 36; trans. Chadwick, p. 151).
[23] Earlier Christian writers had already appropriated the figure of Continence for Christian use, among them the author of *Shepherd of Hermas* and Tertullian. See Pierre P. Courcelle, *Recherches sur les Confessions de saint Augustin* (2nd ed., Paris: Revue des Études Augustiniennes, 1968), p. 192, note 2; and James J. O'Donnell, *Augustine: Confessions* (Oxford: Clarendon Press, 1992), 3:53. What is more interesting is that Augustine had earlier described this figure as the figure of Philosophy (*Contra Academicos*, 2.25–6). I take it as significant that he here changes from "Philosophy" to "Continence."

Augustine, torn by the competing voices, goes off from Alypius a second time, to weep alone. It is now that he overhears the famous command chanted by a voice – a boy's or a girl's, he cannot tell. For once a voice appears to him not as male or female, not as holding a fixed position in the economy of lust, but simply as a child's voice – the voice of one of the children of Continence. The voice seems to come from one of the neighboring houses – or, perhaps, from the "divine house."[24] "Pick it up and read it" – that is the chant. Bewildered at first, Augustine then grasps the command. He rushes inside to find his copy of the letters of Paul. In it he reads, as if at random: "Not in riots and bouts of drunkenness, not in coupling-beds and impurities, not in strife and rivalry, but put on the Lord Jesus Christ and make no provision for the flesh in its desires."[25] Augustine is persuaded at last. He joins the children of Continence: he renounces the possibility of marriage. Or so the *Confessions* would have it.

Augustine's conversion to continence may indeed have left him a moderate defender of Christian marriage for other people, as we shall see in chapter 5. He does not make his conversion a general rule of sexual abstinence after baptism. Some ancient Christian churches did have such a rule. For Augustine, their practice would have seemed too close to the obligatory chastity of the Manichean "perfect," the leaders of the religious group he rejected in becoming Christian. Two qualifications need to be added. The first is that Augustine's espousal of marriage is perfectly consistent in his mind with ardent exhortation to the ideal of chastity. The second is that it did not deter later Christian writers from continuing to argue quite forcefully against married sex and the biological family. The strongest expressions of early invective against families continue to appear in later writers. We expect them in monastic or clerical reformers.[26] They are also to be found in moral writers with more general purposes.

---

[24] *Confessions*, 8.12.29 (ed. Skutella and Verheijen, lines 19–20; trans. Chadwick, pp. 152–3). The variant reading "de divina domo" may be recorded in Rome, Bibl. Victor Emmanuele MS 2099, of the early seventh century. For the problems with the variant, see O'Donnell, *Augustine: Confessions*, 3:62–3.

[25] Romans 13:13–14. The version quoted by Augustine differs in one salient aspect from the main textual tradition of the Vulgate. Where Augustine ends with "in concupiscentiis," the main tradition has "in desideriis." The difference is not unimportant given Augustine's views on rhetoric and desire.

[26] See, for example, the discussion of Bernard of Clairvaux's *Letter 322* and Isaac of Stella's *Sermon 29* in Caroline Walker Bynum, *Jesus as Mother: Studies in the Spirituality of the High Middle Ages* (Berkeley: University of California Press, 1988), pp. 145–6.

Among the many thirteenth-century handbooks of the virtues and vices, one has attracted particular attention as a source for Chaucer's Parson's Tale. The text, known by its opening word as *Postquam*, was written, perhaps by an English Franciscan, "not many years" after 1241.[27] We can take it as a typical medieval compendium on the moral life. What we notice immediately when we turn to the section on "continence" is how unequally divided it is. Topics include the chastity of spouses, of widows, and of virgins, but the chastity of spouses makes up less than 15 percent of the whole.[28] More than twice as much is said about the chastity of widows and four times as much about the integrity of virginity. The praises of marriage and of virginity are equally disproportionate. If there are four reasons why marriage is praiseworthy, some twenty commend virginity.[29] Note also the extremely negative depiction of sex within marriage. It is prey to demonic influences and it invites bestial analogies.

This typical medieval endorsement of virginity as higher and better in so many ways than marriage is answered, of course, by the Protestant Reformers' fierce critiques of professed or professional celibacy and virginity. But it is misleading, I think, to take their critiques simply as a repudiation of the older Christian ideals – however much they wanted to reject what they took to be medieval abuses. Certainly the Reformers' critiques reject many things: the denigration of marriage, the legal structure of vows, the disorder and superstitions of religious communities. But in some of the Reformers, at least, there is a cautious recognition of the old Christian call to a life beyond sex.

Luther's polemics against vows of celibacy or chastity are famously ferocious. Like all effective polemic, they go into battle with every argument they have at hand, without worrying particularly about how the arguments might stand together. The polemics also have different targets in view: Luther's critiques aim rather more at life under vows than at virginity or celibacy. Against vowed life, Luther objects from gospel notions of graced freedom and Christian equality. The specious distinction between universal "precepts" and special "counsels" of poverty, chastity, and obedience creates two orders of Christians where the Lord only intended one. But this is not yet a critique of life beyond sex. Against virginity and celibacy, Luther

[27] *Summa virtutum de remediis anime* (*Summa of the Virtues about Remedies for the Soul*), ed. Siegfried Wenzel, Chaucer Library (Athens: University of Georgia Press, 1984), pp. 11–12.

[28] *Summa virtutum*, ed. Wenzel, pp. 279–325.

[29] Cf. *Summa virtutum*, ed. Wenzel, pp. 279.26–9 with 301.411–303.466.

deploys rather different arguments, which are not so much condemnations
as restrictions. One argument is statistical: it is the assertion that the gift of
a life beyond sex is given by God much more rarely than medieval theology
supposes.

In a letter to nuns written in 1524, Luther claims that "Scripture
and experience both show that among many thousands there is not one to
whom God has given perseverance in pure chastity."[30] Indeed, Luther
goes on to argue that "a woman doesn't have power over herself. God has
made her body to be with man, to bear children and to raise them as the
words of Genesis 1:28 clearly state, and as is made known by the body's
members as ordered by God Himself." Luther here combines a stereotype
of women as sexually voracious with an argument from the design of
human reproductive organs.[31] The argument is generalized to include both
sexes: God has created man and woman to be together "in the married
way." Thus far, the polemic might be taken as a complete rejection of
celibacy – as if the statistics showed that no one in the whole human race
had been given "perseverance in pure chastity." But then Luther advises
that we should feel no shame in being as God made us to be, since most
of us are not given the "high, rare" gift of being otherwise.[32] Here the gift
is given, though very rarely. The gift of a life without reproduction – and
a fortiori without sex – must be as rare as other miracles that suspend the
created order.

In longer texts, Luther deploys a wider range of arguments. For example,
his *Judgment on Monastic Vows* (1521) includes appeals to Christian freedom
and equality, horrified denunciations of monastic vices, candid admissions
of the universality of lust, and reinterpretations of the key scriptural texts.
For all of that, Luther does not condemn the choice not to marry as an
ideal. He argues for it as a positive help to ministry – so long as it is done
freely in faith and not under the coercion of presumption. He agrees with
Paul that "the necessities of this life, the Christian life particularly, are

---

[30]   Luther, letter of August 6, 1524, no. 766 in the *Werke, Kritische Gesamtausgabe*
(Weimar: Herman Böhlau, 1883–), Abt. 4: *Briefwechsel*, vol. 3, pp. 327–8. (This series
of editions will be cited in what follows as "Weimar *Werke*.") See p. 327, lines 22–7,
for this and the quotation following. This letter was not selected for inclusion in the
English translations of *Luther's Works*.
[31]   And not only women. For Luther's respect for the "healthy elemental force of desire"
in both sexes, see Heiko A. Oberman, *Luther: Man between God and Devil*, trans. Eileen
Walliser-Schwarzbart (New York: Image Books, 1992), pp. 275–6. Note that Oberman
quotes a passage in which virginity is again described as a "high and rare grace."
[32]   Luther, Letter of 1524 (Weimar *Werke*, Abt. 4, 3:327:29/31).

carried more comfortably by those who are unmarried and free than by those who are married and bound."[33] Moreover, in a remarkable passage, Luther seems to hold that the good in real chastity cannot be perverted except by being made a temptation to presumption: "Because Satan could in no way turn [chastity] into its opposite, as he did with obedience and poverty, he left it untouched, though he turned it to the greatest evil (*perniciem*)," that is, by making it a temptation to presumption and lust.[34] Here God-given chastity would seem so intrinsically good that it can be perverted only by being made an occasion for another kind of evil.

Now these are only some of Luther's many words on virginity and celibacy. There are others that could be read in an opposite sense. My aim is not to provide a synthetic interpretation of Luther's "view," if he had only one. I want instead to suggest that the old Christian topics of life beyond sex are carried forward even into the Continental Reformers' texts. If the topics were not emphasized by the practice of Protestant churches, that may say more about evolving denominational culture or the need to maintain separation from Rome than about the availability of the topics in authoritative texts. The relation of church words about sex to church institutions for managing sex is always dialectical.

We can take another example of the dialectic – and another cautious recognition of life beyond sex – from Calvin. In the final version of the *Institutes* (1559), Calvin repeats an extended critique of monastic vows, particularly the vow of chastity.[35] He argues from the decadence of the late medieval monastic communities; he also presents, with ample textual support from Augustine, a picture of "a holy and legitimate monasticism."[36] Certainly Calvin means to deny the idea of a "double Christianity," in which some Christians are called to a life of "perfection" in response to special "counsels." He treats as execrable "the pretence that there is some more perfect rule of

---

[33] Luther, *De votis monasticis* (*Judgment on Monastic Vows*), in Weimar *Werke*, Abt. 1, 8:585:28–30, with a translation by James Atkinson in *Luther's Works*, ed. Jaroslav Pelikan and Helmut T. Lehman (St. Louis: Concordia, 1955–76, then Philadelphia: Fortress Press, 1955–76) [cited hereafter as "Luther's Works"] vol. 44 (Philadelphia: Fortress Press, 1966), p. 264.

[34] Luther, *De votis monasticis* (Weimar *Werke*, Alot. 1, 8:587.21–3; trans. Atkinson, *Luther's Works*, 44:267).

[35] Calvin, *Institutes* [1559], 4.13.8 21, in *Joannis Calvini opera selecta*, ed. Petrus Barth and Guilelmus Niesel (2nd ed., Munich: C. Kaiser, 1957–62), 5:244–58. There is a good English version in *Institutes of Christian Religion*, ed. John T. McNeill, trans. Ford Lewis Battles, Library of Christian Classics, vols. 20–1 (Philadelphia: Westminster Press, 1960), here vol. 21, pp. 1261–6.

[36] Calvin, *Institutes*, 4.13.10 (ed. Barth and Niesel, 249.29–30; trans. Battles, 21:1264).

life than that common rule which God has handed down to the whole Church."[37] But Calvin does not deny that there are some who are given this "special gift" by God.

> Those that have it should use it; if at some time they feel themselves troubled by flesh, they should take refuge in him by whose power alone they can resist. If they gain nothing, they should not contemn the remedy that is offered to them. Those to whom the faculty of continence is denied are clearly by the voice of God to marry.[38]

This passage is a critique, not of celibacy as a gift to some, but of celibacy as a legally enforceable vow made by too many. "We disapprove of the vow of celibacy for no other reason that that it is improperly considered worship (cultus), and is audaciously assumed by persons who do not have the power of restraining themselves."[39]

Calvin does strongly commend marriage in these pages. Having defended the ancient monasticism described by Augustine from its modern misprision, Calvin renders his own judgment: "It was fine, having thrown away their resources, to lack all worldly cares, but the pious governance of a household is more pleasing to God where the holy head of it, released from all avarice and free from ambition, and the other lusts of flesh, has as his purpose to serve God in a particular vocation."[40] This would seem to make marriage the higher estate, the way of perfection, but the marriage it means is mostly or entirely free from lust, that is, from sexual desire. A few paragraphs later Calvin will interpret 1 Timothy 5:12 as assuming that the execution of some church offices, at least in certain circumstances, does require celibacy:

> when those widows who were received into a public ministry imposed on themselves a condition of perpetual celibacy: if they afterwards married, we easily understand how, having thrown off all modesty, they became more insolent than befits Christian women. In this way they not only sinned by failing the faith of the Church, they revolted from the common rule of pious women.[41]

---

[37] Calvin, *Institutes*, 4.13.12 (ed. Barth and Niesel, 249.21–3; trans. Battles, 21:1266).
[38] Calvin, *Institutes*, 4.13.17 (ed. Barth and Niesel, 254:25–9; trans. Battles, 21:1272).
[39] Calvin, *Institutes*, 4.13.18 (ed. Barth and Niesel, 256:10–12; trans. Battles, 21:1273).
[40] Calvin, *Institutes*, 4.13.16 (ed. Barth and Niesel, 253.28–32; trans. Battles, 21:1271).
[41] Calvin, *Institutes*, 4.13.18 (ed. Barth and Niesel, 255.34–256.1; trans. Battles, 21:1273).

Calvin leaves room for a call to churchly service in which celibacy is the better state. Celibacy takes on an instrumental or circumstantial goodness.

Calvin's praise for marriage needs to be qualified or specified by reference to his own example, which was a powerful authority in the churches that looked to him for teaching. He was married for only seven years – to a widow with grown children he met after circulating a description of the qualities he sought in a wife. His ideal wife would be more chaste than beautiful, and she would refuse (with him) to enter marriage in the lustful hurry sparked by glimpsed beauty.[42] After his wife's early death, Calvin chose not to remarry, presumably because he judged himself beyond the temptation of incontinence. If he had felt such temptation, he would have been compelled to marry according to his own notions. But Calvin's own example in fact shows that a Christian grows toward a life after sex. It reinforces one reading of the Pauline ideal: marriage should be entered into as a protection against unlawful lusts, but the better life is life beyond sex.

More striking retrievals or reactivations of the old speeches about virginity and celibacy can be found in later Protestant writers. I take just one example. In 1743, John Wesley published a tract, *Thoughts on Marriage and a Single Life*. In it, he argued from Jesus' obscure saying on eunuchs that every Christian believer should remain single and celibate. Wesley rejected a distinction between counsels and commands; he advocated Christian perfection not as the ideal of a professional clergy, but as the demand on every baptized believer. For precisely that reason, he could not restrict the scope of the teaching in Matthew 19:10–12. Continence was a gift given to every person truly converted. What of those already married? They were to continue to fulfill their sexual obligations to their partners with God's help. Still their status was something to be regretted – something less than what Jesus had wanted in his followers.

Wesley's views were not well received even by his own associates.[43] So he was led to publish a revision of his tract, which he did in 1765 under a shortened title, *Thoughts on a Single Life*. The revised tract begins by rebuking those who would denigrate marriage. But Wesley returns to the

[42] John Witte, Jr., *From Sacrament to Contract: Marriage, Religion, and Law in the Western Tradition* (Louisville, KY: Westminster/John Knox, 1997), pp. 106–7.
[43] For the biographical circumstances, and some similar teachings in other groups, Henry Abelove, "The Sexual Politics of Early Wesleyan Methodism," in *Disciplines of Faith: Studies in Religion, Politics, and Patriarchy*, ed. Jim Obelkevich, Lyndal Roper, and Raphael Samuel (London and New York: Routledge & Kegan Paul, 1987), pp. 86–99, at pp. 86–9.

saying on the eunuchs, this time with a more pessimistic reading. It now seems to him that "every man is able to receive it when he is first justified. I believe everyone then receives this gift; but with most it does not continue long. . . . It is not so clear, whether God withdraws it of his own good pleasure, or for any fault of ours. I incline to think, it is not withdrawn without some fault on our part."[44] Everyone receives the gift of continence; most forfeit it by some failing. But for those who can keep it, Wesley has three principal lessons. The first is to "know the advantages" of being unmarried.[45] He lists several dozen, beginning with these: "You enjoy a blessed liberty from the 'trouble in the flesh,' which must more or less attend a married state. . . . You are exempt from numberless occasions of sorrow and anxiety. . . . Above all, you are at liberty from the greatest of all entanglements, the loving one creature above all others."[46] The second lesson is to "prize the advantages" of being unmarried.[47] The third is to be careful about not losing them.[48] Here Wesley adds a series of practical counsels about how to avoid sexual temptation. He is careful to praise marriage and to defend it against its attackers. But he ends with a quiet plea for celibacy: "Upon the whole, without disputing whether the married or single life be the more perfect state, . . . we may safely say, Blessed are 'they who have made themselves eunuchs for the kingdom of heaven's sake'; who abstain from things lawful in themselves, in order to be more devoted to God."[49]

The original ideal of Christian life beyond sex is a persistent ideal. It persists as a topic in authoritative texts, from the Gospels on down. Even in Christian communities where institutions of vowed celibacy or virginity have never flourished or have been fiercely repudiated, the original ideal returns alongside the practice of Christian marriage. We need to consider what the persistence of the ideal means for the attempt to construct a Christian sexual ethic, but not before noticing that the ideal has already begun to produce identities. We need to examine one of these, which is in many ways the most important: the identity of the Virgin Martyr.

---

[44] John Wesley, *Thoughts on a Single Life* [1765], in *Works of John Wesley* (London: Wesleyan Methodist Reading Room, 1872; repr. Peabody, MA: Hendrickson, 1894), vol. 11, p. 458, no. 5.
[45] Wesley, *Single Life*, p. 458, no. 6.
[46] Wesley, *Single Life*, pp. 458–9, no. 6.
[47] Wesley, *Single Life*, p. 460, no. 9.
[48] Wesley, *Single Life*, p. 460, no. 10.
[49] Wesley, *Single Life*, p. 463, no. 15.

The Virgin Martyr

New life beyond sex has been proposed since the early church to men and women. Some of the arguments on its behalf seem to appeal equally to both. Other arguments would have had different resonance for women than for men. So, for example, a life of chosen virginity could have appealed to many women as a kind of emancipation. It freed them from their subordination to the reproductive schemes of various families (their own, their husband's) for a life of spiritual and even political agency. It gave them a distinguished office in the Christian churches. And so on. In these and other ways, the call to virginity could have been more compelling for women than for men.

More generally, too, the flowering of the cult and then the theology of the Virgin Mary provided a challenging alternative to prevailing views of feminine gender. In one way, Marian devotion affirms that only a virgin can stand in privileged relation to Jesus. In another way, it redefines motherhood. The mother of Jesus is a mother unlike any other, a mother who has never been a woman erotically. Again, and especially in its liturgical aspects, it elevates a woman of unusual marital status to a public position very near divinity. No account of the gendered identities in Christian thought or practice can get very far without considering at length the cult and the doctrine about the mother of Jesus. But the identity that is important for us just now is one not exemplified by the Virgin Mary. Although much is made of her suffering beside her son's cross or of her identification with the pains of her spiritual children in the world, Mary did not in fact suffer torture and death. On the contrary, and from early on, some believed that she did not so much die as fall asleep – that she escaped even the pains of ordinary human passing.

By contrast, many of the most prominent virginal women in early Christian writing are the "virgin martyrs." What distinguishes these martyrs from their male counterparts is the emphasis placed in the narrative of their "acts" on their virginity, which is often both the seal of their relationship to the Lord and the provocation to their execution. It can often seem, reading these texts, that the noblest thing a Christian woman can do is to refuse sex with men and then suffer torture for it.

These motifs are apparent in some of the earliest Christian writings, including the New Testament apocrypha. Consider the "Acts of Paul and Thecla," part of the cycle of the apocryphal acts of Paul and the most authoritative source for the life of St. Thecla. This text and others like it circulated early on in the churches, becoming sometimes an occasion for controversy. For example, Tertullian, writing near the end of the second century, rejects an appeal to Thecla's example as justification for the right of women to preach and baptize.[50] If the "Acts of Paul and Thecla" were rejected as non-canonical by authors we now count as orthodox, the cult of St. Thecla spread widely in the early church. It was the cult of a young woman who abandoned her fiancé to follow Paul, preacher of a new kind of "marriage" to Jesus.

The Paul of these "Acts" is the apostle of chastity. Newly arrived in Iconium, he preaches "the word of God about abstinence and the resurrection."[51] He speaks his own beatitudes, 13 of them. Four have to do with sexual abstinence, another two with separation from the world. "'Blessed are the bodies of the virgins, for they shall be well pleasing to God and shall not lose the reward of their chastity.'"[52] While Paul is setting forth this "discourse of virginity," the virgin Thecla refuses to move from her window, fixed by attention to his words. Her mother and her fiancé are concerned, then irritated. Others become alarmed at this apostle who goes about "deceiving virgins so that they should not marry but remain as they are." He warns, "'There is for you no resurrection unless you remain chaste and do not pollute the flesh.'"[53] Summoned before Rome's proconsul by the jilted fiancé, Paul proclaims that he has been sent to rescue his listeners "from all pleasure, and from death, that they may sin no more."[54] The proconsul imprisons him. Thecla bribes her way in to see him by handing over her bracelets and mirror, but she is discovered in the prison cell. Paul is scourged and cast out of the city. Thecla is condemned to be burned in public for refusing to marry her fiancé. She is miraculously saved and manages to find Paul again. Thecla wants to accompany him: she cuts off her hair and begs for baptism. He promises that the baptism will come in time and reluctantly permits her to follow him.

No sooner do they arrive in Antioch than a prominent citizen falls in love with Thecla. She rebuffs him insultingly and is condemned to execution once again. Thecla asks only that "she might remain pure" until

---

[50]   Tertullian, *De baptismo* (*On Baptism*), 17.5, in his *Opera Catholica*, ed. J. G. P. Borleffs, Corpus Christianorum Series Latina, vol. 1.2 (Turnhout: Brepols, 1954), pp. 291–2. For a summary of the complicated problems of attestation and transmission for the "Acts of Paul and Thecla," see Elliott, *Apocryphal New Testament*, pp. 350–3.

[51]   I cite the section numbers of the "Acts of Paul and Thecla" as translated by Elliot in *Apocryphal New Testament*, pp. 364–74.

[52]   "Acts of Paul and Thecla," no. 6 (Elliott).

[53]   "Acts of Paul and Thecla," nos. 11–12 (Elliott).

[54]   "Acts of Paul and Thecla," no. 17 (Elliott).

her confrontation with the beasts of the arena. There she is again saved miraculously – and she uses the occasion to baptize herself in a pool intended to be a means of death. "And there was round her a cloud of fire so that the beasts could neither touch her nor could she be seen naked."[55] Thecla is again released. Disguising herself in a man's cloak, she tracks Paul down, in order to announce that she has received baptism and that she intends to return to her home in order to preach the Gospel.

The story ends differently in different versions. In one of them, Thecla is threatened a final time by a gang of ruffians hired by pagan physicians who resent her ability to perform miraculous cures. The ruffians have been sent to rape her in hopes that her loss of virginity will also mean a loss of healing power. As they are about to assault her, Thecla prays: " 'Deliver me from these lawless men and let them not insult my virginity which for your name's sake I have preserved till now because I love you and desire you and adore you.' "[56] She is protected again, this time by being hidden away in a gap in the rock face. The attempts to make her a martyr finally fail, but only after she has suffered repeated trials.

Thecla's last prayer, her last appeal to the Lord, assumes that her virginity is to be protected by God because it has been dedicated to God. This may be an unsurprising cultural construction in societies familiar with various forms of religious virginity. When the pagan physicians of Seleucia decide to have Thecla raped, they are reasoning on the assumption that her virginity gives her a special claim on the goddess Artemis. So it is not surprising that Christian virgins should be understood – should understand themselves – on analogy to already familiar forms of religious virginity. Christian authors were at pains to deny these analogies, of course, and to specify the churches' virgins as distinctively Christian. So they would argue, for example, that physical virginity is less important than spiritual virginity, which is the full enactment of a distinctively Christian charity. But a more direct way to specify Christian virgins is to insist that they are virgins for the sake of Christ and no one else. In hagiographical and liturgical texts, virgin martyrs are represented as the fiancés of Christ. Suffering martyrdom consummates the betrothal as a marriage.

These notions of marriage to Christ were translated from Greek-speaking Christianity into the Latin West, though not without changes. Ambrose emphasizes marriage to Christ in his work on virgins (written around 390):

---

[55] "Acts of Paul and Thecla," no. 34 (Elliott).
[56] This comes from an appendix without section numbers, as in Elliott, *Apocryphal New Testament*, pp. 372–4, at p. 373.

[The virgin] has brought from heaven what is to be imitated on earth. Nor
has she inappropriately sought her manner of life from heaven, since she has
found a spouse for herself in heaven. Passing beyond clouds, air, angels, and
stars, she has found the Word of God in the Father's breast, and she has
drawn him into herself wholeheartedly.[57]

The individual virgin is identified with the Virgin Church, which is also
Christ's bride, as she is identified with Christ himself considered as moth-
ering virgin.[58] Ambrose also calls up more particular marital images. The
individual virgin should remind herself, for example, that God is the true
judge of beauty.[59] If her parents oppose her, she knows that she has a rich
husband, who will provide from his father's treasure.[60] Most of all, the
individual virgin should know that if she must become a victim, she will
do so as the bride of an ultimately powerful Lord. As Ambrose writes of
Agnes: "As a bride she could not have hurried to the wedding chamber
more than, as a virgin, she rushed gladly to the place of suffering, her head
adorned not with braids, but with Christ."[61] Christ is himself the wedding
crown of the victim-virgins, his wives. All of the goods of marriage are
redefined by Ambrose so that virgin martyrs may receive them – and
receive them most fully.

The erotic images that link the virgin martyr to Christ are clear enough in
the unadorned "acts" or in the theological commentary of Ambrose, clearer
still in some more ambitious hagiographical writing. Consider two lives from
Prudentius's *Peristephanon*, a sequence of poems on particular martyrs. The
sequence contains a "hymn" for St. Eulalia and a "passion" of St. Agnes.
In the hymn, Prudentius foreshadows his lesson at once: Eulalia, whose
"members" were "not destined for the marriage chamber," found sweetness
in the flames of the pyre.[62] A more striking description of virginal suffering
comes when Prudentius narrates the tortures before Eulalia's execution. She
has gone to extraordinary lengths to appear before the Roman governor in
order to rebuke his idolatry. The governor reminds her of what she is giving

---

[57]   Ambrose, *De virginibus* (*On Virgins*), 1.3.11, in Migne *PL* 16:202B. There is an English
version in *Some Principal Works of Ambrose*, trans. H. De Romestin, Nicene and Post-
Nicene Fathers, ser. 2, vol. 10 (repr. Peabody, MA: Hendrickson, 1995), here p. 365.
[58]   Ambrose, *De virginibus*, 1.5.22, 1.6.31 (Migne *PL* 16:205C-D, 208B-C).
[59]   Ambrose, *De virginibus*, 1.6.30, 1.7.37 (Migne *PL* 16:208A, 210B).
[60]   Ambrose, *De virginibus*, 1.12.62 (Migne *PL* 16:217A-B).
[61]   Ambrose, *De virginibus*, 1.2.8 (Migne *PL* 16:201B; trans. De Romestin, p. 364).
[62]   Prudentius, *Peristephanon* (*Crowns of Martyrdom*), 3, lines 18, 13–15, as in *Prudentius*,
vol. 2., trans. H. J. Thomson, Loeb Classical Library (Cambridge, MA: Harvard University Press, 1953).

up in provoking his justice by refusing even token obeisance to the state's gods. She is forsaking not only the pleasures of marriage, but the promise of future children and the long love of her family and friends. Eulalia spits at the governor and begins to destroy the pagan altars. The executioners seize her, gouging her flesh to the bone with a metal hook. Eulalia takes these wounds as the name of Jesus cut into her body: "'Look, you are writing on me, Lord. Let me read these letters, Christ, which record your victories! The drawn blood's redness itself speaks the holy name.'"[63] Eulalia's virgin body is pierced by an instrument that writes Jesus' name into her own blood. Her torture completes her espousal to Jesus.

If the violently erotic imagery of Eulalia's piercing is still not clear enough, turn to Prudentius's recasting of the martyrdom of Agnes. He presents her already being cajoled and threatened for refusing to worship idols.[64] The pagan judge reasons that while it may be easy for Agnes to scorn life, she does still value her virginity. So he orders her sent to a brothel, where young men will rush to enjoy her. In the event, almost everyone avoids her. The one man who does gaze at her lustfully is struck blind by heavenly fire. Frustrated, enraged, the judge orders a soldier to kill her with a sword. Agnes replies with a remarkably crude taunt:

> I rejoice that a man like this comes to cost me my shame in death – like this, savage, cruel, a violent warrior, and not some languid, tender, and effeminate ephebe, dipped in perfume. This lover, this one at last, I confess, pleases me. I will go to meet his approaching steps, and I will not reject his hot desires. I will take all of his blade into my breasts and pull his sword's power deep into my chest. And so, married to Christ, I will leap over all the clouds of the sky, higher than the ether.[65]

The passage is almost pornographic. In it, Agnes lavishly eroticizes the violence done to her as the final gift of her virginity to Christ. She is married to Jesus in being tortured for her refusal to give her body to anyone else.

The erotically charged imagery might be considered just the personal tic of Prudentius if it did not occur in so many other texts. It is also approved by public worship. In typical medieval liturgies, for example, fragments of the story of Agnes are chanted at the giving of the veil to new nuns. The same liturgies are full of nuptial imagery – indeed, the giving of the veil is itself copied from Roman marriage ceremonial. The liturgical recollection

---

63 Prudentius, *Peristephanon*, 3, lines 139–40.
64 Prudentius, *Peristephanon*, 14, lines 15–20.
65 Prudentius, *Peristephanon*, 14, lines 69–80.

transfers violent suffering from martyrdom to asceticism, from the relatively brief suffering of torture to the lifelong suffering of penances and mortifications. The transfer is fully incorporated into celebrations or explanations of women's religious life. The connection of virginity at once to spiritual betrothal and physical suffering has persisted in the Catholic church well into modern times.

The identity of the virgin martyr hardly passes down unchanged through centuries – like an unchanging text in an ideal liturgy. On the contrary, the identity is constantly reformulated as the institutions housing it are built up, changed, replaced in response to new needs. Christian institutions for women's virginity have included desert communities, splendid villas, rich and sprawling estates for the Benedictines, small and deliberately poor convents for the Franciscans, anchor-holds, *Béguinages*, the "Sisters' Houses" of the *Herrnhuter*, Shaker communes in America, and charitable institutions of so many kinds. The ideal of a community of unmarried and ascetical women remains in the Christian texts and practices as a possibility waiting to be retrieved. It is retrieved, even where there is no institutional support for it. When a young Florence Nightingale tried to imagine her future life, she thought of establishing "something like a Protestant Sisterhood, without vows, for women of educated feelings."[66] If Miss Nightingale seems a silly example of the Protestant Virgin, a more serious one could be found in Susanna Wesley or many foreign missionaries. Examples closer to hand can be found today in the "pillars" or "church ladies" of many congregations.

Even the ideal of virginity as suffering can be transplanted into much less exotic settings than the Mediterranean under the Romans. In his *Rule and Exercises of Holy Living* (published in 1650), Jeremy Taylor situates holy virginity within a comprehensive teaching on chastity as it is found in all the states of Christian life. A protégé of Archbishop Laud and supporter of both James I and James II, Taylor must be considered "high Anglican" and so perhaps suspiciously close to Roman Catholic traditions. Still, it is worth hearing his text as a remarkable retrieval of an ancient Christian identity. Taylor is careful to begin with chastity as a general virtue for all Christians. He is equally deliberate in praising marriage. But Taylor's highest praise is for voluntary, religious virginity:

> a life of angels, the enamel of the soul, the huge advantage of religion, the great opportunity for the retirements of devotion; and being empty of cares, it is full of prayers: being unmingled with the world, it is apt to converse

---

[66]   As quoted in Lytton Strachey, *Eminent Victorians* (London: Penguin Books, 1986), p. 113.

with God; and by not feeling the warmth of a too-forward and indulgent nature, flames out with holy fires, till it be burning like the cherubim and the most ecstasied order of holy and unpolluted spirits.[67]

Doubtless Christian virginity is "more excellent than the married life, in that degree in which it hath greater religion, and a greater mortification, a lesser satisfaction of natural desires, and a greater fullness of the spiritual."[68]

A citation immediately following to Revelations 14:4 might make it seem that these virgins are or could be male, but when Taylor comes to give practical rules for "virginal chastity," the pronouns turn feminine: "For a virgin, that consecrates her body to God, and pollutes her spirit with rage. . . ."[69] We must understand all of the rules to apply to women – to women who have become like angelic men. So we must understand that the asceticism they prescribe is the trace of the ancient virgin's martyrdom. Taylor teaches the virgins to cultivate "a singular modesty," which requires that they be ignorant of "the distinction of sexes, or their proper instruments."[70] They are not to know the difference of male and female genitals, much less how they function. Taylor's virgins are to be "retired and unpublic," else they will forfeit some of the "severity, strictness, and opportunity of advantages" in their way of life.[71] Their circumstances would be "a misery and a trouble, or else a mere privation," unless they were redeemed by spiritual purpose.[72] The holiness of virginity continues to reside in a kind of suffering – though a much more ethereal and less pornographic suffering that we were forced to witness in Prudentius.

Underneath or alongside the institutional changes or the shifts in theological depiction, it is just possible to note some recurring features of the role of the Virgin Martyr. The first has to do with virginity. Identity as a virgin depends on the body; it can be forfeited by a single, physical act. Once forfeited, it cannot be regained. In this way virginity places enormous stakes on particular bodily motions. It endows them with enormous spiritual significance. The virgin's heavenly crown can be lost forever by a single act of intercourse – and perhaps by something less. It is not clear, for example, whether a woman could maintain her "physical virginity" and still forfeit her spiritual identity as a virgin – either by physical acts short of

---

[67] Jeremy Taylor, *Holy Living*, 2.3, as in *Whole Works of the Right Rev. Jeremy Taylor, D.D.* (London: Henry G. Bohn, 1850), vol. 1, p. 424, col. b.
[68] Taylor, *Holy Living*, 2.3 (1:424b).
[69] Taylor, *Holy Living*, 2.3, Rule no. 4 (1:427a).
[70] Taylor, *Holy Living*, 2.3, Rule no. 2 (1:427a).
[71] Taylor, *Holy Living*, 2.3, Rule no. 3 (1:427a).
[72] Taylor, *Holy Living*, 2.3, Rule no. 1 (1:426b–7a).

intercourse or by sharp desire. The identity is enormously fragile, then, and in constant need of reinforcement.

The second recurring feature of the identity appears in the confrontation with martyrdom. In her audacious courage, the virgin martyr acts against or beyond her nature as an innocent girl or woman. The writers of the older hagiographies stress that she has the "manly" virtues of courage, endurance, combative intelligence, and fierce eloquence. In one passage, speaking on behalf of virgins generally, Jerome says, "my task is without sex."[73] We might say, more provocatively, that it is a task or project of reversing sex. Acts and attributes that are stereotypically gendered male can be attributed – in eminent degree – to a female. The young woman who is supposed to be before sex can cross over into the role of the opposite sex. Often enough she dresses and acts like a man in order to accomplish her "manly" purposes.

The third recurring feature links virginity to martyrdom and especially to the reinterpretation of the martyrdom as the consummation of the virgin's betrothal to Christ. If the virgin's identity depends absolutely on avoiding even a single sexual act, her identity also permits her to be described with the most erotic language and in relation to a figure whose sexuality is normally outside of speech altogether – namely Christ himself. The young woman who must avoid sexual acts or lose who she is can nonetheless be described in the strongest sexual terms – in relation to the man–God who is usually deemed beyond sex.

There are other recurring features in the identity, but these three already suggest my principal point. "Virgin Martyr" is one of the oldest and most potent of Christian sexual identities. It may even be that this identity serves as a sort of model or prototype for other kinds of identities in the moral theology of sex. The Sodomite or Witch may well contain some rather simple inversions of the identity of the Virgin Martyr, while the Angelic Monk and Pure Priest might be in part male imitations of it. But if the identity of the Virgin Martyr is a sort of model, it is by no means static. On the contrary, it is intrinsically transitory (because always threatened) and it is filled with curious tensions (reversals of gender roles and of taboos about sexual speech). We ought to learn from this authoritative example that the sexual identities of Christian theology are anything but static. Indeed, it may be that they are inevitably points of disconcerting change.

The identities constructed and distributed by Christian ethics are always being repeated with variation – in the same way and at the same time that traditional texts are. The many traditions of Christian moral texts provide an enormous reservoir of words in favor of sexual purity. These words attack sexual acts, their causes and effects. They also present identities that are

[73] Jerome, *Epist.* 22, 18.3 (ed. Hilberg 167.17; trans. Mierow, p. 150).

discovered or destroyed by sexual acts. The words wait to be brought back into speech – to be spoken again in unpredicted situations. The words wait to project their identities – into unfamiliar institutional or social contexts. In this way, the identities are like topics in authoritative texts. They are sets of words subject to continual revision. They are scripts performed and reperformed, with smaller or larger adjustments. The rhetoric of religious identities – like the rhetoric of scriptural texts – has extraordinary power to name sexual acts and suggest sexual identities across time, but never in exactly the same way.

Living with Sex

Our ears ringing with so many reiterations of the ideal of life beyond sex, we might be tempted to ask two pointed questions. First, how many alternative ideals might we find within the Christian traditions? Second, can a religious tradition that so prized early on an ideal of life beyond sex ever have much to say about sexual life?

To the first question, an obvious reply might be to point to the slow and yet rich developments in the Christian teachings on marriage. We will sample those teachings in chapter 5 in order to see how far they do embody alternative ideals. But we must recognize already that Christian marriage was justified against claims of virginity (rather than apart from them). It is not clear how far Christian marriage is an alternative ideal and how far it is a derivative ideal. So we might ask again, more strongly: Were there in early or medieval or reformed Christianity no radical altern- atives to the ideal of life without sex, no unabashed affirmations of the goodness of sex as part of human life?

The answer to this question will depend entirely on how tightly you draw the circle of "Christianity." We cannot talk about "Christian" ideals of celibacy, chastity, or virginity without admitting that the most significant alternatives to these ideals have been excluded from the churches as anti- Christian, that is, as heretical. Beginning with the Corinthian "libertines" of Paul's first letter, many individuals and groups have been ruled out of communion or church membership for advocating different ideals of Christian sexual behavior. Many of these "heretics" typically considered themselves to be faithful followers of Jesus. They didn't see contradictions between their views about sex and their faith in the Lord. The judgment that their views are un- or anti-Christian is the judgment of the orthodox, that is, of the victors in the doctrinal struggles.

We know very little about these "heretical" views and then mostly through the unreliable accusations of their opponents. The orthodox not only pass judgments, they write the histories. (That is what it means to win a doctrinal victory.) What is more important, the victorious orthodox usually control the means of textual transmission. If we do not now have many Christian writings that advocate alternate ideals of sexual behavior, that is because the writings were systematically destroyed – in very good conscience – by the defenders of orthodoxy. Think how different our picture of "Gnosticism" was before the recovery of the texts from Nag Hammadi. Think how different our views of the historical range of Christian teachings on sex might be if we found a library of writings by the dozens of heretical groups tarred over the centuries with charges of sexual indecency.

As it is, we are left to reconstruct the views or practices of these groups by trying to read through the highly colored accusations against them. This is particularly dangerous because charges of sexual indecency became part of the standard charges to be leveled against any heretical group. Whatever else was said against the words or deeds of a heretic, sexual charges could be tacked on for good measure. If celibacy or virginity were the Christian ideals, then evidently any anti-Christian must espouse or practice their opposite – seduction, adultery, polygamy, sodomy, pederasty, bestiality. Charismatic male preachers were typically assumed to corrupt the women or men who were their followers; female mystics must of course be copulating with each other or with devils. Charges of "unnatural" sex proved particularly popular in polemic against heretical groups or their leaders. In consequence, it is often impossible to dissociate the actual sexual teachings of dissident or minority groups from the sexual charges brought against them in orthodox denunciation. For the main narratives of church history, heresy implies sexual deviance and sexual deviance implies heresy.

Scholars sometimes try to distinguish fact from polemical accusation by relying on their intuitions of veracity. Epiphanius describes a practice by the fourth-century Gnostics in which the heretics, after copulating or masturbating, would lift ejaculated semen to the heavens in an obscene Eucharist. One modern scholar thinks that this has "a ring of truth," and yet a very similar story is told by Cyril of Jerusalem of the Manichees.[74]

---

[74] Epiphanius, *Panarion (Against Heresies)*, 26.11, in *Epiphanius*, vol. 1, ed. Karl Holl, GCS, vol. 25 (Leipzig: J. C. Hinrichs, 1915), pp. 288–9/92. Malcolm Lambert, *Medieval Heresy: Popular Movements from the Gregorian Reform to the Reformation* (2nd ed., Oxford: Blackwell, 1992), p. 14, seems to refer to this passage. But compare Cyril of Jerusalem, *Catecheses ad illuminandos (Catechetical Instructions)*, 6.33, in Migne *PG* 33:597, for a strikingly similar description. The passage is skipped over prudishly in the English version of Edwin Hamilton Gifford, Nicene and Post-Nicene Fathers, second series, vol. 7 (repr. Peabody, MA: Hendrickson, 1995), pp. 42–3. He relegates the offending words to a Greek footnote.

Long reading in a particular genre of sources can sometimes give scholars an uncanny sense for what is factual and what polemical. It does not give infallibility. "Intuitions" about sources remain too often projections of one's own views about what kinds of sex are permissible or impermissible for Christians. For example, scholars who are squeamish about same-sex relations generally are squeamish about them in historical accusations of heresy.

The accusations against heretics allege more than genital acts. Sexual deviance is often equated with gender deviance – that is, with the violation of socially dictated gender roles. From the condemnation of women who act "against nature" in Romans 1 on, Christian polemic has often conflated strong women with sexually sinful women. Such women must also be heretics or the dupes of heretics. For a woman to claim a role of public leadership in the churches was taken often enough as a sign of her doctrinal unreliability – and a confession de facto of her sexual proclivities. So we face here the same circularity in the evidence encountered just above. A group that advocates different gender roles – and especially roles of authority for women – is by that very fact a group to be suspected of heresy. Hence a group suspected of heresy may also be suspected of advocating deviant notions of gender. The same must apply in reverse to men: heretics must be corrupters of women and effeminate seducers of men. Perhaps that is why charges of same-sex activity are a recurring feature in Christian heresiography – against the Gnostics and the Messalians in the fourth century, the Paulicians of Byzantium in the late ninth century, the Bogomils of the eleventh and twelfth centuries, the Cathars of the high Middle Ages, the Lollards in fourteenth- and fifteenth-century England (they elegantly reversed the charge), the Adamites around 1520 in Prague, the English Methodists as early as 1732, and papist priests by Protestant pamphleteers from the Reformation on.[75] For good measure, charges of gender deviation are typically accompanied by charges of orgiastic incest, the abuse of children, and so on.

---

[75] For the Paulicians and Bogomils, see Janet Hamilton and Bernard Hamilton, *Christian Dualist Heresies in the Byzantine World c. 650–c. 1450* (Manchester and New York: Manchester University Press, 1998), pp. 96 and 228, respectively; for the Cathars and Adamites, see Lambert, *Medieval Heresy*, pp. 111 and 336–7, respectively; for the Lollards and their reversals, see Carolyn Dinshaw, *Getting Medieval: Sexualities and Communities: Pre- and Postmodern* (Chapel Hill, NC: Duke University Press, 1999), pp. 55–99; for the early Wesleyans, see Abelove, "Sexual Politics," p. 94; for a sample of anti-papist polemic, Winfried Schleiner, " 'That Matter Which Ought Not To Be Heard Of': Homophobic Slurs in Renaissance Cultural Politics," *Journal of Homosexuality* 26:4 (1994): 41–75, at pp. 49–54.

Something similar, if not so lurid, seems to be true of the so-called "heresy of the Free Spirit" in the later Middle Ages. In 1312, the Council of Vienne convicted this "abominable sect" on multiple counts, including the teaching that sexual intercourse was not sinful when nature impelled one to it.[76] But the evidence we have, including "heretical" theological treatises like Marguerite Porete's *Mirror of Simple Souls*, suggest that this teaching was a gross misunderstanding of a rather subtle doctrine about the freedom of a soul close to God, a soul long habituated in a life of virtue. In other cases, it may be clearer that a "heretical" group did actually espouse sexual or marital arrangements prohibited by the dominant Christian norms or their civil enactments. Still, the orthodox judges were hardly fair in representing the theological justifications offered for these arrangements. In the early Anabaptist movement, for example, some groups espoused the dissolution of old marriages and the making of new ones under the direct guidance of the Spirit.[77] Because these changes were made without recourse to civil courts or church authorities, they constituted adultery or polygamy. They were also interpreted by the orthodox as acts of unbridled lust – doubtless inspired by demons. For the Anabaptists themselves, the "Spirit marriages" seem to have been a sincere and often arduous attempt to place every act of sexual intercourse under the direct inspiration of the divine voice.

Groups that espoused alternative principles for judging sexual acts were excluded first from church membership and then from church history. Similar exclusions can be seen in the ways that particular denominations treat the teachings or histories of other denominations. After so many exclusions, the range of moral principles available to "orthodox" or denominational theologians is quite small – and completely reinforced by the approved historical narratives. But then we feel the full force of the second question posed at the start of this section: Where is a religion that begins with such a strong critique of human sexual life to find principles for constructive teaching about it?

This question is usually sidestepped. One way of getting around it is to argue that the anti-erotic elements in Christianity were imported from outside – from other religious groups, or from pagan philosophy, or from ascetical communities. This reply forgets how indelibly ideals of celibacy

---

[76] For a summary, Lambert, *Medieval Heresy*, pp. 184–7; for much more extended treatment, Robert E. Lerner, *The Heresy of the Free Spirit in the Later Middle Ages* (Berkeley: University of California Press, 1972).

[77] I follow the account in Lyndal Roper, "Sexual Utopianism in the German Reformation," *Journal of Ecclesiastical History* 42 (1991): 394–418, especially pp. 398–402.

and virginity are written into the most authoritative Christian texts. We could not remove them from Christianity except by rewriting the New Testament. Another way of sidestepping the question is to say that these ideals are deeply inscribed in early Christianity, but only as the result of transient historical circumstance (say, the expectation of the imminent eschaton or the civic disruptions consequent on the collapse of the Roman system). This reply begs the question of the general applicability of Christian moral teaching. If the earliest Christian ideals about sex were determined by transient historical circumstances, what can we learn from those ideals – we who live in obviously different circumstances?

A religious impulse to virginity or celibacy would seem to provide a very unstable basis for the moral evaluation of sexual acts. Renunciation provides no satisfying criteria for permissible forms of appropriation. "Just say 'No'" doesn't seem to offer much instruction about when to say "Yes." Yet "orthodox" Christianity did find principles for constructing any number of detailed moral evaluations of sexual life. These evaluations were often enough condemnations of sexual sins, but even as condemnations they proved enormously resourceful in analyzing and categorizing human sexual desires and acts. Precisely because of their mistrust of human sexuality, many Christian moralists have, during two millennia, shown themselves astute catalogers of its varieties. They have given sex a seriousness that a more indulgent religious tradition might have denied it. Indeed, Christian theology has succeeded in demarcating the sphere of the sexual in the modern sense of the term as a special and separate sphere of moral consideration. Behind its thousands of particular judgments on sexual sins, behind its ever more expansive institutions for investigating and controlling genital acts and their prologues, Christian churches have been compiling an enormous vocabulary for sexuality. It is important to remember that some of the first and most powerful motivations behind the compilation are negative, prohibitory. It is also important to remember how much speech has issued from those original negations. What can a religion that begins with the ideal of a life beyond sex have to say about sex? Enough to fill libraries over centuries.

Where exactly has historical Christianity found principles for such speech? Have they been discovered from inside or have they come from outside? Are principles of reproduction or the nature of reproductive organs or the social centrality of marriage Christian principles or principles borrowed by Christianity from outside, from natural science or philosophy or law? In following these and other questions, we are trying to understand not just how Christianity could say so much, but what kind of speech it was offering when it did so.

Chapter 4

Crimes against Nature

We hear the terms "crimes against nature" or "unnatural acts" used so often as names for particular kinds of sexual acts that we forget their theological origins. The terms appear in English and American law, in biographies or historical narratives, and even in news reports. Until recently, they also figured in medical and psychiatric textbooks, not to say in public health pamphlets and books of candid advice for newlyweds. But the notion that certain sexual activities especially or uniquely violate nature is a theological claim constructed over centuries of Christian exegesis and argument. The same exegeses and arguments produced the overtly biblical category "sodomy" – though fewer and fewer English speakers remember that "sodomy" ought properly to be capitalized. It was coined as a name for the sin of the inhabitants of Sodom that provoked God to destroy them (according to Genesis 19). As theological categories, "crimes against nature" and "sodomy" share a genealogy that sometimes identifies them, sometimes distinguishes them. Neither category can be understood without looking to parts of that genealogy.

In this chapter, I begin with a simplified story about the genesis of the two categories. My purpose will be to show how a set of sexual acts got to be grouped together in Christian ethics as *the* crimes against nature. I will then describe the further steps by which "unnatural" acts were placed under arguments about "natural law." Finally, we will look in more detail at some typical theological speeches about distinct types of "unnatural" acts. Throughout the chapter, I will for clarity's sake often use contemporary terms to describe the acts under discussion. Remember that there are risks in that kind of clarity. The precision and literalness of our terms cannot be projected back into older schemes of names. For that matter, our way of figuring particular acts often differs in interesting ways from older schemes. To take a single example: In the neo-Latin of seventeenth- and eighteenth-century handbooks of moral theology, what we call politely "fellatio" (still using Latin) is most usually called *irrumatio*. For us, the "active" partner in fellatio is the person "sucking," while the person "getting sucked" is "passive." In the older texts, the person actively performing *irrumatio* is the person actively inserting his penis into the mouth of his (preferably female) partner. This reversal is interesting, not least because the older term seems to preserve the male prerogative of activity and so to project a patriarchal matrix onto this kind of oral sex. In one sense, then, it is not wrong to substitute the more familiar "fellatio" for *irrumatio* when talking about these texts. In another sense, this "translation" has completely reversed the gender expectations of the older term.

If you find yourself somewhat shocked to read details of one kind of oral sex in an introduction to Christian ethics, you are going to be quite agitated by many of the paragraphs that follow. The "development" of Christian sexual ethics has been a struggle between two motives. One theological motive wants to fill gaps in the canonical scriptures or moral traditions by specifying particular sinful acts as precisely as possible. This motive pushes for a ranked and detailed classification of sexual sins. In contrast, the second motive wants to cover sexual matters with a more and more perfect silence. Far from seeking more graphic descriptions of sexual organs and their deeds, this motive backs away from them into vaguer allusion or horrified silence. The two motives intertwine. You can find both in a single author or work. You can also see that one provokes the other. A tense silence will suddenly give way to a flood of speech. A long labor of classifying particular sins will be cut short by a revulsion that ends in a (temporary) silence. We ourselves experience the alternation of two motives when we go back and forth between clinical objectivity about sex and squeamishness over talking about such things at all in church contexts. If we can be squeamish about parts of our bodies and how they behave, we are sometimes even more squeamish about parts of Christian speech that refer to them.

We have to overcome both kinds of squeamishness in order to think seriously about the Christian ethics of sex. We also have to pay attention to different genres or forms of speech. As we have seen, Christian speeches about the ideal of a life beyond sex often take the form of elegy and ex-hortation – of utopian writing. Some Christian speeches about "unnatural acts" look more like invective or bitter satire. Others – and the more important – resemble legal prohibitions or punishments. In fact, much Christian writing about "unnatural" sex has the look of a criminal law or its bureaucratic application by a police agency.

"Bureaucracy" and "police" are partly metaphorical and partly not. Many Christian societies have created and then maintained agencies for discovering and punishing certain sexual acts. The agencies have operated within the churches and alongside them, with their own powers to punish or with the help of the "secular arm." When they have not sponsored actual agencies, Christian groups have spoken in the styles of the courts and the police. They have written Christian moral theology as if it were a criminal code ready for enforcement.

The "enforcement" of moral theologies of sex is itself curiously metaphorical – or ironic. Christian bureaucratic speech does not so much interpret what already happens as it imposes interpretations on what might otherwise be constructed quite differently. The interpretations configure acts in a particular way. They also reach behind acts to identities. In Christian speeches about "unnatural acts," we can watch the projection of sexual sin-identities. Christian eulogists of a life beyond sex displayed the glory of the Virgin Martyr. Christian persecutors of "unnatural" sex will display the horror of a whole troupe of grand sinners. Bureaucratic speech in moral theology strives to impose identities on the flickering variety of human acts and motives. It is not enough to persuade the righteous that a sin-identity "fits" what is being done by sinners. Sinners have to be persuaded to perform their identities – that is, to present their lives in conformity with the identities. A Sodomite is supposed to be a certain sort of person. The Christian who is committing sodomy has to become that sort of person for the moral theology to be convincing.

You might see in this bureaucratic regulation of identities a sort of compromise between specifying acts in detail and concealing them by silence. Christian speeches can limit the need to specify acts by invoking an identity. You may have to specify acts somewhat in order to narrate a sufficiently vivid portrait of a sin-identity. Once the identity is established, specifying acts becomes less important. Once moral theology knows who a Sodomite must be, it can be increasingly silent about what Sodomites actually do. Sodomy is what the Sodomite does.

From Sodomitic Acts to the Sodomite's Identity

Forget whatever you think you know about which acts constitute "sins against nature" or "sins of Sodom." It is bound to be too restrictive. The two categories have included, in one author or another, *every* erotic or quasi-erotic act that can be performed by human bodies *except* penile–vaginal intercourse between two partners who are not primarily seeking pleasure and who do not intend to prevent conception. Every other erotic act, desire, or wish has been deemed a sin against nature by one Christian theologian or another. Moreover, a certain variable subset of the prohibited acts and desires, especially those between members of the same sex, have been counted as the preeminent sin against nature. They have been judged such a direct affront to God's creative purposes that they merit the severest legal punishment so that God does not destroy the city or region in which they are committed.

It is not self-evident that we should group together some sexual sins as eminently unnatural. In fact, it took several conceptual steps over a number of centuries before certain sexual acts could be counted egregious violations of nature. Not coincidentally, these steps were part of a general program for ordering Christian moral teaching. Sexual sins were both an occasion and an urgent motive for reducing the accumulated exhortations, counsels, and decrees to something like an articulate proclamation of enforceable laws. The general ordering is too lengthy and too episodic an accomplishment to be narrated as a single story. But we can hear some of the episodes by which Christian theologians specified a set of acts as the unnatural sin of sodomy – as the deeds of that anti-natural figure, the Sodomite.

The genealogy of the Sodomite's acts begins with a misreading or overreading of Paul in Romans 1. We have already seen that Paul there uses a broad notion of what is beyond or in excess of nature, perhaps borrowed form Stoic or Hellenized Jewish moralists. Paul applies this notion first to unspecified sexual acts or socioerotic relations between women (1:26), and then by implication (he does not repeat the phrase) to acts or relations between men (1:27). If Paul does mean to refer to particular sexual acts, there are two cautions to be noted in drawing inferences about them. The first is that he chooses not to specify the acts. The second is that he never claims that they are the most important acts against nature.

Paul does not need to be thinking of particular acts or relations here, because the genre of his moral speech does not require it. He is using a pattern of exhortation familiar enough from Jewish or gentile moralists, a pattern related to synagogue sermons or popular philosophic diatribes. There is no need to specify acts in such a speech. Indeed, it is better not to do so, because any effort to delimit particular actions would only distract from the moral sweep of the persuasion. Better to let the hearers or readers decide for themselves, in the secret spaces of their guilty hearts, which of their acts are being condemned. The point is not to engage in case analysis, but to move the listeners to an embracing resolution of reform, a wholehearted turning back to God. So the genre of Paul's exhortation discourages the naming and delimiting of acts – even if he had particular acts in mind.

Later writers felt the need for genres other than exhortation or diatribe when dealing with sex. Many of the genres required a greater specification of particular acts. So the next step was for Christian interpreters to connect Romans 1 with their misreading or overreading of the story of Sodom in Genesis 19. The "sin of the Sodomites," now understood as some kind of sex between men, was arbitrarily linked to what Paul says about acts "against nature," even though Paul never refers to the story of Sodom and the story of Sodom never speaks of nature. We can see this link in many texts, but very influentially in Augustine's *Confessions*, 3.8.15.[1] Augustine does not, on a strict reading, equate the sin of Sodom with the sins of lust that he mentions, but he does associate them, if only as regards the punishment they deserve. The association was enough to make Augustine's passage decisive encouragement for conceiving church law as prohibition and punishment. The story of Sodom suggests that there are very particular crimes (as particular as a geographical point) that must be prevented in order to avoid divine rage. The lesson of Sodom is not so much about sex as about the urgency of avoiding whatever (sexual) acts will provoke divine wrath. In this way, the story encourages Christians to draw up a sexual code backed by severe punishments.

Even as Augustine wrote, legal genres were asserting themselves quite explicitly in Christian sexual ethics. The link between Sodom and Romans 1 is also found in early collections of church law. We find it most consequentially in the later legislation of the Christian emperor Justinian. Indeed, Justinian's *Novella* 141, promulgated in 559, explicitly connects the sin of the Sodomites with the Pauline passage, condemning as "sacrilegious and unholy" acts so far beyond nature that no animal commits them.[2] This criminalization of all male–male acts is the work of a Christian emperor, and it invokes scriptural authority when it punishes them with death. But even in Justinian, the acts that constitute the sin of the Sodomites are not precisely defined.

Here we may appreciate how difficult it is, even in the genres of law, to specify sexual acts in any morally coherent way. Often Christian writers do not attempt to refer to acts, on the plea that doing so would be obscene or provocative. They deploy instead broad terms of uncleanness or horror. When specific terms for acts do appear, their reference is often unclear, as

---

[1]   Compare Augustine, *De civitate Dei* (*City of God*), 16.30, ed. Bernardus Dombart and Alphonsus Kalb, Corpus Christianorum Series Latina, vol. 48 (Turnhout: Brepols, 1955), 535.305, where the sin of Sodom is identified as "raping" or "assaulting males" (*stupra in masculos*).

[2]   Justinian, *Novella*, 141, in *Corpus iuris civilis*, vol. 3: *Novellae*, ed. Rudolfus Schoell and Guilelmus Kroll (8th ed., Berlin, 1963; repr. Hildesheim: Weidmann, 1993), pp. 703–4.

we have seen. What really do *fornicatio* or *porneia* mean in the early Christian texts? What acts, committed how frequently, in what circumstances, make one a *molles* or *malakos*? What does one have to do exactly to merit the label *arsenokoitês*? Many Christian texts, not least in the New Testament, imply that you are already supposed to know the answers to such questions – and that to ask is itself a sign of sinfulness. Perhaps so. Perhaps detailed instruction about sexual matters is meant to be passed down within Christian communities by living word and holy example. It can still be noted that refusing to specify sexual acts relieves one of a very difficult task.

Even texts that want to be very specific in categorizing or punishing acts can turn out to be both vague and contradictory. Consider the so-called "penitentials," the early books of penance elaborated in the Latin-speaking church at least from the seventh century on. These penitentials were first compiled in Irish and Anglo-Saxon monasteries for the use of confessors. So they typically group together certain sins in order to assign them graded penances. This project proved enormously influential. Penitentials in more or less their original form went on to several centuries of popularity throughout Western Europe. They were then incorporated into larger patterns for ordering the whole of moral theology. In this way, they are an important, if often overlooked, model for the work of much later moral theology, both Catholic and Protestant. Indeed, the main project of the penitentials – which is to make the schemes for judging sins rational – has remained a methodological preoccupation for Christian ethicists.

Beginning with the early penitentials, we find mentions of fornication "in the sodomitic manner" or "style." One text specifies this "manner" by an allusion to the language of Leviticus 18: it consists of one man having "female intercourse" with another.[3] Related texts describe the same acts as "unnatural" or else contrast "natural" fornication with "sodomitic" fornication.[4] The emphasis here is on men, but there are also passages that speak specifically about women committing acts with other women. In some penitentials, women are said to "fornicate" with one another and to use "machines" on one another.[5] But their sins are not usually called "sodomitic." In the

---

[3] Ludwig Bieler, *The Irish Penitentials*, Scriptores Latini Hiberniae, vol. 5 (Dublin: Dublin Institute for Advanced Studies, 1963), p. 102 (Penitential of Columbanus).

[4] Bieler, *Irish Penitentials*, p. 60 (Preface of Gildas), p. 220 (Bigotian Penitential).

[5] For example, Bede 3.23–4 and Ps.-Theodore 16.4, 18.20, as in F. W. Hermann Wasserschleben, *Die Bußordnungen der abendländischen Kirche* (Halle: Graeger, 1851; repr. Graz: Akademische Druck- und Verlagsanstalt, 1958), pp. 223, 574, 581. For an ampler selection of texts, see Pierre J. Payer, *Sex and the Penitentials: The Development of a Sexual Code, 550–1150* (Toronto: University of Toronto Press, 1984), p. 138.

theology of unnatural sex, as in moral theology generally, women are often reduced or excluded – when they are not figured as particularly malignant.

If you compile passages on these kinds of sex from the different penitentials, you can notice two things. The first is that the penitentials are naming acts rather than defining them. They enumerate various kinds of intercourse tersely, even technically, on the assumption that the reader will know how to connect the names with situations being confessed or denounced. The other thing to notice is that the penitentials offer no explanations for ranking sins in terms of their seriousness. The same sin can take very different penances in different texts, and even a single text will often assign penances for different varieties of an act without comment, much less argument. So even these rather specific texts, which make even some contemporary translators squeamish, leave much to the reader, both by way of interpreting and reconciling.

One very important effort to standardize the penitentials on sodomitic or unnatural sex was a broadside written around 1050 by Peter Damian, renowned monk and sometime cardinal. This *Gomorran Book* or *Book of Gomorrah* authoritatively introduces and perhaps coins the term "sodomy" in an attack on sexual sins within the clergy. Apologizing for his candor, Peter Damian describes the sin of sodomites by combining four types of male–male sex from the penitentials: masturbation, mutual masturbation, copulation between the thighs, and copulation "in the rear." He identifies this "most abominable and most shameful vice," this worst of all crimes, with the specific sin of the Sodomites, the specific sin condemned in Leviticus 18, and the specific sin between men in Romans 1.[6] What is much more important, Peter Damian connects his synthetic definition of sins with a sin-identity. He wants to fix the vagueness and incoherence of the penitentials by referring individual acts to a vividly depicted identity. Indeed, Peter Damian introduces his enumeration of the acts by saying that they are what sodomites do. They are the acts of sodomites alive in his own day, the acts of a persisting identity. Peter further calls their particular crimes "demonstrably against nature," "against the law of nature," and the exact opposite of "natural appetite."[7] Theirs is sin against nature in the fullest

---

[6]   Respectively, Peter Damian, *Liber Gomorrhianus* (*Gomorran Book*), *Epistola 31*, as in *Die Briefe des Petrus Damiani*, vol. 1, ed. Kurt Reindel, Monumenta Germaniae Historica: Die Briefe der deutschen Kaiserszeit, vol. 4 (Munich: MGH, 1983), p. 287, line 1, and p. 289, lines 6–7. There is an English version in Peter Damian, *Letters*, vol. 2, trans. Owen J. Blum, The Fathers of the Church: Mediaeval Continuation (Washington, DC: Catholic University of America Press, 1990).

[7]   Peter Damian, *Liber Gomorrhianus* (ed. Reindel, 298.21, 307.10, 313.18).

possible sense of that phrase. The sins of the Sodomite, now named in some detail, have become the most outrageous violation of nature.

By synthesizing the definition and connecting it to an identity, Peter has made significant advances over the penitentials. This does not mean, of course, that he has exhaustively specified the acts in question. On the contrary, note three gaps in Peter's list. First, the list ignores many acts that later theologians will include among unnatural acts – not only the whole range of acts we call "oral sex," but same-sex kisses and caresses designed to arouse. Second, Peter's list is clearly intended to apply only to men. The sins are not considered in relation to women or to male–female couples. Third, Peter makes no effort to delimit acts by degree or frequency. For him, a single act of solitary masturbation is as much sodomy as a lifetime of male–male copulation. There is nothing like a ranking of virtues and vices or an analysis of human acts as such within which to situate Peter's severe judgment on unnatural acts.

Peter Damian does not provide a comprehensive specification of sins against nature. He does turn our attention away from the sins and toward the sinner. According to Peter, whoever does the acts is a Sodomite. A Sodomite's soul is Sodom in miniature – a city of exile, of death, over which fiery clouds always rain cinders. Indeed, the Sodomite seems to concentrate within himself every sin – in just the way that the Virgin Martyr possessed every gift of grace. The Sodomite may in fact be partly constructed by variation on that older identity or opposition to it. The Virgin Martyr could forfeit her identity by a single act, but so long as she retained her virginity, she was authorized both to reverse certain gender roles and to speak erotic words to a prohibited person, namely, Christ, who has become her husband. Peter Damian's Sodomite can forfeit clerical office and incur lifelong punishment for a single act, but does not seem to gain identity in that act. The Sodomite already has his identity; the act only discloses it. The sodomitic identity compels a reversal of gender roles (in same-sex desire or behavioral effeminacy), as it compels the speaking of certain erotic words to a prohibited person – namely, another man. For both the Virgin Martyr and the Sodomite, individual acts destroy or disclose a comprehensive identity, one that articulates itself in every aspect of social encounter. Each identity is importantly cut off from ordinary human society to be taken into a special community – the Virgin Martyr with the chorus of her sister saints, the Sodomite with the dark remnants of the destroyed city.

The description of the Sodomite is supposed to be a prelude to ministry. Peter Damian's stated rhetorical purpose in many passages is to convince sodomites to turn themselves in for punishment by expulsion from clerical

office and life imprisonment. Of course, it sometimes seems in Peter, as in
other Christian writers, that the identity of the Sodomite is irreformable.
The Sodomite is the very figure of the soul beyond the possibility of effective
repentance. So we may suspect that Peter's urgent desire to enter into a
dialogue with the Sodomite has other motives. One of them, I argue, is to
persuade an individual to take on the sin-identity, to agree to speak the
lines of a moral script.

By "script" I mean the ways in which Peter's words impose not just
terms for self-description or self-evaluation, but the role for a personage,
the stage directions for an identity. Similar scripts for the Sodomite can be
found in a number of Christian genres – in sermons and scriptural interpretations, treatises and compendia of cases, confessional interrogatories
and inquisitorial trials. What runs through these genres is the power of
words to elicit and enforce the varying performance of identity-motifs.
The scripts for the identities include much more than discrete sexual acts,
however named or described. Caught up in a cosmic narrative of rebellion
against God, the Sodomite is compelled to seek damnation, to seek it in
the blackened city of companion sinners, to obey absolutely the demonic
compulsions of the identity, and to produce its truth not only in actions,
but in words of self-identification.

By speaking of these identities as roles with scripts, I don't mean to
trivialize them. The theology of "crimes against nature" was rather more
than a theatrical game for theologians. It was a matter of law in a double
sense. The teaching was not only elaborated in legal forms, it was handed
over to courts, both ecclesiastical and civil. The court systems became
increasingly interested in finding and punishing such crimes. Crimes against
nature or crimes of sodomy fell between church courts and civil ones, not
least because clergy and members of religious communities who committed
them could in theory claim an exemption from civil prosecution. Yet there
were also and increasingly civil laws against them. Some of these laws (as
with Justinian's *Novella*) present themselves as efforts to legislate Christian
moral convictions. Others preceded Christianity. Some of the ethnic groups
that were Christianized during the European Middle Ages brought with
them their own taboos and punishments for sexual activities.

Medieval theological writers often remark that civil laws against sexual
crimes were harsher and less flexible than church laws. But church and civil
authorities collaborated frequently enough in the prosecution of sodomites.
A campaign of popular preaching could lead to a civic crusade; an upsurge
of civic asceticism could shame the clergy into reform. Beginning in the
thirteenth century, increasingly powerful civil governments attempted
to gain control over prosecutions of sodomy or sin against nature on the

pretext either that it was a danger to cities or that it was not being pursued vigorously enough by the church courts. In 1432, for example, the republic of Florence created a special magistracy to "root out of [this] city the abominable vice of sodomy, called in the holy scriptures the most evil sin."[8] Where special offices were lacking, city councils or courts took it upon themselves to pass statutes and to contest the jurisdiction of church courts, even in cases involving priests or monks.

It might be objected that civil legislators – whether Justinian or the Florentine magistrates – don't belong in a history of Christian sexual ethics. After all, they aren't theologians and they may well be importing non-theological or even non-Christian materials (say, ethnic prejudices). There are two answers to this objection. The first is that it is not so easy to separate among Christian speakers the theologians from the non-theologians. Justinian and the Florentine magistrates certainly understood themselves to be quoting or applying authoritative theology. Conversely, theologians often use the evidence of Christian civic legislation in making arguments for the gravity of "unnatural acts." The second reply to the objection is that it is equally hard to pick out a "distinctively Christian" teaching in actual Christian societies. We may wish for a clear line between the holy and the unholy, the sacred and the secular. No such line is drawn down the streets of "Christian" cities. Nor can we make presumptions about where we ought to look for "distinctively Christian" teaching in a society that purports to regulate sex according to Christian revelation. If we come to such a society already claiming to know what is distinctively Christian, then we may be able to pick out quickly just the features that agree with what we already know. Of course, if we come already knowing, we have nothing to learn – except perhaps how unhappily the pure Christian truth gets mired in the streets of real cities.

The cities contain both the words and the regimes of criminal enforcement. If Christian moralists had always to engage with the genres and procedures of legal texts, Christian morality also exercised itself through bureaucracies with police powers. These exercises of power are not a historical sidebar. They are a recurring situation in the development of Christian ethics. We can deplore the entanglement of Christian ethics with the policing of civic morals or we can applaud it. What we cannot do is pretend that Christian judgments about "unnatural" sexual acts were developed in tranquil freedom, entirely apart from ethnic customs, civic politics, or the growth of larger and larger structures for enforcement.

[8]   Michael Rocke, *Forbidden Friendships: Homosexuality and Male Culture in Renaissance Florence* (New York: Oxford University Press, 1996), p. 5.

Unnatural Acts and Natural Law

The entanglements of the civic with the theological is nowhere more evident than in the application to sexual sins of arguments from "natural law." The application is tangled enough when it is carried out carefully by the best theologians. It becomes much more dangerously tangled when these theologians are read sloppily or polemically. For example, one of the most famous and most influential teachings on natural law can be found in Thomas Aquinas. His texts retain considerable authority for church teachings on sex – and not only for Roman Catholics. The problem is that the very different things Thomas says about "crimes against nature" and "nature law" are confounded because it is assumed that natural "law" is like human criminal "law." It is worth tracing out this assumption in the example of Thomas because it will disclose some common fallacies in the rhetoric of natural law arguments, Thomistic and non-Thomistic alike.

Thomas's most deliberate discussion of what we would call sexual sins comes in the middle of his masterpiece, the *Summa of Theology*, under the vice of *luxuria*, a vice opposed to chastity, which is part of the virtue of temperance. *Luxuria* means for Thomas a self-indulgent excess of pleasure in what he calls "venereal acts," that is, "the acts of Venus," the Roman goddess associated with erotic love. It is remarkable and important that Thomas does not use here anything like our category of the sexual, much less of sexuality (whether homo- or hetero-). He does not have such categories. He has only a euphemism that requires reference to a pagan goddess.

What makes *luxuria* sinful for Thomas is that it "dissolves" human reason in animal pleasure, that is, in the pleasure associated with the animal activity of copulation. Animal pleasure in copulation he condemns as far beneath human rationality. This kind of natural – the natural as bestial and irrational – is not something that human beings should want to imitate. Thomas next tells the reader that there are six kinds of *luxuria*: simple fornication, adultery, incest, deflowering a virgin (*stuprum*), abduction for sexual purposes, and "the vice against nature." There are many troubles in this traditional list, but the only pertinent one concerns the meaning of the last phrase. "The vice against nature" turns out to include a number of different acts: "uncleanness" or "softness" (which we would call masturbation), "bestiality," the "sodomitic vice," and any genital contact between man and woman other than vaginal intercourse in an approved position. Let me emphasize: masturbation, fellatio, cunnilingus, variant postures in heterosexual intercourse – on Thomas's account, these are all equally "against nature." Why? Because they are contrary to the "natural order of the venereal [i.e., sexual] act that is appropriate to the human species."[9] These acts are "against nature" because they are against the "natural order" of human copulation, as regards partner or organ or posture.

In replying to a counter-argument, Thomas emphasizes the seriousness of these sins by borrowing a passage from Augustine. Thomas paraphrases the argument in this way: "just as the order of right reason is from the human, so the order of nature is from God himself. And so in sins against nature, in which the very order of nature is violated, an injury is done to God himself, who gives order to nature."[10] What is peculiar about the remark is that the same syllogism can be constructed about any sin whatever. For Thomas, every vice or sin is against created nature, hence against God's plan. Why then is this group of sins singled out? Thomas has suggested earlier in the *Summa* what we mean when we single out one vice as "*the* vice against nature." In an aside within the discussion of "natural law," Thomas writes that "the sleeping together of men" is said especially to be a vice against nature because it goes against the "mixture" (*commixtio*) of men and women that is natural to human beings and animals.[11] This brief remark resonates strongly with other passages where the "vice against nature" is seen as a violation of the fundamental purposes of human reproduction.

Same-sex copulation belongs, then, to a group of vices that are characterized by their opposition to the "natural" purpose and manner of human copulation. This produces the odd conclusion that most of the observed range of human sexual activity is against nature. But note more importantly that the use of the word "natural" here cannot simply be equated with natural law. For Thomas, "natural law" is not a cumbersome way of talking about nature. It is first of all "law" in his particularly ample sense, that is, common teaching about how human beings ought to live. Thomas says that natural law is "participation by the rational creature in eternal law" by means of which the rational creature has "a natural inclination to its appropriate act and end."[12] Natural law is how human beings experience or understand their created tendency to seek after God. It is how they are taught by God to seek after God. For Thomas, "lower animals" act in certain ways, according to what we now call instinct, without understanding how their actions are related to their ends. By contrast, human beings do somewhat understand their own deepest impulses toward a highest goal. They recognize these impulses as their natural share in God's creative plan for human

---

[9] Thomas Aquinas, *Summa theologiae* (*Summa of Theology*), 2–2.154.11.
[10] Thomas Aquinas, *Summa theologiae*, 2–2.154.12, reply to 1.
[11] Thomas Aquinas, *Summa theologiae*, 1–2.94.3, reply to 2.
[12] Thomas Aquinas, *Summa theologiae*, 1–2.91.2.

life. It is a natural share in the sense that it goes along with human nature. You do not have to be a Christian, much less a Christian in a state of grace, in order to share in this teaching of God's plan for human life.

This does not mean, however, that each of us has an inner rule book that we can consult to settle questions about sexual morality. For Thomas, the natural law is, at best, an abstract and incomplete guide to action. We need the human laws of the society in which we are raised in order to complete natural law, because human law offers particular conclusions drawn from the "common and indemonstrable principles" of natural law.[13] But Thomas knew as well as any medieval theologian that human societies disagree sharply about how human beings ought to act. He himself mentions cases in which whole societies teach their members to do things that he thinks contrary to natural law. Given the diversity of societies, the contradictions in the history of moral conventions, is there any kernel of natural law that every human being shares? Perhaps there is, but that kernel will not be enough to direct us individually or to make us agree collectively.[14] In practical matters, agreement about principles and about the shape of moral reasoning is no guarantee of agreement about practical conclusions. Indeed, the more particular the case, the more difficult it is to arrive at a conclusion on which all will agree. Alternately, the more specific a norm or precept proposed in ethics or law, the more liable it is to justified exception. In many particular cases, the right course of action cannot be regularly agreed, even among virtuous people.

This insufficiency of natural law becomes the starting point for Thomas's arguments in the *Summa* on the need for a divine law, that is, for an explicit teaching about human conduct revealed by God. Because natural law participates in God's eternal plan only "according to the proportion of the capacity of human nature," God generously teaches a more articulate law, the divine law that is eminently contained in the Old and New Testaments.[15] We are able to "fulfill" the natural law only after God's revelation. The content of natural law only becomes clear with the handing down of the Old Law, the law of Moses. The content of natural law only becomes practicable with the gift of grace in the New Law – whether we are talking about justice or about "unnatural" sex.

Many of the "natural law" arguments we hear today do not rise to the level of misreadings of Aquinas. They are rather loud assertions pretending to be common sense or, what is worse, natural science. But even in more

---

[13] Thomas Aquinas, *Summa theologiae*, 1–2.91.3, reply to obj. 3.
[14] Thomas Aquinas, *Summa theologiae*, 1–2.94.3.
[15] Thomas Aquinas, *Summa theologiae*, 1–2.91.4, reply to 1.

serious efforts to make "natural law" arguments against certain sexual acts, we can hear how easily Christian theology can slip from rich conceptions of law as divine self-disclosure to poor conceptions of law as imposed ideology or criminal code.

Read in medieval contexts, Thomas Aquinas's remarks on the sodomitic vice are remarkable for their restraint. He says nothing about the vice's particular acts or its social and spiritual consequences. Indeed, we should be struck by what seems the disappearance in Thomas of the melodramatic figure of the Sodomite. Thomas seems to have replaced this figure with that of the person who suffers the vice of *luxuria*. The Sodomite gives way to the Intemperate. As a whole, Thomas's *Summa* quite deliberately replaces more specific and lurid sin-identities with more general vice-identities. The vice-identities are then further specified as identities to which the moral teaching of law and grace is directed. Thomas seems less interested in eliciting the performance of scripts of particular sin than of scripts of learning what God teaches through nature, the virtuous city, and divine law. This is a remarkable reorganization of Christian sexual teaching. It is also remarkably unsuccessful in the history of Christian morals. Thomas's readers, including the most sympathetic, refused his general principles for reorganizing identities in order to use his texts piecemeal in support of the old identities. The teaching on "natural law," instead of being the beginning of another conception of moral identity, became instead a way of shoring up the identities already in place. We need to watch more closely how identities are staged in relation to three kinds of prohibited acts – same-sex couplings, masturbation, and oral sex.

Same-Sex Desire, or Identity in Community

Medieval theological speeches after Thomas are hardly brief and rarely restrained. They want above all to describe the identity of the Sodomite as a rebellious sinner and universal traitor, a living insult to God's creative generosity and a constant threat to the survival of human society. In order to give substance to the charge of treason, they rely increasingly on the notion – already suggested in Peter Damian – that sodomy founds a demonic sect or community.

We get a repulsed description of sodomitic community in one of the most characteristic of late medieval speeches about sodomy. It comes in the *Summa theologica* of the Dominican Antoninus, archbishop of Florence. Completed shortly before 1459, this *Summa* invokes Thomas Aquinas as the preeminent authority in regard to sodomy. But if Antoninus quotes bits of Thomas, he certainly does not imitate Thomas's restraint in teaching about sodomy. On the contrary, Antoninus here builds an entire "Scholastic" sermon against sodomy around a scriptural verse that he artfully subdivides into topics and then richly supplements with illustrative stories or *exempla* – all in order to warn the reader about sodomitic communities.

The Scriptural *thema* of the sermon is a verse from Psalm 82: "Who were destroyed at Endor, who became dung for the ground."[16] With this verse, Antoninus emphasizes the destruction of Sodom, as he suggests the sodomites' unnatural fondness for excrement. But he also and quite deliberately likens sodomites to a political and ethnic community, to the tribe of Midian, with their "captain" and their "king." Sodomites have a homeland, which is forever marked with the signs of their sin. It is utterly sterile, "unnatural": its air stinks of sulfur, its produce tastes of ash.[17] But while the Midianites perished at Endor, sodomites did not die at Sodom. Antoninus finds them again in the pride of the ancient Greeks and Romans. Not only the pagan poets, but also the conquering pagan emperors were sodomites.[18] Indeed, pagan culture seems to be characterized as sodomitic. Antoninus repeats from Jerome the story that God almost refused to become incarnate in a creature or a time given over to this vice. All sodomites had to die instantly on the night of Christ's birth.[19]

Still they reappeared – and reappear. Antoninus finds sodomitic association not only in history, but in the present. It is an association that begins, for example, when older men, besotted by luxury, persuade adolescents to sin with them. More generally, keeping company with sodomites can expose a whole "society" (*societas*) to contagion.[20] One person carrying the vice can infect a whole city. That is why God killed off the infants and the innocent in Sodom, a bloody (though ineffective) quarantine. Sodomites can only be corrected when caught young and isolated from contagious contact. Those who do not correct the vice in their children, relatives, and subordinates are themselves worthy of execution. Unchecked, unpunished, sodomy becomes impudent: sodomites will commit their crimes in public, as if they were not sins. This means that there will soon be more of them – a

---

[16]   I translate from Antoninus's quotation of the Vulgate, Ps. 82:10 (83:10 in the modern numbering), at *Summa theologica*, pars 2, titulus 5, caput 4, in *Sancti Antonini Archiepiscopi Florentini Ordinis Praedicatorum Summa Theologica* (Verona: Typographia Seminarii, Augustinus Carattonius, 1740; repr. Graz, 1959), col. 668B.

[17]   Antoninus, *Summa theologica*, 2.5.4, cols. 671E–672E.

[18]   See the mentions of Julius Caesar, Octavian, in Antoninus, *Summa theologica*, 2.5.4, col. 668D–E.

[19]   Antoninus, *Summa theologica*, 2.5.4, col. 670D.

[20]   Antoninus, *Summa theologica*, 2.5.4, col. 673B.

growing colony of the ancient city repopulating itself from the cities of the present. For Antoninus, as for many other Christian writers, sodomitic sex is less horrifying than the sodomitic identity, which in turns is less horrifying than the sodomitic community. The specification of private sexual acts here goes over into the specification of the public characteristics of the identity. Indeed, as the identity gains demonic power, it begins to act out in public what before had only been suspected in private.

The Protestant Reformation changed much in Christian sexual morals, but it did not change the teaching on sodomites and their communities. Indeed, the social commitments and polemical engagements of Protestant writers tended to exaggerate the features of the sodomy. So far as they wanted to replace what they saw as the confessional's emphasis on an accounting of particular acts, they underscored the horror of sodomy as a state of sin. So far as they wanted to attack the institutions of vowed celibacy in the priesthood and the religious life, Protestant writers made more vivid their depictions of the shared horrors resulting from unnatural sex.

Reformation polemics made the figure of the priest-sodomite a fixed and familiar one. If Luther often used Sodom as a general figure of corruption, he sometimes linked it quite pointedly with the question of monastic chastity.[21] Calvin, in the *Institutes*, makes the infamous practices of monasteries and convents an argument against institutionalized vows of chastity. Sometimes he seems to allege heterosexual sins, as when he writes that "you will barely find one in ten [monasteries] which is not rather a brothel (*lupanar*) than a holy place of chastity."[22] But a little further on the sexual crimes seem to have become worse:

> if I am silent, experience speaks: it is not unknown with how much obscenity almost all monasteries are filthy. If some seem more decent and modest than others, still they are not chaste, since the evil of impurity impels and is contained within. So God, by horrible examples, punishes the audacity of men, when, forgetting their weakness and repudiating nature, they attempt what is denied to them [namely, continence], and contemning the remedies [namely, marriage] that the Lord has gave into their hands, trust that they can overcome the disease of incontinence by proud obstinacy.[23]

---

[21] For example, only one of Luther's mentions of Sodom in *De votis monasticis* seems to me to allude to male–male sex even indirectly. He there quotes Ezekiel 16:49–50 and goes on to describe arrogance and luxury as threats to monastic chastity. See Weimar *Werke*, 8:650–1; cf. trans. Atkinson, *Luther's Works*, 44:370–1.

[22] Calvin, *Institutes*, 4.13.15 (ed. Barth and Niesel, 252; trans. Battles, 21:1270).

[23] Calvin, *Institutes*, 4.13.21 (ed. Barth and Niesel, 258:19–28; trans. Battles, 21:1276).

Here "against nature" refers to vows of continence undertaken without divine calling. But it is not hard to hear in it the suggestion that monasteries conceal those who sin "against nature" in the more traditional sense.

Later Protestant polemicists could be less restrained. They often presumed that Catholic clergymen and members of religious orders would be sodomites, as they argued that sodomy followed inevitably from the unnatural arrangements of mandatory celibacy and all-male or all-female communities. In the Netherlands, one Calvinist divine likened Rome to "an abominable bordello of sodomitic love," while another proclaimed that enforced celibacy had produced "a hundred thousand sodomites."[24] It was with particular relish that Protestant writers trumpeted the sodomy of celebrated Catholic counter-Reformers such as Giovanni della Casa.[25] Even those who led the Catholic campaign to reform the church of Rome succumbed to the traditional sins of the Roman clergy.

If sodomy was an attribute of papal religion, and if the papacy was at war with Protestant governments, then sodomy should be construed as simultaneously a form of apostasy and of rebellion. So it was. In England, sodomy recurs as a fixed attribute of the treasonous and heretical Papist.[26] A charge of sodomy was thus immensely useful as a political weapon. It implied and followed from a charge of treason. The usefulness of the charge had long been known.[27] Indeed, in creating the category of "sodomy," Christian theology created a new technology for Christian political warfare. What other allegation of secret behavior could so excite popular hatred while giving ample legal grounds for deposition from clerical or political office and seizure of personal or institutional property? But so far as Reformation polemic affixed the sin of sodomy to papism, it intensified the power of the charge. It became now more than ever a triple threat – an accusation of personal filthiness, of shared heresy, and of high treason.

With the rhetoric surrounding sodomy now so highly charged, it became curiously fantastic. The ideal Sodomite was seen as belonging to another realm – one far beyond ordinary experience. To say this in reverse: the Sodomite had to be kept out of ordinary experience, because the attributes

---

[24] Theo Van der Meer, *Sodoms zaad in Nederland: Het onstaan van homoseksualiteit in de vroegmoderne tijd* (Nijmegen: SUN, 1995), p. 372.

[25] Schleiner, "'That Matter,'" pp. 49–54.

[26] Alan Bray, *Homosexuality in Renaissance England* (expanded ed., New York: Columbia University Press, 1995), pp. 19–21, 26, 29, 52.

[27] For a reflection on some other political cases outside the church, see James A. Brundage, "The Politics of Sodomy: Rex. V. Pons Hugh de Ampurias (1311)," in *Sex in the Middle Ages*, ed. Joyce Salisbury (New York: Garland, 1991), pp. 239–46.

affixed to the Sodomite did not correspond to ordinary experience. At the same time, and however fantastic the identity of the Sodomite was becoming, the need to fight treasonous sodomites effectively required legal specification of sodomitic crimes. Moral theologians had to supply classifications to the growing modern bureaucracies for policing morals. The bureaucracies were both Protestant and Catholic, both "secular" and "religious" (so far as that distinction can be made in early modern Europe). The bureaucracies required old silences to be broken and old vagueness to be filled in. All sorts of bold questions had to be asked and answered. For example, was it really possible for women to commit a complete or "perfect" act of sodomy? This question was pushed both by the need to specify acts and by the construction of the identity – which had remained male (indeed clerical) in both the theological and the popular imagination.

Consider the enormous *Cursus theologiae moralis* elaborated by the Discalced Carmelites of Salamanca between 1685 and 1715. In the treatise on the sixth and ninth commandments, they devote a whole section or *punctum* to sodomy. Thomas Aquinas's definition is their starting point.[28] It is unfolded with casuistical precision: sodomy is coupling (*concubitus*), which distinguishes it from masturbation. It is coupling not with the proper sex, which distinguishes it from all other species of luxurious coupling. So the distinguishing difference of sodomy, according to the "Salmanticenses" (as they were called), is the gender of the partner, or "supposit", as they like to say. But is a woman coupling with a woman the "true sin of sodomy"? Yes, indeed, under Thomas's definition, and it is to be punished as sodomy, that is, by burning. The authorities further concur in holding that one discovers the perfect crime of sodomy whenever one woman "inseminates" another, in or out of the vagina, with or without an "instrument" (that is, a dildo or other device).

A slightly different answer is given by a text that would fix Catholic moral theology well into our own century. The text is the *Moral Theology* of Alphonsus Liguori, first definitively assembled in 1757. Alphonsus comes to the question of sodomy within his treatise on the sixth commandment, in a section on the species of *luxuria* consummated against nature.[29] He first repeats the received distinction between two kinds of sodomy. Imperfect

---

[28] "Salmanticenses," *Collegii Salmanticensis Fratres Discalceatorum Cursus theologiae moralis* (Venice: Nicolaus Pezzana, 1724), 6.7.5.1, 6:162b, para. 77.

[29] Alphonsus Maria de Liguori, *Theologia moralis*, 3.4.2.3, in *Sämtliche Werke des heiligen Bischofes und Kirchenlehrers Alphons Maria von Liguori*, Abteilung 3: *Moraltheologische Werke*, ed. Michael Haringer (2nd ed., Regensburg: Georg Joseph Manz, 1879), vol. 10, p. 38, no. 466.

sodomy is male–female copulation outside the approved organ or "vessel." Perfect sodomy is same-sex copulation, which may be distinguished as active and passive. But we already know, even if Alphonsus did not immediately remind us, that there is a "great question" about which acts constitute sodomy. Some believe that it is copulation with the inappropriate sex, others copulation in an inappropriate vessel. Both opinions are probable and each highlights one kind of deformity. Alphonsus himself finds the second opinion more probable and more widely approved. But his real work comes in a series of inferences from the approved definition.

The first inference is that there can be true sodomy between woman and woman, though Alphonsus admits that it is not entirely improbable to regard this as a sort of "improper sodomy, since there cannot be perfect copulation between women."[30] Alphonsus's second inference is that any coupling or touching of bodies with a person of the same sex constitutes "true sodomy," no matter what parts of the body are involved. The only mitigating circumstance to be mentioned in confession is the absence of ejaculation or pollution. Alphonsus's third inference is that male–female anal intercourse is "only imperfect sodomy, distinct in species from perfect [sodomy]."[31] He then adds a question about whether oral sex is also a distinct species of sodomy. The answer: "irrumation" in the mouth of a woman is to be regarded as "inchoate copulation." In the mouth of a man, it is sodomy. He does not make mention of what we would call cunnilingus: all of his oral sex requires a penis.

Technical definitions were used by the bureaucracies to police the identities. Technical moral teaching about women and sodomy did not much alter the identity of the Sodomite, either in theological or popular imagination. Up through the nineteenth century, the theologian's Sodomite remains what he was in the eleventh century, a man – and too often a churchman. We ought to learn from this not only that technical correc-tions can be slow in changing powerful identity-motifs, but also that the theological identities reach much further and last much longer than the proof texts or argumentative principles from which they are supposed to derive.

Theological identity-motifs may even outlast theology itself – or the transfer of power from churchly to secular bureaucracies. Michel Foucault is notorious for arguing that the category of "homosexuality" was invented in the nineteenth-century and that it differed in significant ways from categories for same-sex desires or actions that had gone before. Foucault's

---

[30] Liguori, *Theologia moralis*, 3.4.2.3 (ed. Haringer, p. 40).
[31] Liguori, *Theologia moralis*, 3.4.2.3 (ed. Haringer, pp. 40–1).

argument is subtle and usually misunderstood.[32] It ought to be connected with a theological suggestion he makes in the same text. He suggests that we can discern the birth of the modern notion of sexuality in the kinds of surveillance practiced within seminaries, religious colleges, and convents since the Counter-Reformation.[33] Modern sexuality was churched *before* it was born. Foucault himself describes a series of extensions by which the monastic discipline of chastity was applied to larger and larger groups – to the clergy as a whole; then to all religious, male and female; then to pious laypeople; then to laypeople simply.[34]

The extension can be traced as well into the "Homosexual," which is in at least two ways still a theological artifact. First, quite obviously, the rhetoric of sodomy is hardly extinct. It survives literally in any number of Christian communities. It survives concealed in others: where the term "sodomy" has recently been abandoned in favor of "homosexuality," as in Vatican statements, the rhetorical logic of the older term persists. The category of "homosexuality" brings some of its own ideas, some of its particular legal and medical logic, but it has to fit these within a logic of definition and condemnation set in place long before it was coined. More-over, second, the "Homosexual" remains a theological artifact because Christian rhetorics of identity enforcement were infused into the category from the very beginning – in ways that Foucault does and does not admit. It may be that the identity of the homosexual pervert really is just a variation on the much older theological category of the sexualized sin-identity. We will be able to go further with this notion as we add another of the old and new sexual identities, that of the self-abuser.

Masturbation, or Identity in Solitude

The exemplary scriptural sin of masturbation was supposedly performed by a man, though it is in fact difficult to understand how exactly an urgent concern for masturbation found a footing in the Christian Bible. The passage most often cited – the passage that gives masturbation its theological name – seems to be concerned in fact with another sin. In Genesis 9:8–10, Onan

[32] For a masterful interpretation and elaboration of it, see David M. Halperin, "How to Do the History of Male Homosexuality," *GLQ: A Journal of Lesbian and Gay Studies* 6 (2000): 87–123.

[33] Michel Foucault, *Histoire de la sexualité*, vol. 1: *La volonté de savoir* (Paris: NRF/Gallimard, 1976), p. 142 (trans. Hurley, pp. 107–8).

[34] Foucault, *Histoire de la sexualité*, 1:29 (trans. Hurley, pp. 20–1).

is commanded by Judah to fulfill the obligation of levirate marriage by impregnating his deceased brother's wife so that his brother's line might be continued. (Onan's brother has been killed by God for unspecified wickedness.) But Onan is unwilling to fulfill the obligation because he knows that any resulting children will not be counted as his offspring. So he "spills his seed" on the ground whenever he goes to copulate with his brother's wife. For this disobedience to marriage law, God kills Onan.

Now the sin or crime in this passage is not the "spilling of seed," but the refusal to provide offspring for the dead brother. Moreover, it is not at all clear from the passage that Onan "spills his seed" by what we would call masturbation. The fact that he does this just when he goes to impregnate his brother's wife suggests that the "spilling" is withdrawal at the point of ejaculation. Certainly there is no explicit condemnation of masturbation elsewhere in the Torah, though there is the claim that any ejaculation renders a man temporarily unclean (Leviticus 15.16–17). Even so, these three verses in Genesis were taken by many Christian theologians as warrant for condemning masturbation as "Onanism."

The other scriptural passages that are traditionally cited by Christians as condemnations of masturbation are vaguer still. In one of Paul's sin-lists, which we encountered above, we find the term *malakoi*, that is, "the soft" or (more figuratively) "the weak" or "the corrupt" (1 Corinthians 6:9). Modern exegetes have quarreled over whether this refers to "passive" male homosexuals, male homosexuals generally, the effeminate (whatever that might mean), or (male?) masturbators. The quarrels are endless because the passage gives no evidence for concluding them. So, too, with Pauline references to "uncleanness" (Galatians 5:19–21, Colossians 3:5–6, Ephesians 5:3). These are so unclear, so general, that they can be made to refer to anything that does or ought to make one ashamed. Many Christians seem to have been ashamed about masturbation – or to have been ashamed that they were not sufficiently shamed by it. So it is perhaps not surprising that many Christian exegetes have understood Paul to be referring in these passages to masturbation – or, rather, to male masturbation, since female masturbation that did not involve penetration seems always to have been a confusing subject for these male authors.

From these sparse scriptural beginnings, masturbation went on to an extraordinary history in Christian ethics, a history that linked it especially with the dangers of solitude – the solitude of the monastic cell or the convent garden or the child's bedroom, but also the solitude of the sinner's remembered past or fantasized future. But with masturbation, as with the other unnatural acts, the theological history is often one of allusion and concealment, of saying much less than enough to be clear. One scholar concludes from a meticulous survey that the first explicit description of solitary masturbation doesn't appear in Christian writing before the sixth century.[35] Earlier passages either speak euphemistically or combine masturbation with other forms of sexual activity. For masturbation, too, as with the other unnatural acts, the most explicit discussions concern men rather than women. Long after we have clear descriptions of male masturbation, female masturbation is often undistinguished from other genital activity between women. Women's sexual life remains remarkably vague to the male writers of moral theology.

Christian monastic communities have long stigmatized male masturbation as one of a range of prohibited sexual actions. It figured as a dangerous disruption of the quest for purity. We have already seen something of the shape of this ideal for Christian religious communities. We can now situate the preoccupation with masturbation in it. Let me use as an example the *Ladder* of John Climachus (c.579–c.649), a book that still retains great authority for Orthodox communities. In the *Ladder*, monks are urged to attain a state in which no body, no beauty, causes erotic "stirrings."[36] The beginning of chastity is the refusal to consent to erotic thoughts or nocturnal emissions. The middle stage is freedom of erotic dreams and their consequent emissions, though erections may still occur (e.g., from overeating). The last stage of chastity is to be free even from erections.

Under such ideals, overt sexual acts will obviously be condemned. Monks are tempted to overt acts by devils who seek to murder their souls by entrapping them in unnatural sins. These unnatural sins include masturbation, a particularly cunning temptation for monks who spend much time in solitude: "opportunity for lapses" lie "everywhere." John Climachus applies the teaching of Anthony the Great, the type of monastic founder, who "knew well that the sin of fornication does not require the availability of another body."[37] The cell is a place of great risk for this temptation, and bedtime the riskiest hour. Casual contacts can also feed the mind: "with the eye alone, with a mere glance, by the touch of a hand, through a song

---

[35]   See the summary of conclusions in Giovanni Cappelli, *Autoerotismo: Un problema morale nei primi secoli cristiani?*, Nuovi saggi teologici, vol. 23 (Bologna: Edizioni Dehoniane, 1986), pp. 255–63, particularly the characterization of the sixth-century change on p. 263.

[36]   John Climachus, *The Ladder of Divine Ascent*, trans. Colm Luibheid and Norman Russell, ed. Richard J. Payne, Classics of Western Spirituality (Mahwah, NJ: Paulist Press, 1982), Step 15, p. 172.

[37]   John Climachus, *The Ladder of Divine Ascent*, Step 15 (trans. Luibheid and Russell, pp. 174–5).

overheard, the soul is led to commit a definite sin of unchastity without any notion or evil thought."[38] The monk must wage constant warfare against the demonic seductions. A defeat in the battle bring serious consequences. If John does indeed include masturbation as a kind of fornication, he elsewhere cites a conciliar canon that punishes fornication with seven years' exclusion from communion.[39]

The severity of the punishment may surprise. It is connected no doubt to the special status of the monk as God's athlete, as an angel on earth. But it is also due to the fact that masturbation is a symptom for Climachus of spiritual diseases that particularly afflict the monk. He abandons marriage to dwell in a complicated solitude. It can take opposite values. On the one hand, Climachus emphasizes the dangers of the desert or the cell. On the other hand, he praises solitude in some cases as a remedy for thoughts that might lead to masturbation or involuntary pollution. (A monk who was troubled by fantasies at a dinner excuses himself as if to go to the toilet. He goes, in fact, to compose himself outside.) The most dangerous solitude is the solitude of inner reverie – the solitude of private memory or fantasy, the solitude that is the necessary effect of individual consciousness. So too the outward act of masturbation is only the sign of sexual sins committed inwardly, in memory and fantasy.

In trying to cure or to penalize these erotic thoughts, these invisible masturbations, Climachus cites a classification of the degrees of mental sin. It corresponds to and partly explains the degrees of physical arousal already discussed. The classification that Climachus uses is only one of a large number of schemes for distinguishing and judging the mind's sexual acts. From the early Egyptian monasteries to the early modern confessional, Christians have been concerned to analyze sexual fantasies according to a number of criteria, such as intensity, duration, resistance to efforts at repression, extent and consequence of physical effects. Many of the analyses were interested in assessing the degree of the sinner's consent. A weak sexual image immediately resisted was probably not wanted – hence, not culpable. An erotic epic deliciously elaborated in order to produce repeated physical excitements certainly was wanted – and seriously culpable. These analyses would eventually make up that large branch of sexual ethics concerned with what Latin speakers called *delectatio morosa* and English speakers "impure thoughts."

[38] John Climachus, *The Ladder of Divine Ascent*, Step 15 (trans. Luibheid and Russell, p. 183).
[39] John Climachus, *The Ladder of Divine Ascent*, Step 15 (trans. Luibheid and Russell, p. 177).

The concern was not only with consent to fantasy or culpability for it. As Climachus has shown, the frequency, intensity, and effect of sexual fantasy were taken as an important indication of one's degree of spiritual progress. Monks who committed no outward sins of unchastity could still be sinning inside, afflicted by memories or fantasies that they did their best to resist or repress. The spiritual warfare waged by demons fastened on the body, but also on the memories and anticipations of a private mind in a body. The body could and should be mortified to prevent its succumbing to masturbation. The mind had somehow to be deprivatized in order to resist those thoughts. So monastic life developed more and more subtle techniques for placing the mind in the presence of God, or the Virgin Mary, or the saints. In all of these ways, masturbation was connected in monastic life with the much larger surveillance of unruly bodies and selfish souls.

Monastic preoccupations with masturbation entered the main ethical traditions not just as high ideals, but as penitential codes that covered all kinds of Christians. In the Irish and Anglo-Saxon penitentials, for example, we see a wide range of punishments for single acts of masturbation. They are typically graded by age and church status. In one text, an adult monk who "defiles" himself is ordered to do penance in confinement for one year. Shorter sentences are given for young men ("twenty years") and for boys ("twelve years").[40] Another text assigns a penance of two years for adults; another, three years for those ordained or under vows.[41] The so-called "Ambrosian" penitential also mitigates the penalty for those with less education, while the text attributed to St. Columbanus makes mention of the masturbator's marital status.[42]

In the Latin penitentials, masturbation is regularly connected or confused with other sexual crimes. For example, the same text of Columbanus juxtaposes masturbation and bestiality.[43] That juxtaposition is not unusual: "fornication with oneself" is often treated in the same paragraph as "fornication with an animal." The *Penitential of Cummean* reads: "He who sins with a beast shall do penance for a year; if by himself, for three forty-day periods; if he has [clerical] rank, a year; a boy of fifteen years, forty days."[44]

---

[40] Bieler, *Irish Penitentials*, pp. 66–7, no. 2 (Synod of North Britain); cf. pp. 114–15, no. 6 (Cummean). See also, for a finely graded list, pp. 598–9, nos. 3–7 (Ps.-Theodore).

[41] Respectively, Bieler, *Irish Penitentials*, pp. 68–9, no. 8 (Synod of Grove of Victory), though the English translation prudishly omits the details; pp. 100–1, no. 10 (St. Columbanus).

[42] Bieler, *Irish Penitentials*, pp. 102–3, no. 17 (St. Columbanus).

[43] Bieler, *Irish Penitentials*, pp. 100–1, no. 10 (St. Columbanus).

[44] Bieler, *Irish Penitentials*, pp. 114–15, no. 6 (Cummean).

It is not clear what exactly makes the connection. It may be that the sins are linked as illicit ejaculations, as sins (putatively) condemned in the Old Testament, or as sins likely to be committed in solitude.

Medieval Latin theologians link masturbation not only with bestiality, but with sodomy. We have already seen that masturbation appears first in Peter Damian's list of the things that sodomites do. Somewhat later, he emphasizes the unnatural dangers of solitary sodomy by telling a cautionary tale. There was a hermit who was tricked by the devil into thinking that semen was not different from any other bodily superfluity.[45] Just as he blew his nose when congested, so the monk masturbated whenever he felt the tickle of desire. On his death, the hermit was seized by demons in full view of his monastic companion. The companion, knowing the man's practice of the virtues but not his sexual crime, despaired that anyone could attain salvation. An angel stood by to explain that the departed hermit had befouled all of his good deeds by the unrepented sin of uncleanness.

Peter Damian's judgment on the gravity of masturbation was not generally shared. Even when acknowledging receipt of the *Gomorran Book*, Pope Leo IX demurred from the conclusion that a single act of masturbation ought to be grounds for deposition from priestly office. Again, however much the penitentials disagree about the exact penalties for any particular sin, they generally agree in assigning much lighter penances to solitary masturbation than to male–male sex. Still others seem to have assumed that male masturbation would lead to mutual masturbation, which would lead on to simulated or real intercourse. Robert of Sorbonne, for example, writing in the 1260s or 1270s, says that the confessor can give this sort of warning: "It is the custom of sodomites to show each other their male parts (*virilia*), and they know each other by this sign, and it is most vile to become like the sodomites."[46] But Robert adds immediately that this is best said only to those who desire women vehemently and who have often sinned with women. Other masturbators, the less virile, are apparently at risk of sliding all too quickly from masturbation to exhibitionism to sodomy.

Once discovered, the sin of masturbation had to be condemned harshly and with compelling arguments. The condemnations may sometimes seem exaggerated. In Robert of Sorbonne, again, no advice is given about how

---

[45]   Peter Damian, *Liber Gomorrhianus* (ed. Reindel, 1:319.3–12).

[46]   On Robert and his confessional booklet, see Mark D. Jordan, *The Invention of Sodomy in Christian Theology* (Chicago: University of Chicago Press, 1997), pp. 104–5. I translate here from the text printed as a work of William of Auvergne in *Guilielmi Alverni . . . Opera omnia* (Paris: A. Pallard, 1674; repr. Frankfurt am M.: Minerva, 1962), 2:2321b–2b.

to interrogate the penitent about masturbation. The penitent spontaneously admits to have ejaculated by touching his "nature" with his own hands. The confessor is to reply as follows:

> You sinned most seriously, and it seems more serious to sin by doing this than by knowing one's own mother; for it is more serious to know a relation than to know a stranger, and the closer the person is as relation the more serious the sin done with that person. So someone who pollutes himself in this way sins most seriously.[47]

Quite ingeniously, Robert makes one's relation to oneself the worst case of incest. Because you are closer to yourself than to anyone else, having sex with yourself is the worst kind of incest – worse than copulating with your mother. A similarly exaggerated argument is found in the *Compilation* of Peter of Poitiers (c.1216), who compares the masturbator to a hermaphrodite who plays both male and female roles with himself/herself.[48]

These relational analyses of masturbation may be amusing or appalling, but they ought not to conceal the logic at work in the main medieval accounts. Theologians view masturbation mainly as deliberate self-pollution. Involuntary pollution is troubling enough, as we can see in the continuing discussion of nocturnal emissions. But voluntary pollution adds, in the medieval imagination, an extra horror. The closest medieval analogy would be, to adapt a suggestion from Dyan Elliott, a sort of voluntary menstruation.[49] If menstrual blood is conceived as intrinsically defiling (and it was), then voluntary menstruation would be doubly so. Semen outside of its proper place is conceived as polluting: wasted semen, like menstrual blood, is the by-product of failed fertility. Moreover, since semen is on many medieval medical accounts a kind of distilled blood, it is easy enough to transfer blood taboos onto it.

We recover here something of the logic that makes "spilling seed" the best moral description of masturbation. But this logic can have the unintended consequence of diminishing the seriousness of female masturbation. If women do not have seed, then they cannot spill it. It would seem then that women cannot commit the sin of Onan. Whatever sin there is in female masturbation is some less serious sin of physical pleasure. Female

---

[47]   I translate again from the text printed as a work of William of Auvergne in *Guilelmi Alverni . . . Opera omnia*, 2:2321b–2b.

[48]   Peter of Poitiers, *Compilatio praesens*, ed. Jean Longère, Corpus Christianorum Continuatio Mediaevalis, vol. 51 (Turnhout: Brepols, 1980), pp. 18–19.

[49]   Elliott, *Fallen Bodies*, pp. 27–9.

masturbation would, on this logic, be in the same moral class as lascivious kissing or lewd touching. But this also means that a change in the view of women's role in conception will also change the evaluation of female masturbation.

We can see this clearly enough within early modern Catholic theology – in that most authorized of commentaries on Thomas's *Summa*, the explanations and defenses of Thomas de Vio, Cardinal Cajetan.[50] When Cajetan comes to comment on Thomas's q.154 a.11, the article on vice against nature, he lists six "doubts," that is, six topics in need of elaboration. In a number of these, he is trying to specify how exactly the category of sodomy articulates with sex differences. But he adds to these, in the next article, an "arduous doubt" about how "masturbation and sodomitic vice" can be mortal sins in women. The answer that he wants to give is that mature women do indeed have "seed" and can waste it just as men do.[51] The change in medical teaching extends the full force of the moral judgment to women's masturbation or to sexual acts between women. It applies as well to certain acts between married partners. The fifth doubt of the previous article has asked whether it is against nature for a man to get a woman to emit her seed, that is, to attain orgasm, without emitting his own. Cajetan's answer is Yes, on the grounds that bringing about emission in a man or a woman under conditions that do not allow conception is just the definition of sin against nature.

Reformation and Counter-Reformation theologies inherited these large and contradictory discourses about masturbation. Sometimes masturbation appears as an emblem for the private sins of the most spiritual. Sometimes it appears as the prelude to same-sex sin, that is, to sodomy. In some texts, it is the dreadful wasting of human seed; in others, the weakness of the young and ignorant. These themes seem to me to cut across the divide between Catholic and Protestant theologians. You can find many Catholic theologians of the modern period who analyze more and more detailed cases of masturbation with a view to confessional practice, but you can also find Protestant casuists who have other ends in view. If many Protestant writers reject the confessional's preoccupation with the numeration and recitation of individual acts in favor of a more psychological analysis, so

[50] The commentary is printed in the Leonine edition of Thomas's *Summa*, that is, in Thomas Aquinas, *Opera omnia iussu impensaque Leonis XIII. P. M. edita*, ed. members of the Order of Preachers, vols. 4–12 (Rome, 1882–) [cited henceforth as "Leonine *Opera*"]. Cajetan completed his commentary on the moral part of the *Summa* in 1517.
[51] Thomas Aquinas, *Summa theologiae*, 2–2.154.12, "Commentaria Cardinalis Caietani," sects. 20–1 (Leonine *Opera* 10:252a–b).

do many Catholic writers. In both Catholics and Protestants, we watch the extension of the moral supervision into more and more areas of the life of the laity. We have already seen Protestant and Catholic authors adopting notions of virginal purity to the new circumstances of bourgeois life. We can also see them adopting monastic doctrines of dangerous solitude.

More striking in the wake of the Reformation is the emergence of a clearer identity for the masturbator. We see it most clearly in the great medical campaign against masturbation begun in the eighteenth century. The campaign has many causes and stretches forward into our own time. It is often interpreted as an important indication of the increasing regulation of human sexual life by medical and legal bureaucracies – a regulation with which we are all intimately familiar. But the campaign was supported from its origins by theological reasonings and church authority. This is plain enough in a notorious English treatise that many treat as a founding charter of the campaign against masturbation – the booklet *Onania*, first published in London around 1710.[52]

Now *Onania* is in many ways simply a work of quackery. It is an advertisement for the author's therapies against "abominable practice." Still, the medical argument is framed by a theological one. Before the title page labels masturbation an "abominable practice," it calls it a "heinous sin." Indeed, the title page quotes the end of the story of Onan from Genesis 38:9–10. The first sentence of the Preface reinforces the message:

> The Sin of ONAN, and GOD's sudden Vengeance upon it, are so remarkable, that every Body will easily perceive, that from his Name I have derived the running Title of this little Book; and tho' I treat of this Crime in Relation to Women, as well as Men, whilst the Offence, is SELF–POLLUTION in both, I could not think of any other Word which would so well put the Reader in Mind both of the Sin and its Punishment at once, as this. (p. iii)

The treatise goes on to interpret the story from Genesis, not least by supporting it with a number of other scriptural passages (pp. 3, 30). It invokes theological authorities, not least by quoting at length from Jeremy Taylor

---

[52]   On the work's history and relation to other English and Continental treatises, see Roy Porter, "Forbidden Pleasures: Enlightenment Literature of Sexual Advice," in *Solitary Pleasures: The Historical, Literary, and Artistic Discourses of Autoeroticism*, ed. Paula Bennett and Vernon A. Rosario II (New York and London: Routledge, 1995), pp. 75–98, especially pp. 82–6. I quote here from the much expanded eighth edition of *Onania* published in 1723, repr. in Anonymous, *Onania, or the Heinous Sin of Self-Pollution, with A Supplement to the Onania*, ed. Randolph Trumbach (New York and London: Garland Publishing, 1986).

(p. 2). It reprints letters in which desperate readers ask for God's help – and the author's – in combating the dreadful sin. Whatever medical quackery there is in *Onania* is quackery in the costume of moral theology.

Christian children and adults have exerted tremendous effort to curb masturbatory impulses. The modern control of masturbation is the complement and continuation of medieval campaigns against sodomy. The Sodomite traditionally was a person who naturally created unnatural networks. He (or perhaps she) was the member of a tribe that reached down through history. The Onanist is precisely not the member of a tribe. He or she is a solitary sinner who destroys a body by spending too much time in the mind, in solitary fantasy. The war against sodomy attacks sexual sin in its political networks. The war against masturbation attacks it in its psychological solitudes. To do so, the church and the state need a bureaucracy that reaches into every dangerous place: the schoolyard, the dormitory, the gymnasium, the open field. It must create sites for instruction and therapy: the classroom, the Sunday school, the doctor's office, the scout troop. We can begin to see here how fully correlated are sexual identities and the bureaucracies erected to regulate them – that is, to elicit and punish their performances.

At the same time, there is a curious delay in fixing the theological identity of the Masturbator. In patristic and medieval times, the identity merged with that of the Sodomite or dissipated into the more general problem of desire. In both Protestant and Catholic reformers, the sin is caught up in growing programs of control, but not immediately conceived, not fully scripted. It is really only in the last three centuries, with the fuller transfer of power over sex from church to state, that we can clearly picture, first, the Onanist and, then, the Self-Abuser or Masturbator. We may begin to wonder here about why it is that certain acts or states are attached earlier than others to fully elaborated theological identities. We may also wonder whether there are some sexual acts that Christianity hasn't yet scripted into full identities.

Oral Sex, or Acts before Identity

The last of the unnatural acts mentioned by Thomas Aquinas was "sleeping together" with someone of the opposite sex in other than the natural way, either by using an improper instrument or by using certain "monstrous and bestial manners."[53] Improper instruments are not what are now called "sex toys." They are parts of the body not meant for *concubitus*, such as

[53] Thomas Aquinas, *Summa theologiae*, 2–2.154.11, corpus.

hands, anuses, and mouths. Readers have traditionally taken Thomas to be referring euphemistically to a series of prohibited heterosexual acts, including mutual masturbation, anal intercourse, and oral sex.

Thomas's teaching is hardly revolutionary. He is merely repeating what a number of earlier authors say. There may be condemnations of oral–genital activity as early as Augustine; there certainly are by the time of Alphonsus Liguori. We have already seen heterosexual fellatio condemned in the later Catholic casuists as fully unnatural, if not fully sodomitical. Indeed, it is only too easy to condemn oral sex by appealing to any of a number of principles invoked in condemnations of same-sex copulation or solitary masturbation. This kind of activity spills seed without procreative purpose. It produces extreme physical pleasure. It does not respect gender differences, and so might be taken as a prelude or inducement to same-sex copulations. Given so many different ways of making the condemnation, it is not surprising that fellatio and cunnilingus were universally condemned in Christian writers, when they were mentioned at all.

Indeed, what is interesting about judgments on oral sex is not that they are negative, but that they show the unstable interaction of the principles behind the judgments. They show, in other words, how the multiplicity of different principles begins to work against the category of the unnatural act. They also show the difficulty in approaching a theology of sexual sins without identity. This may be clearer if you conceive of the teaching about unnatural acts as the uncertain result of the interaction of a number of convictions – which is to say, of a number of anxieties. One anxiety is to prevent same-sex copulations from disrupting the division of the sexes and all the gendered expectations that follow from it. Another is to regulate private pleasures so that they don't derail the spiritual or psychological development of the individual. Yet another anxiety is to insure that sexual pleasure will encourage procreation rather than detract from it.

These anxieties have now to be mapped onto the set of possible human sexual actions. But the anxieties don't match up with actions in any obvious way. The same sexual action can be described differently under the impulse of different anxieties. Sometimes this will be a matter of which circum-stances are considered morally important. For traditional Christian moralists, a man being fellated by a man is not engaged in the same act as a man being fellated by a woman. The acts will be different again as we adjust the marital status of the partners. At other times, the interaction of the anxiet-ies will lead to different judgments of severity. A boy masturbating will be described differently depending on whether we are worried principally about his fantasy life, his possible attractions to other males, or his usefulness to the reproduction of the species. At yet other times, what matters is the interaction of the anxieties and the prevailing medical models. A girl masturbating will be judged differently by one anxious about reproduction depending on what view of the female role in reproduction is endorsed.

The interplay of these anxieties in relation to acts shows us something important about the category of unnatural acts. The problem in it is not in the end with the incoherencies and instabilities of "unnatural." It is with the notion of sexual acts. Christian ethics always stutters in speaking about specific unnatural acts. It has never been very fluent in describing them, much less in defining them. One reason for this is that theology's anxieties cut across the realm of sexual acts – as if in search of something else. It seems to have been searching for identities. The troupe of varying Christian sex-identities rescued theology from stuttering through analyses of unnatural acts. As these sex-identities have faded or mutated into secular models, the problem of classifying and specifying acts has returned to Christian theology with a vengeance. The difficulty we now feel in speaking convincing arguments about "unnatural" sex cannot be blamed on just the growth of modern medicine or the spread of liberal notions about self-fulfillment. We understand it better as a loss of the grand Christian rhetorics within which sin-identities made sense of acts by organizing them. When we try to pull the acts away from the identities, we find that they don't make much sense. Of course they don't. They never did without identities.

This loss of coherence in specifying "unnatural" acts is closely connected to the loss of conviction produced by appeals to natural law. Christian condemnations of unnatural acts were not meant to work without Christian sin-identities; arguments from natural law were not meant to work outside of an ideal pedagogy of virtuous family, just city, and luminous divine revelation. Natural law arguments about sex are not detachable from the Christian narrative of a progressive divine teaching through history. Christian classifications of sexual acts as unnatural are not detachable from the slow elaboration in theology of the sin-identities that give them sense by giving them scripts.

Chapter 5

Marriage Acts

After exhortations to the ideal of virginity, in spite of the solicitations of crimes against nature, we come at last to Christian marriage. We come to it at last, though so many theological discussions of the ethics of sex begin with it. The preceding chapters have wanted to show why that typical order must be reversed. To assume as obvious that "God made sex for marriage" is to miss how hard Christian theology has worked in order to make the claim obvious. If Christian believers and Christianized societies take for granted that married sex is the only normal sex, it is because they are urged every Sunday to take it for granted. They have judged all other forms of sex immoral and even unnatural in part because notions of morality and nature have been constructed to produce that judgment.

When we approach Christian marriage through the ideals of virginity and the invectives against the unnatural, we can perhaps see that marriage was constructed within Christianity as the only place left for sex. Marriage was meant to protect sex both from the ideals and from the invectives. To say this differently: marriage shelters some sexual activity from an otherwise absolute critique of sexual pleasure. In this chapter, we will examine the kinds of theological speeches that provided shelter. We will be concerned to see how they construct a protective boundary between moral sex and immoral sex, between married sex and everything else. We will also want to understand how that boundary restricts speech about the sex within marriage.

The principles of selection that I have used throughout must be applied most ruthlessly. There are too many topics in the library of Christian discourses. Historically Christians have asked of marriage: Is it permissible? Is it desirable? If it is permissible and desirable, what is it for? Who performs it? When exactly has it been fully performed? With whom can it be performed? Is its performance a central religious rite like baptism and the Eucharist?

Can the performance be repeated (in case of bereavement)? Can it be dissolved (without death)? These questions become topics for whole subfields in
theology. Consider, for example, the different elaborations of the criteria for
eligibility to enter into a marriage – criteria of age, consent, physiological
capability, sexual inexperience, church membership, spiritual condition, and
freedom from earlier obligations. Remember the analyses of the sequence
of promise ("engagement"), public ritual, and private consummation. Recall,
again, the elaborate Christian prohibitions against incestuous marriage,
which have excluded not only quite remote biological relations, but also a
number of forms of spiritual "kinship." The dialectic of theological motivations and social expectations stands out in the simple listing of these topics.
That dialectic becomes ever more complicated as Christian churches enter
differently evolving social structures. We should also remember that the
dialectic developed hesitantly and in dependence on civil institutions.
Christian churches were slow to make a place for their own marriage rites,
and slower still to develop any theological account of marriage.[1]

Our concern here is with a more restricted and basic question. We are
concerned not with marriage as a whole, but with marriage as the only site
of permissible sex. We want to sample theological speech that constructs
permission for married sex, not least to understand why it must pass over
many topics in silence. We want, then, to understand how the identities of
Christian Husband or Christian Wife are and are not sexual identities like
the others we have already seen.

Justifying Sex by Justifying Marriage

Augustine has told us in the *Confessions* of the decisive role that the
reading of Paul played in his conversion. When he obeyed the voice in
the garden and took up the book to read, he read those Pauline verses
through which he was able to accept the grace of continence.[2] Paul's effect

---

[1] For the slow development of Christian marriage, see Philip Lyndon Reynolds, *Marriage in the Western Church: The Christianization of Marriage during the Patristic and Early
Medieval Periods*, Supplements to Vigiliae Christianae, vol. 24 (Leiden and New York:
E. J. Brill, 1994); for medieval constructions of the canon law on sexual acts in and out
of marriage, see James A. Brundage, *Law, Sex, and Christian Society in Medieval Europe*
(Chicago: University of Chicago Press, 1987); for a classification of Christian "models"
of marriage, especially from the Reformation to the present, see Witte, *From Sacrament
to Contract.*
[2] Augustine, *Confessions*, 8.12.29 (ed. Skutella, rev. Verheijen, 131.31–6; trans.
Chadwick, pp. 152–3).

on Augustine was not unusual. Many Christians were and are moved by reading the canonical letters. Augustine's effect on the reading of Paul was unusual − and still is. Augustine has fixed a certain reading of Paul for generations of later readers. The moral theology of what we call western Christianity − the medieval "Catholic" church and all the European churches descended from it − is strictly inconceivable without Augustine. His influence is particularly strong in Christian sexual morality. It is also ambivalent. Augustine's writings are unruly, both extravagant and contradictory. A superbly rhetorical writer, he composes dialectically and always with a view to some particular persuasion. I remain very suspicious of attempts to synthesize a global moral teaching out of Augustine's texts. Augustine himself certainly did not favor syntheses. So I turn to a very particular booklet by Augustine − one that was widely quoted by later theologians and canon lawyers. It happens also to be a work thoroughly dependent on Paul, especially the Paul of 1 Corinthians 7. The booklet is Augustine's *On the Marital Good* (written in 401). It is known more commonly as *On the Good of Marriage.*

Augustine's purpose in the booklet is rather more complicated than the title might suggest. At first glance, it seems that he aims to establish that marriage is not intrinsically sinful. Christians can enter into marriage for the sake of procreating children and in order to enjoy the special bond between husband and wife. Christian marriage is a *sacramentum*, a holy oath or bond, which cannot be broken once it is undertaken. Christians should give their bodies to one another as if they did not own them, to open the way for children and to fight off the temptations of lust.[3] At the same time, Augustine repeats that celibacy is the preferable state. He argues at length that Christians live under very different conditions from those of the Old Testament patriarchs. The patriarchs were obliged to marry and to beget numerous children in order to build God's Chosen People and hasten the coming of the Messiah. There is no such need for numerous children in the Christian church. Indeed, it would not be a bad thing if every Christian were to be celibate. Universal abstinence would hasten completion of the City of God and the coming of the end of time.[4]

---

[3]   Augustine, *De bono coniugali* (*On the Marital Good*), 6.6, ed. Josephus Zycha, Corpus Scriptorum Ecclesiasticorum Latinorum, vol. 41 (Vienna: F. Tempsky, 1900). There are several English translations, of which the most accessible is probably that by Roy J. Deferrari in *Saint Augustine: Treatises on Marriage and Other Subjects*, Fathers of the Church: A New Translation (New York: Fathers of the Church, 1955).

[4]   Augustine, *De bono coniugali*, 10.10 (ed. Zycha, 201.10−13; trans. Deferrari, p. 23).

Augustine's purpose is really a set of purposes, and the purposes pull at one another. Marriage is a defensible concession to human weakness (though the strong will not need to avail themselves of it). Marriage is for the sake of procreation, which increases God's people (though procreation is no longer commanded as it was at the time of creation, and ceasing to procreate would hasten the Lord's return). Marriage is for companionship and the fullness of human society (though a higher companionship and a more perfect society can be found in "spiritual friendships" or monastic communities). Each assertion is balanced by a contrary assertion, each concession by a condescension.

In these claims and counterclaims, Augustine responds to 1 Corinthians 7, that primer for Christian discourse about sex. In that passage, Paul does offer a justification for Christian marriage, but it is not the same justification that Augustine wants to construct in his booklet. The Pauline text justifies monogamous marriage as an antidote to *porneia*, that is, to (unspecified) sexual sin: "Because of *porneia*, each man should have his own wife and each woman her own husband" (1 Cor. 7:2). Spouses are to "give" intercourse to each other as payment of a debt (7:3) in order to avoid demonic temptation directed at weakness of will (7:5). Those who cannot control their desire can marry without sin (7:36, 7:37). They *should* marry if they are not controlling themselves, because "it is better to marry than to burn" (7:9).

Paul's words in this chapter, taken by themselves, present marriage as a concession to uncontrolled or uncontrollable desire. Indeed, Paul himself labels his recommendation not to abstain from sex in marriage except by mutual consent an "allowance" or "counsel" rather than an "injunction" or "command" (7:6). Augustine can simply quote Paul up to this point. Augustine, too, regards marriage as a concession to desire. He too wants to present marriage as a way of life inferior to virginity or celibacy. He wants further to justify marriage as companionship. He can find some support for that claim in Paul's descriptions of mutual exchange. What Augustine cannot find in 1 Corinthians 7 is an argument for marriage from procreation. He cannot find it because it is not there.

Children are mentioned in Paul's chapter only once, in an aside to a discussion of (non-Christian) marriages contracted before one partner converts (7:14). The Apostle does not refer to children when he describes the benefits of marriage. He does not consider them when he is talking about its cares. In 1 Corinthians 7, men and women appear as married or unmarried, as spouses or celibates, but not as fathers and mothers. For that matter, Paul invokes parent–child relations in the whole letter chiefly as metaphors for spiritual relations within the Christian community. The most important "children" for this letter are the Corinthian Christians considered as Paul's spiritual wards (4:14–15). They are also "infants in Christ" who are not ready for adult food (3:1–2). They are, at the same time, Paul's "brothers and sisters" (from 1:10 on). Paul's paternity is preaching the Gospel; his family, his children, and his siblings are other Christian believers. The family of spirit displaces the family of flesh. Perhaps that is why Paul does not mention merely fleshly children in his discussion of marriage. The only individual child who appears in the chapter's immediate context is the man who is having sexual relations with his father's wife (5:1), and he is to be expelled from the Christian community.

Whatever the motives behind it, Paul's silence about child rearing creates a gap in the argument that Augustine needs to fill. He fills it by asserting that children are among the goods of marriage. He can then use the criterion of procreation as a way to limit sex in marriage further even than Paul does in 1 Corinthians 7. Augustine wants to stigmatize whole classes of excessive or unnatural sexual acts within marriage. He can now do so by classifying them as non-procreative. At the same time, more delicately, Augustine wants to suggest that licit sexual activity even within marriage is always open to corruption, always on the border of decent Christian living. The highest state, the most admirable one, is the state of Christian continence, and any Christian who can keep continence should.[5] So Augustine limits the appeal to procreation as soon as he makes it.

Proper sexual relations between husband and wife must satisfy a set of criteria that are not obviously connected with one another. First, most obviously, there is the criterion about the character of the marriage: it must be monogamous and permanent. There is no possibility of remarriage before death and no permission for adultery even by mutual consent.[6] Augustine does remark, in regard to the Israelite patriarchs, that polygamy "is not against the nature of marriage," but he does not apply the notion to Christian marriage.[7] Second, there is a criterion of reproduction. Marriage makes youthful lust honorable by using it for conceiving children; so nothing must be done to prevent births. Childless marriages are still marriages only if the partners have not taken to steps to make themselves childless.[8] Of course, the desire to have children in the ordinary way is itself suspect. "In our day, . . . no one perfect in piety seeks to have children except spiritually."[9] A third criterion in Augustine's booklet is what might be called a criterion of justice or obligation. It is captured by the Pauline metaphor of the fleshly

5   Augustine, *De bono coniugali*, 8.8 (ed. Zycha, 199.6–17; trans. Deferrari, p. 21).
6   Augustine, *De bono coniugali*, 3.3, 5.5, 15.17, 4.4, generally and respectively.
7   Augustine, *De bono coniugali*, 17.20 (ed. Zycha, 213.17–18; trans. Deferrari, p. 34).
8   Augustine, *De bono coniugali*, 3.3, 5.5, passim.
9   Augustine, *De bono coniugali*, 17.19 (ed. Zycha, 213.2–3; trans. Deferrari, p. 34).

"debt" that married persons "owe" one another.[10] A husband or wife may not deny reasonable requests for sexual intercourse, though a wife or husband must deny requests for sex against nature.[11] Finally, fourth, there is a criterion of temperance or self-restraint. Married couples should strive to limit intercourse to what is necessary for procreation and should look forward to an early cessation of sexual activity by mutual consent.[12]

The criteria cut across each other in particular cases. A young married couple, fired by lust, may engage in penile–vaginal intercourse much more than is required for procreation. In time, this excess will be curbed, first by their becoming mother and father, then by the decrease of sexual desire in age. But how are Christians to judge newlywed ardor? On the one hand, it is sinful to want excessive intercourse and a greater sin to do it. On the other hand, preventing illicit intercourse and especially adultery in some way excuses the sin. Evil habits push the married to excessive copulation, but the good of their marriage pardons the sins they commit – so long, that is, as the "sins" do not violate the criteria of monogamy and permanence or of reproduction or of natural acts. Augustine renders an equally complex judgment on the question of consensual abstinence within marriage. It is good for a married couple to reach an agreement about refraining from sexual activity. "Continence from all intercourse (concubitus) is certainly better than that marital intercourse which is for begetting children."[13] But it is imprudent for one partner in the marriage to impose abstinence unilaterally.

Augustine's judgments on sex within marriage cannot be reduced to any set of simple formulae. Much less can they be summed into a single "answer." I do think it important to test any interpretation of them against the rhetorical shape of the work in which they occur. At the beginning of On the Good of Marriage, in one of his apparently artless digressions, Augustine tries to imagine human life without death. He confesses himself uncertain how we might have reproduced if we had not sinned. The bodies of our first parents "merited the condition of death [only] by sinning, nor can there be copulation except of mortal bodies."[14] Augustine reasons with one hypothesis that procreation was given to us only because of death, in order to make up the void in human nature. Or perhaps, he continues, the original human bodies were somehow animal without being mortal. They would have been transformed into immortal bodies through obedience to spirit.

[10] Augustine, De bono coniugali, 4.4 (ed. Zycha, 191.17–19; trans. Deferrari, p. 13).
[11] Augustine, De bono coniugali, 11.12 (ed. Zycha, 204.6–8; trans. Deferrari, p. 25).
[12] Augustine, De bono coniugali, 3.3, 11.12, passim.
[13] Augustine, De bono coniugali, 6.6 (ed. Zycha, 195.23–4; trans. Deferrari, p. 17).
[14] Augustine, De bono coniugali, 2.2 (ed. Zycha, 188.8–9; trans. Deferrari, p. 10).

There would then have been new generations, but not the aging of the old. Augustine catches himself. We do not know which of the hypotheses is correct. We do not know what God intended for sinless human bodies. We do know, and Augustine repeats, that there would not have been any death without sin. Our urgent need to procreate is linked from the beginning with our original sin.

On the Good of Marriage ends with an extended consideration of the Hebrew patriarchs and their marriages. The consideration is in part a defense of the marriage of the patriarchs against the Christian endorsement of celibacy over marriage. How could the scriptures present us with holy figures who are married – who, indeed, are polygamous? Augustine replies by pleading historical changes (such as ancient underpopulation) and by urging that we Christians cannot know what virtues of self-restraint were exercised by the patriarchs. At no point does Augustine concede that marriage is for Christians a choice equal to the choice of life without sex. Indeed, the last chapter of his booklet not only urges couples to agree on marriage without sex, it ends with an exhortation to perseverance in those who have chosen virginity. The good of marriage is framed by hypotheses of life without reproduction and by persuasions to the choice of virginity.[15]

In his dialectical rereading of 1 Corinthians 7, Augustine makes theological room for sexual activity in Christian life. The space is small and well guarded. With Paul's text in hand, Augustine also fixes a number of the topics for theological discussion of married sex. From these topics, I choose three: procreation, marital lewdness, and adultery as linked to remarriage. These will serve as our points for sampling Christian discourses about sex in marriage. Before turning to them, I want to draw out some preliminary conclusions about the Christian identities for married partners.

Sex in marriage is the only approved space in Christianity for sex. Sex outside of marriage is counted serious sin. So it would seem that Husband and Wife would be the most sexual of approved Christian identities. But sex within marriage escapes sin only so far as it satisfies a complex set of criteria. These criteria are meant to remove from sex the sinfulness of unbridled lust, the effects of disordered *eros*. Moreover, they are meant in many Christian writers to move the spouses beyond sex – to contain it by making it a thing of the past, a shameful and youthful excess. So Husband and Wife are identities for containing and getting beyond sex. In this sense, they are in much of Christian tradition anti-erotic identities. They give us a contrast, in fact, for the identity of the Virgin Martyr. The Virgin Martyr can never have sex, but she earns by abstinence the privilege of

---

[15]   Augustine, *De bono coniugali*, 26.34–5, passim.

reversing gender roles and eroticizing her relation with Christ. The Christian Husband and Wife are permitted to have sex, but they can do so only by de-eroticizing it and by fully inhabiting their gender roles. Husband and Wife must have natural sex, that is, sex in which the man is man and the woman, woman. They must also have procreative sex, through which Christian Wife becomes Mother and Husband, Father.

The Procreative Rule

In his booklet *On the Good of Marriage*, Augustine does not make procreation the only end of marriage. He does make it an indispensable end of marriage, one that cannot be neglected or contradicted without destroying the marriage itself. Since he confines sexual activity to marriage, and since he judges that procreation must be an end for married sex, procreation provides a rule for judging sexual acts. This was an old rule in Christianity even when Augustine wrote – and an ambiguous one. If procreation is a rule for judging sex, it has never been the only rule, as Augustine makes perfectly clear. The actual or possible fertility in adultery or fornication cannot be used to justify those acts. They must be excluded by another rule, the rule that confines sex to marriage. We could summarize this by saying that procreation is a necessary and yet insufficient justification for sexual relations among Christians. But this summary would conceal more than reveal. Procreation is better understood as a rule that always needs other rules. We have seen that in Augustine. We can see it more clearly if we turn to a less familiar text by an author not so deeply embedded in every discussion of marriage among western Christians. The author is Clement of Alexandria, who provides several of the most detailed discussions of married relations in the early churches. I take the discussion from Clement's *Pedagogue* (written around 190), a book intended to lead Christians through the school of self-control in dozens of different situations – including marriage.

The *Pedagogue* starts its discussion of sexual matters by stating the procreative rule: "the goal is child-making (*paidopoiia*), the end having beautiful children."[16] Clement follows the statement with the first of many analogies to the cultivation of crops. But the decisive restriction has already been made in the words just before the principle of procreation: "We must now examine the appropriate time for copulation by married people, since for married people the goal is child-making, the end having beautiful children."

---

[16] Clement of Alexandria, *Pedagogue*, 2.10.83.1, as in *Le pédagogue, II*, trans. Claude Mondésert, ed. Henri-Irénée Marrou, Sources Chrétiennes, vol. 108 (Paris: Éditions du Cerf, 1965).

The repetition of "married people" makes clear that procreation cannot be discussed except within marriage. Which rules justify that restriction? There are at least three in Clement's text, and they should be considered a supplement to Augustine's criteria for licit married sex. The first rule here is the now familiar rule of self-control, that is, the claim that sexual activity can only be permissible if it is kept to a strict minimum. The second is a rule of social order, that is, the claim that sexual excesses are contagious, progressive, and rapidly destructive of social harmony. The third is a rule of purity, that is, the judgment that certain substances are polluting.

Clement introduces the additional rules within an animal allegory. This kind of allegory was common enough in ancient philosophy, and Clement relies on pagan accounts for (alleged) details about the animals' habits or anatomy. The particular allegory is suggested to him by Hebrew prohibitions against eating meat from the hyena or the rabbit.[17] The hyena is prohibited, Clement explains, because its curious anatomy encourages sterile copulations between members of the same sex. We are taught by this to avoid anal intercourse specifically and same-sex relations generally. So far the allegory reinforces the rule of procreation. The rabbit is prohibited, Clement continues, in order to teach us "to abstain from violent desires and uninterrupted couplings, from unions with pregnant females, from lasciviousness and pederasty, from adultery and promiscuity."[18] Intercourse with a member of the same sex or during pregnancy can be condemned on the rule of procreation, but the other sins on the list might all be fertile. They have to be condemned with another rule. That rule is a requirement of self-mastery. Clement supports it with both biblical and philosophical authorities, from Plato and the Stoics. The critique of excess in sexual relations is a critique of pleasure. "Pleasure (*hêdonê*) just by itself, even if contained within marriage, is against law, against justice, and against reason."[19] Pleasure or overpowering desire (*epithumia*) is a feverish tyrant that leads to a host of maladies, especially to the sickness of promiscuity, which is "common and vulgar and impure."[20] Opposed to promiscuity is the Christian practice of self-control or self-mastery (*sôphrosunê*).[21]

In this praise of self-control, we see Clement invoking the rule of purity. It figures more explicitly in other passages. For example, he rejects intercourse

---

[17] Leviticus 11:5–6. Clement's version must have said "hyena" where modern versions mention another animal, perhaps the rock badger (NRSV).

[18] Clement of Alexandria, *Pedagogue*, 2.10.88.3 (Mondésert).

[19] Clement of Alexandria, *Pedagogue*, 2.10.92.2 (Mondésert).

[20] Clement of Alexandria, *Pedagogue*, 2.10.93.2 (Mondésert).

[21] Clement of Alexandria, *Pedagogue*, 2.10.97.2 (twice), 2.10.100.2 (Mondésert).

during menstruation on grounds that one shouldn't "dirty" the essence of semen with bodily impurities, since that essence has the capacity to become a human being.[22] Again, Clement compares the fornicator to a cadaver: "What is holy, as is evident, refuses to be dirtied."[23] A city in which debauchery is performed is, even for the pagan poets, a city "full of impurities."[24]

A city, indeed. Here Clement invokes yet another rule, a rule of social order. Sexual pleasure is against the law and against justice: it produces bastard children, as it commits injustice by taking another's spouse.[25] Again and again in these pages Clement proscribes activities using terms of order: Christians should avoid what is illegal, unjust, irrationally disordered. In an earlier section, he had summarized his condemnations of obscene language or behavior by invoking social propriety and law: human genitals deserve respect rather than shame, but they become obscene when they act contrary to the law. It is then that they deserve both disrespect and punishment.[26] "Law" has many meanings here. It refers to scriptural commands or to the regularities of nature. It also refers to the common law of all civilized people, to the norms of good society. We are constrained by these norms to avoid not only obscene displays of bodily parts, but even words that refer to them. A rule of good order stands ready to guide us in erotic matters where the rule of procreation might fail.

A rule of procreation just by itself would not prohibit unmarried sex or even adultery. Indeed, it might be used as an argument for sex outside of marriage in certain cases – say, where a fertile woman found herself married to an infertile man. If nature has made our genitals for reproduction, why let nature's purposes be frustrated by such a misalliance? For Clement, as for other Christian authors, the rule of procreation is checked or corrected in these cases by rules of self-control, social order, and purity. The rules lead him to reinterpret important scriptural passages. Chief among these is the original blessing pronounced immediately after the creation of human beings: "Be fruitful and multiply" (Genesis 1:28). Clement interprets this restrictively: "The Lord wants humankind to 'multiply,' but he does not say 'be promiscuous,' and he does not want us to give ourselves to pleasures as if we were born for coupling."[27]

---

[22] Clement of Alexandria, *Pedagogue*, 2.10.92.1 (Mondésert).
[23] Clement of Alexandria, *Pedagogue*, 2.10.100.1 (Mondésert).
[24] Clement of Alexandria, *Pedagogue*, 2.10.98.3–94.1 (Mondésert), quoting the "Sibylline Oracles."
[25] Clement of Alexandria, *Pedagogue*, 2.10.91.1 (Mondésert).
[26] Clement of Alexandria, *Pedagogue*, 2.6.52.2 (Mondésert).
[27] Clement of Alexandria, *Pedagogue*, 2.10.95.2 (Mondésert).

The rule of procreation does not work alone. It requires correction by other rules. It must also presuppose some particular model of human reproductive physiology. For Clement, semen is the active principle of generation, while the woman contributes only matter – indeed, matter that rapidly becomes "impure" and is rejected by the body in menstruation. Many other Christian authors have relied on similar accounts that privileged the male's biological role. They have also adopted physiological evaluations of sexual intercourse. For Clement, again, as for much of ancient and medieval medicine, sexual intercourse and especially male ejaculation weakens the body. Christians should exercise self-control not only because it is good morals, but because it is good medicine.[28] Many other Christian authors have asserted medical reasons for restricting application of the rule of procreation.

The rule of procreation doesn't work alone, but it can be combined with various principles to produce opposed views of marriage. It works well, as we have seen, with ascetical suspicions of marriage. It can work equally well with ardent defenses of marriage or with claims that marriage is a general obligation for Christians. This ought to suggest that theological analyses of the purpose of marriage are not the same as analyses of the purpose of sex in marriage. A theologian can emphasize marital friendship or the married estate or the marriage covenant and still use the procreative rule to restrict sex in marriage.

Christian theology not only restricts sex to marriage, it restricts sex within marriage. Again, theological justifications of marriage have hardly ever given general license for sex within marriage. Most Christian theologians have shared the conviction that marriage provides only a limited justification for sexual intercourse. Certainly it provides no justification for the pursuit of sexual pleasure in its own right. Moreover, so far as it emphasizes that permissible sex is procreative sex, it gives sex a purpose entirely apart from pleasure. Sex is supposed to be about children in the future, not about pleasure in the present. For this kind of traditional theology, whatever eros might threaten the roles of Wife and Husband is supposed to be transmuted into the officially anti-erotic roles of Mother and Father.

Marital Debt and Married Lewdness

In many ways, the theology of Christian marriage has been the effort to promote sex without eroticism. It has wanted both to limit the kinds of

---

[28] Clement of Alexandria, *Pedagogue*, 2.10.94.2–4 (Mondésert).

sex that married Christians could have and to extend means of surveillance or accountability into the sexual activity of marriage. We have already encountered the strongest limitations on married sex, which were closely connected to the ideals of virginity or celibacy. One limitation expressed itself as the argument that married sex is never entirely free from sin, hence that it ought to be reduced to the absolute minimum. Another limitation was the claim that the best Christian marriages would tend as soon as possible to be marriage without sex, "white marriages," as they have come to be called. Neither of these notions is uncontroversial within Christian history, but each recurs with some frequency. On my reading, they recur even in authors who are described as the champions of Christian marriage.

Luther provides a telling example. We have already heard some of his thundering judgments against priestly celibacy and vows of chastity in general. The judgments are often linked to praise for human fertility within marriage. Indeed, historians of the Protestant Reformation often speak of the way in which the movement elevated marriage as a means of moral education and sanctification. The Reformers promised "a religion of wedded life and a politics of the control of marriage."[29] Luther himself is especially credited with a "vigorously affirming, naturalistic attitude to the sexual functioning of the body."[30] I am not sure that his texts are quite so unambiguous.

From early to late, Luther does indeed emphasize in numerous passages not only that God instituted marriage, but that "God has created man and woman so that they should come together with pleasure (*Lust*) and love, willingly and gladly with all their hearts. And bridal love or the will to marry is a natural thing, implanted and bestowed by God."[31] The divine providence extends down to the particular couple: God must be the one to unite particular husband with particular wife.[32] God has already exercised special care in establishing the estate of marriage. As Luther writes in the *Large Catechism*, "God has also most richly blessed this estate above all others,

---

[29] Lyndal Roper, *The Holy Household: Women and Morals in Reformation Augsburg* (Oxford: Clarendon Press, 1989), p. 15, summarizing the promises in order to dissent from the usual historiography about their effects on women.

[30] Roper, "Sexual Utopianism," p. 398.

[31] Martin Luther, *Von Ehesachen* (*On Marriage Matters*), in Weimar *Werke*, Abt. 1, 30/3: 236.10–12. Compare the translation by Frederick C. Ahrens in *Luther's Works*, vol. 46 (Philadelphia: Fortress Press, 1967), p. 304. The phrase "Lust und Liebe" is repeated at the end of the same paragraph (236.22).

[32] Martin Luther, *Ein Sermon von dem ehelichen Stand* (*A Sermon on the Estate of Marriage*), in Weimar *Werke*, Abt. 1, 2:166–7, with a translation by James Atkinson in *Luther's Works*, vol. 44 (Philadelphia: Fortress Press, 1966), p. 8. Compare *Von Ehesachen*, Weimar *Werke*, Abt. 1, 30/1:213–24; trans. Ahrens, *Luther's Works*, 46:276–7.

and, in addition, has bestowed on it and wrapped up in it everything in the world to the end that this estate might be well and richly provided for."[33] Still, these praises of married sex or marriage itself are in some ways Utopian – or, rather, Edenic. Luther speaks more darkly in an early sermon, which he took care to issue in an authorized version:

> If Adam had not fallen, the bride and groom would have been the loveliest thing. But now this love is not pure either, for clearly a married partner desires to have the other, yet each seeks to satisfy his desire with the other, and this corrupts this love. . . . And the temptation of the flesh has become so great and consuming that marriage may be likened to a hospital for the sick, which keeps them from falling into graver sin.[34]

Better to marry than to burn, as Paul had said. Better to confine your lust within marriage than to let it run wild in fornication or adultery or unnatural copulations.

Lust confined is still lust. As Luther says in the *Large Catechism*, "Flesh and blood remain flesh and blood, and the natural inclination and excitement go on without pause or obstacle, as everybody sees and feels. In order, therefore, that it may be easier in some degree to avoid unchastity, God has commanded the estate of matrimony, that every one may have his proper portion and be satisfied with it."[35] Marriage redeems lust in the sense that it extracts one "proper portion" of sex as not necessarily unchastity, not necessarily sinful. Marriage draws a boundary around one small portion of sex so that it can be excused. Indeed, marriage makes of it a duty. Luther in the early sermon: "The wicked lust of the flesh, which nobody lacks, is a marital obligation and is not damnable when done within marriage, but in all cases outside the bond of marriage, it is deadly."[36] Sex in marriage is not necessarily sin, so long as it is done with moderation – which is the decisive qualification. From the same sermon: "A man must master himself and not make a dung heap and sow's sty of his marriage."[37]

---

[33] Luther, *Deutsche Katechismus* (*Large Catechism*) [1529], Sixth Commandment, in Weimar *Werke*, Abt. 1, 30/1:161, with an English translation in *Book of Concord: Confessions of the Evangelical Lutheran Church*, ed. Robert Kolb and Timothy J. Wengert (Minneapolis: Fortress Press, 2000), p. 414.

[34] Luther, *Von dem ehelichen Stand* (Weimar *Werke*, Abt. 1, 2:167–8; trans. Atkinson, *Luther's Works*, 44:9).

[35] Luther, *Deutsche Katechismus*, Sixth Commandment (Weimar *Werke*, Abt. 1, 30/1:162; *Book of Concord*, p. 415).

[36] Luther, *Von dem ehelichen Stand* (Weimar *Werke*, Abt. 1, 2:168; trans. Atkinson, *Luther's Works*, 44:10).

[37] Luther, *Von dem ehelichen Stand* (Weimar *Werke*, Abt. 1, 2:169; trans. Atkinson, *Luther's Works*, 44:11).

A marriage becomes a sow's sty when the spouses use it to wallow in their lusts. That is because, on Luther's early and late views, human sex as we now experience it is fallen sex. It is deformed by selfish, disorderly desire. Copulation by itself, outside marriage, does not constitute a bond so much as a defilement. The copulation of two lovers who make secret promises brings shame on both, and especially the woman if her lover abandons her. On common views that Luther paraphrases without denying, a woman's "most precious treasure," her "honor," is irrecoverably forfeit and she has been "defiled" and rendered "worthless."[38] Nor can any justification be expected when the illicit union satisfies the rule of procreation by producing a child. "Among us [German Christians], womanly honor is regarded as more important than any fruit of the body, and a girl who has slept with someone can hardly regain honor, and there is great danger that she may even become common [i.e., a prostitute]."[39]

Luther is, with Augustine, one of the most rhetorically gifted of Christian theologians. He says contradictory things in different places because he is addressing diverse audiences or pursuing alternative kinds of persuasion. With Augustine, he also grows from, into, and through different theological accounts. Many readers think, for example, that there was a major change in Luther's views on marriage around 1523, after which he emphasized the role of marriage in building faith. My aim here is not to agree or disagree with these more comprehensive readings of Luther. I want only to show how the old, theological suspicions of married sex can reappear even in Luther. In the passages I have cited and others like them, Luther's "vigorously affirming, naturalistic attitude" toward sex seems to come to this: God created men and women to marry each other for pleasurable procreation and companionship. The Fall corrupted them to such an extent that even the best marriage between Christians has to maintain a kind of guard against the insinuations of lust. Sex within marriage can be excused. Indeed, it can serve a number of good ends, both physical and spiritual. Still, this does not mean that our sex is now "intrinsically" good. On the contrary, it is marriage that redeems it from its fallen condition. Sex outside of marriage is coarse, filthy, defiling, demonic. So too is immoderate sex within marriage – and perhaps sexual desire itself as we know it since the Fall.

Calvin, who is hardly ever described as "naturalistic," reactivates the old topics of suspicion in his exposition of the commandment against adultery.

---

[38] Luther, *Von Ehesachen* (Weimar *Werke*, 216:34; trans. Ahrens, *Luther's Works*, 46:280). See also Weimar *Werke*, 226.7–8, *Luther's Works*, 46:292.

[39] Luther, *Von Ehesachen* (Weimar *Werke*, 225:35–7; trans. Ahrens, *Luther's Works*, 46:291).

He emphasizes that marriage is a prophylactic against lust: "the conjugal union itself is ordered to be a remedy for necessity, that we not break out into unrestrained lust (*libido*)."[40] But the "sum" of the commandment is that "we must not be dirtied by any filth (*spurcitia*) or lustful intemperance."[41] The commandment against adultery is thus applied as much within marriage as without it. "For if the decency of marriage veils the shamefulness of incontinence, it ought not necessarily be made a provocation to it."[42] Calvin's image of the veil in this passage is ambiguous. A veil conceals the dangerously attractive face of a woman from the public gaze. So, too, marriage conceals incontinence so far as it confines it to the marriage chamber. But not every act can be performed in that chamber. Spouses should remember that they do not have a general permission for sexual indulgence. On the contrary, "they are admonished that [their union] must not be filthied by intemperate and dissolute lust."[43] A little later, commenting on the tenth Commandment, Calvin extends the principle to thoughts, that is, to the very character of mental desire. God forbids any taint of concupiscence in our affection for another person – presumably including our spouses.[44]

Calvin uses the image of covering sex elsewhere. He does so at length in a sermon on Deuteronomy 5:18 delivered on July 2, 1555.[45] The scriptural text is the second version of the Commandment against adultery, which in itself would call for remarks on marital discipline. More interestingly, a wedding was performed right before the sermon was preached.[46] So Calvin naturally enough applies that Hebrew law to the daily practice of Christian marriage. Now marriage is a "remedy" given by God to those who cannot abstain from sex. It is a remedy so far as it forestalls divine judgment on sex. Even though "intemperance of the flesh" is vicious and damnable in itself, properly ordered sex within marriage is not judged as a vice. Marriage is a "covering" that prevents the sin from being imputed before God. In a prayerfully sought, properly performed, and temperately lived marriage, the vice of fleshly desire is "covered and

---

[40] Calvin, *Institutes*, 2.8.41 (ed. Barth-Niesel, 381.18–20; trans. Battles, 20:405).

[41] Calvin, *Institutes*, 2.8.41 (ed. Barth-Niesel, 381.3–6; trans. Battles, 20:405).

[42] Calvin, *Institutes*, 2.8.44 (ed. Barth-Niesel, 383.12–14; trans. Battles, 20:407).

[43] Calvin, *Institutes*, 2.8.44 (ed. Barth-Niesel, 383.11–12; trans. Battles, 1:407).

[44] Calvin, *Institutes*, 2.8.50 (ed. Barth-Niesel, 388–9; trans. Battles, 414–15).

[45] Jean Calvin, *Sermons sur le Deutéronome* (*Sermons on Deuteronomy*), Sermon 8 on Verse 5.18 (July 2, 1555), as in his *Opera quae supersunt omnia*, vol. 26, ed. Guilielmus Baum, Eduardus Cunitz, and Eduardus Reuss, Corpus Reformatorum, vol. 54 (Brunsvigae: C. A. Schwetschke, 1883), cols. 334–6.

[46] Calvin, *Sermons sur le Deutéronome*, col. 338.

hidden, and is not at all taken into account."[47] "Let us learn to cover ourselves with this honorable cloak (*ombre*), if we have need of it; so that our crimes will not be cursed, and condemned before God, and before his Angels; and even so let us fear this horrible judgment, which is pronounced against all adulterers and the promiscuous (*paillards*)."[48]

To this point, the images of covering would seem to work as the image of the veil did. Something sordid – namely, sexual intercourse – is concealed by marriage so that it is not "imputed" or "counted" in God's moral judgment of the individuals involved. Only once in the wedding-day sermon does Calvin say something stronger: "The covering of marriage is for sanctifying what is polluted and profaned; it is for cleaning what is dirty and filthy in itself."[49] In this use of the image, it can seem that Calvin is suggesting something more than concealment, namely, a sort of baptism of sex by which it too is redeemed. But I think a more careful reading will show that he means "cleaning" and not baptism. The disfiguring dirt and filth are cleaned off by marriage in the sense that they are no longer visible. But intemperance is still dirty and filthy in itself.

Here another sense of the image becomes important. When theology draws a boundary around sex within marriage, it can seem that all the danger remains outside. But in fact Calvin emphasizes throughout this sermon that there are frightening dangers within. It is not enough for the Christian to avoid sex with persons outside of the marriage. The Christian must be ever vigilant not to commit adultery within the marriage, with her or his own spouse. Marriage covers sex only so far. Marriage is not to be a bordello. It is not a license for all sorts of sexual activity with one's spouse. On the contrary, its moral protection is constantly threatened, from within and without. At any moment, an act of sexual excess can strip back the covering and show the depravity of human desire. Calvin's roles for Christian Husband and Wife necessarily contain the promptings for other, uglier scripts – the script for the double Adulterer, the Adulterer outside the marriage bond and the Adulterer within it – the Lascivious Spouse.

Now some very good readers of Calvin would want to put the accent elsewhere. John Witte, for example, has argued that Calvin's spare justification of marriage in the *Institutes* and his negative views of it as a remedy or concession are early and inherited views. Witte finds in later letters, legal opinions, and other genres a more mature Calvin who establishes a "covenant model" of marriage in which the beauties of reciprocal love are

[47] Calvin, *Sermons sur le Deutéronome*, col. 342.
[48] Calvin, *Sermons sur le Deutéronome*, col. 343.
[49] Calvin, *Sermons sur le Deutéronome*, col. 343.

given due respect.[50] Certainly there are passages in which Calvin describes married companionship and the well-ordered household around it in almost lyrical terms. But in these passages, as in so much of Reformation writing, the nicest things said about marriage are said precisely not about married sex. Indeed, these passages in Calvin are typically bracketed by cautions of the kind we have just been examining. More interestingly, Calvin never saw fit to revise his "glum" views on marriage in the *Institutes*.[51] They appear intact in the 1559 edition, from which we have quoted them. Then, too, language of the marriage "covenant" is often qualified by Calvin, as if he were hesitant to use it except as a metaphor. In the wedding-day sermon on Deuteronomy, for example, Calvin introduces the term "covenant" with a double qualification: "But if we may make a comparison, it is not without reason that Marriage is called a Covenant of God."[52] Calling marriage a "covenant" is a comparison to be made "not without reason." Even if it were a covenant simply and fully, it would still not provide covering for the inherent intemperance of our sex.

Remember in all of this that Calvin and Luther are rightly counted among the most important theological *defenders* of marriage. They endow marriage with a dignity that it did not often have in patristic or medieval texts, as they insist that it is perfectly compatible with ministry and church leadership. Still they are compelled to accompany every permission for married sex with cautions against any abuse of the permission. The combination of permission and caution can remind us of what we do not find in Christian theology, ancient or medieval or Reformed: we do not find advice to married couples on how to have more pleasurable sex. Christian theology does not offer anything like an *ars erotica*, a teaching on the cultivation of sexual acts.

Foucault suggests in one place that Christianity is responsible for directing "Western" cultures to seek *scientia sexualis* in place of an *ars erotica*, that is, to want a knowledge about sex rather than an art of sex.[53] The contrast

---

[50]   Witte, *Sacrament to Contract*, especially pp. 108–12.

[51]   Compare Witte, *Sacrament to Contract*, p. 110: "Calvin had come a long way from his earlier glum description of marriage as 'a good ordinance, just like farming, building, cobbling, and barbering.'" But the quotation is found verbatim in the 1559 edition of the *Institutes*, that is, in the edition produced after Calvin's turn to the covenant marriage.

[52]   Calvin, *Sermons sur le Deutéronome*, col. 335.

[53]   Michel Foucault, "Sexualité et pouvoir," in *Dits et écrits 1954–1988*, ed. Daniel Defert and François Ewald, vol. 3: *1976–1979* (Paris: NRF/Gallimard, 1994), pp. 556–7; cf. the English translation by Richard A. Lynch, "Sexuality and Power," in *Religion and Culture: Michel Foucault*, ed. Jeremy R. Carrette (New York: Routledge, 1999), pp. 118–19.

seems to me much exaggerated, but still suggestive. We should notice how little positive instruction Christian theology has traditionally given about married sex. There is no Christian "pillow book" or *Kama Sutra*, no Christian saints are revered for attaining the vision of God through disciplined erotic refinement. The sex that Christians are permitted in marriage – and it is the only sex they are permitted – is defined chiefly by negations. It is not unnatural, not deliberately sterile, not unchaste, and so on. "Good" sex is defined as not being one of the many kinds of "bad" sex.

An obvious objection to this line of thought has to do with the conditions placed on those authorized to speak Christian theology. So long as theology is written by (nominal or real) celibates, it is not likely that we are to get helpful advice about how to enjoy married sex more fully. Celibate theologians are normatively supposed to know of sex what they hear in the confessional. But then it is more striking that the Protestant Reformation did not produce a Christian *ars erotica* either. The explosion of Reformation marriage books and sermons did not produce a "marriage manual" in the colloquial sense. On the contrary, the churches of the Reformation seem often to have instituted better policed sexual morality, a morality that raised the stakes on public or private expressions of the erotic.

There are various ways to understand this historical result. You can argue, for example, that the introduction of married clergy actually resulted in a more complete clerical control over married sex. It brought marriage under more intense theological scrutiny. Or you can argue that Protestant theologians were anxious to show that their approval of marriage was not due to moral laxity – that they had not gone slack just because they were getting married. Or you can place the tighter regulation of sexual matters within a narrative about the Protestant "rationalization" of all spheres of daily life, from the economic to the erotic.

Without dissenting from these explanations or the dozens of others that have been offered, I would suggest another way of understanding why the Reformation often seems to have tightened theological restrictions on sex within marriage. The great Reformers were impassioned readers of the scriptures. Much of their writing is scriptural exegesis – marvelously attentive readings of whole books of the Christian Bible. Reading the scriptures, they reactivated the rhetorical topics in them, including the topics concerned with sex. They then faced the challenge that generations of earlier readers had faced: sexual topics in the New Testament are few and laconic. Where they do speak of sex, they tend to speak negatively. They speak not instruction or encouragement for better sex; they speak warning or prohibition against sexual pleasure. We read lists of sexual sins and cautions against the power of sexual excess. The severity of scriptural speech on sex can be felt particularly around the topic of adultery.

Adultery and Remarriage

One sin involving sex is named explicitly in the Ten Commandments: the sin of adultery. Indeed, it seems to appear twice, once as act and once as desire or intention.[54] The prescribed punishment for committing adultery was death for both parties.[55] In the canonical gospels, Jesus uses the first of these commandments to extend the judgment on all sin from act to intention. "You have heard that it was said, 'You shall not commit adultery.' But I say to you that everyone who looks at a woman with lust has already committed adultery with her in his heart."[56] Adultery can stand, then, as a type for all sins – or at least all sins of a certain kind. We have just seen one good example of how this logic worked in the later tradition: Calvin repeatedly reads out of the Commandment a universal prohibition against sexual excess, even in marriage. He allegorizes adultery so that it comes to include all sorts of inappropriately erotic activity, including many activities that married partners might want to do with each other. For Christian theology, "adultery" becomes a perfectly general term of sexual condemnation. There are good reasons for its being used in that way, but we need to turn instead to the narrower and more literal sense of adultery, that is, to sexual relations by married partners with persons outside the marriage. We need to take "adultery" in its simplest sense.

What is sinful about adultery conceived narrowly? Christian scriptures offer at least two explanations. The first is that adultery is a violation of property rights – especially of male property rights over women. This would seem to be the sense of the second mention among the Commandments: "You shall not covet your neighbor's house; you shall not covet your neighbor's wife, or male or female slave, or ox, or donkey, or anything that belongs to your neighbor" (Exodus 20:17 NRSV). The verse might seem at first more crudely concerned with property than it is, so far as it places a wife second after "house." But here "house" probably has the sense of household, so that the enumeration that begins in the second clause expands what is meant by the first clause. Still the commandment seems to prohibit desire for a neighbor's wife as part of what belongs to the neighbor. In

---

[54]   Exodus 20:14, 20:17, Deuteronomy 5:18, 5:21.
[55]   Leviticus 20:10; Deuteronomy 22:22.
[56]   Matthew 5:27–8.

1 Corinthians 7, the notion of property becomes a symmetrical, mutual ownership or dominion. "For the wife does not have authority over her own body, but the husband does; likewise the husband does not have authority over his own body, but the wife does" (7.4). Here the offense of adultery is an offense against the dominion of the other partner and not just or principally the husband's control of his wife.

We can connect this to a pair of implications from Paul's notion of sex as a "debt" that is to be paid between spouses. The more positive implication of the image is that one spouse cannot rightly break off sexual relations without serious cause – and then, so Paul says and many Christian theologians insist, only for a short time. Because marriage has been provided as a remedy for disordered desire, the remedy ought not to be rashly neglected. There is also a more troubling implication of the image: married intercourse is a compulsory medication to be administered to one's partner with one's body. Refusing sex is refusing medicine, and refusing medicine is a quick way to lead your partner into the delirium of unlawful desire, that is, of adultery.

There can appear to be something of a circle here. The debt is to be paid in order to avoid adultery. But one thing that makes adultery particularly horrible is that it robs the non-adulterous spouse of what belongs to him or her – namely, the payment of the conjugal debt. The "debt" is conceived in relation to the already existing threat of adultery, that is, to the assumption that the only permissible sex must be monogamous. Marriage is a specific remedy for lust so far as it provides one and only one person as a sexual partner with whom approved sexual acts can be regularly performed. One spouse cannot unreasonably deprive the other of that remedy because doing so will deprive the partner of all licit sex, of every remedy. This might lead in turn to your being deprived of your remedy. I don't mean to suggest that the logic of the debt is crassly self-seeking. I do want to point out that the assumption behind the argument is already the assumption that the only moral remedy must involve one partner. Arguments for the marriage "debt" are a tacit inference from the threat of adultery, that is, from the repudiation of the possibility of sex outside of a monogamous relationship.

A second explanation for the sinfulness of adultery regards it as a betrayal of commitment. In Jeremiah, for example, adultery is interchangeable with prostitution as an image of idolatry. "Because [Israel] took her whoring so lightly, she polluted the land, committing adultery with stone and tree" (3:9 NRSV amended). Here, as in Hosea, adultery becomes the symbol of faithlessness, of broken promises, and betrayed trust. The Lord God has been faithful to Israel, but Israel continually deserts God to worship other gods and to break divine law.[57] Paul picks up this association, as we have seen, in 1 Corinthians 6:9. More generally, adultery comes to be associated with lying or deceit, as in Proverbs 2:16.

These scriptural themes are elaborated and combined by the theological traditions. In Aquinas, for example, adultery is assigned to the genus of *luxuria*, the sins of sexual self-indulgence. Along with the other sins of that genus, it is sinful because it is a disordered excess of pleasure. Adultery is distinguished from the other sins of the genus so far as it is an offense against the mutual dominion of marriage, the power that the husband has over the wife.[58] But Thomas tries to escape the circle of possession arguments by grounding the claim of monogamy in the exigencies of child rearing. Children are raised best, he argues, in a permanent and monogamous relation of one man and one woman. Hence adultery is also damaging to the children of the marriage(s) of the adulterer(s).[59]

Luther reads the Commandment against adultery as one of a series dealing with any kind of injury to one's neighbor. After murder, adultery is the most grievous injury, because it is an injury to "his wife, who is one flesh and blood with him, so that we cannot inflict a greater injury on him in any good that is his."[60] This would seem to be just the logic of the wife as property. But Luther immediately explains that the universal requirement for marriage among the ancient Israelites meant that adultery was the most common form of unchastity among them. So a Commandment against adultery is in effect a commandment against unchastity. For Calvin, as we have seen, the substance of the Commandment against adultery is a general prohibition of lustful excess: "God loves chastity and purity."[61]

Christian theologians have understood adultery in these different ways – as a sin against possession, against unity, against honesty, against continence. They have also been constrained by the gospels to regard it as grounds for the dissolution of a marriage. They have thought about adultery in relation to divorce. Jesus himself speaks of adultery in that way: "Whoever divorces his wife and marries another commits adultery against her; and if she divorces her husband and marries another, she commits adultery" (Mark 10:11–12). Now it is an important fact in the history of Christian theology that this saying is reported in two different ways. Luke agrees with Mark in this simple

---

[57]   See, for example, Hosea 2:3; cf. Jeremiah 23:10.

[58]   Thomas Aquinas, *Summa theologiae*, 2–2.154.8, reply to obj. 3.

[59]   Thomas Aquinas, *Summa theologiae*, 2–2.154.8, body of the article.

[60]   Luther, *Deutsche Katechismus*, Sixth Commandment (Weimar *Werke*, Abt. 1, 30/ 1:160; *Book of Concord*, p. 413).

[61]   Calvin, *Institutes*, 2.8.41 (ed. Barth and Niesel, 381.3; trans. Battles, 20:405).

version (Luke 16:18). Paul, too, seems to apply a similar principle (Romans 7:2–3, 1 Corinthians 7:10–11). But Matthew reports the saying with an important exception: "anyone who divorces his wife, except on the ground of unchastity, causes her to commit adultery" (5:32, to which compare 19:9). The difference in versions has been the source of sharp disagreements among Christian groups, but those disagreements ought not to obscure what is the same in all the versions. Jesus names unchastity in a spouse as the only grounds for divorce. It is the particularly dangerous acid that dissolves a marriage.

Once in Matthew and again in Mark the context supplies a reason for Jesus' precept:

> have you not read that the one who made them at the beginning "made them male and female," and said, "For this reason a man shall leave his father and mother and be joined to his wife, and the two shall become one flesh"? So they are no longer two, but one flesh. Therefore what God has joined together, let no one separate. (Matthew 19:4–6; cf. Mark 10:6–9)

Husband and wife become "one flesh" in marriage. The choice by either or both to find another spouse cannot undo that union. So adultery is an act of violence against the joined flesh of wife-and-husband.

Much of the traditional Christian horror of adultery would seem to be connected to this conviction that the sexual union of man and woman can be indescribably intimate. That same conviction would seem to show itself in a concern that unions be properly "consummated" by sexual intercourse in order to be really marriages. Theologians have argued at length about what kinds of impotence or other inability to have sex in a husband would be grounds for declaring that a marriage had never taken place – or that a wife could seek to find another, more potent husband. At the same time, and even in the same texts, Christian theologians have always found ways to qualify the force of the argument of one flesh.

To begin with, the argument only works for married copulation, not for copulation generally – and certainly not for unnatural copulations. Mere coupling between a man and a woman does not make one flesh. Something more by way of agreement and perhaps public profession is required. Many Christian theologians have understood this unity not as a result of the simple intention or promise to marry, but rather of a free consent to common life. In his influential anthology of theological sources, Peter Lombard stresses that it is not the sexual act, but the uncoerced and reasonably informed declaration of an intention to share life that makes for a marriage. If someone who has made such a declaration copulates with another and even begets children outside the bond, the person is to be recalled to the original partner.[62] Luther, who mocks the tortuous complexity of church law about marriage, agrees with this much: a public declaration of marriage ought in most cases to take precedence over private promises and secret copulation.[63] So the conviction of one flesh is qualified first by what seems a concern for public order in the making of marriages.

Second, Christian theologians have also recognized a variety of reasons for allowing the one flesh of marriage to be dissolved. Some have used the concession in Matthew to justify separation of spouses after adultery. Others have used narrower scriptural texts. In 1 Corinthians 7:12–16, Paul urges converts to Christianity to stay with their unbelieving spouses so long as they can do so peacefully. If the unbelieving spouse leaves, the new convert is not bound by the marriage. This became known in the tradition as the "Pauline privilege," and it is still used in Catholic canon law to justify disregarding some marriages contracted before a person's baptism. The "Petrine privilege" allows a Christian to separate from a spouse in order to take up the ministry of proclaiming the Gospel. In Catholic canon law, this has served as a warrant for allowing couples to separate if both husband and wife enter religious life.

I am not foolish enough to try to summarize Christian debates on annulment, separation (without remarriage), and full divorce (with the possibility of remarriage). I can perhaps say that historically most Christian groups, even those that have permitted divorce on certain specific grounds, have been reluctant to dissolve marriages. I can also note that there is an ancient Christian prejudice against remarriage, even after the death of the spouse. We can see this in 1 Timothy 3:2: "Now an overseer [later construed as "bishop"] must be beyond recrimination, married only once, temperate. . . ." Why "married only once"? The immediate reply would be, because that is a proof of temperance. Indeed, the author of 1 Timothy here echoes a widely shared ancient ideal according to which it was more respectable for persons, and especially women, to seek marriage only once. A fuller reply would suggest that the space opened for sex in Christian marriage is also limited in this way: You only get one chance at it.

[62] Peter Lombard, *Sententiae in IV libris distinctae*, 4.27.8.8, ed. members of the Collegium S. Bonaventurae (Grottaferrata: Collegium S. Bonaventurae, 1981), p. 428; 4.27.10.3, p. 431; cf. 4.28.1.2, p. 432.

[63] Luther, *Von Ehesachen*, First and Second Articles (Weimar *Werke*, Abt. 1, 30/3:207.1–4; trans. Ahrens, *Luther's Works*, 46:267). Luther's answer here is not unqualified. In his analysis of various cases, he allows considerable leeway in how they ought to be handled in practice.

The idea of "one flesh" can be quite beautiful, but it has never been taken as the Christian ideal in all its beautiful strictness. Fornication and adultery did not make "one flesh"; ignorance or coercion could prevent "one flesh" from being made even in marriage; conversion or vocation could rend the "one flesh" of marriage. In some Christian groups, adultery could also tear the "one flesh" in such a way that the guiltless partner could be permitted to go on to another union. So "one flesh" is not the complete logic of Christian monogamy and indissolubility. "One chance" might express that logic more fully. This limit-in-time, this limit of contingent personal history, seems to me another of the strong boundaries that Christian theology builds around the space of marriage.

Considering the boundaries together, we might draw two conclusions for the chapter. The first is that Christian theologians have been very reluctant to abuse God's offer of a remedy for uncontrollable desire in marriage. If God has graciously given the sexual remedy, we should certainly not take it for granted. We should realize that the remedy is very particular – as regards partner, acts, desires, intentions, and effects. The permission creates only a small and anxiously patrolled space within which Christians may have sex. Indeed, we might want to ask whether Christians haven't been considerably more anxious in accepting God's gift than God was in giving it.

The second conclusion follows from this. In Christianized societies, Wife and Husband often seem to be sexual identities only ambiguously. They are sexual so far as they are gained and lost by sexual acts. In the main theological traditions, Wife and Husband are as fragile an identity as that of the Virgin Martyr. The married Christian is given limited permission for sex, but the permission only puts her or him at greater risk for losing the identity. Adultery threatens from without and within. A single sexual act can cause the loss of the identity and, in many of the older traditions, can prevent one from ever seeking the identity in a different marriage. Being a Christian Wife or Husband, like being a Virgin Martyr, is performing an identity that can bring honor, but that also exposes one to the daily possibility of deadly defeat in the warfare against desire.

In this way, Wife and Husband are sexual identities that are also anti-erotic identities. In the main theological traditions, marriage contains lust in order to extinguish it. It can be extinguished when the married couple practice sex only for the sake of children and community or when they give up sex by mutual consent. There is room for sex in Christian marriage, but it is both small and temporary. Wife and Husband are meant to become Mother and Father, and perhaps Sister and Brother.

Chapter 6

Attack upon Christendom

We have sampled some of the enormous library of Christian speeches around three topics central to sexual morality. In the usual kind of historical narrative, now would be the time to draw summary conclusions. Many Christian writers do draw historical conclusions, arguing from an "unbroken" tradition or a "unanimous" judgment of the Christian past to sexual rules for the present. We have seen enough of historical variation to be skeptical of such arguments. Still, we might be struck by the stability of certain condemnations across Christian groups – condemnations of female–male intercourse outside of marriage or of same-sex genital relations of any kind. We might be struck as well by the violence with which the prevailing condemnations have been enforced in churches and societies that have called themselves "Christian." We might be tempted finally to infer that our finding certain proscriptions in a large number of Christian discourses means that they must be distinctively Christian – must derive directly from the Gospel. Does that inference hold? Haven't we seen enough to make us wonder whether these proscriptions recur so regularly not because they are an essential part of the Christian message, but because they are motivated by persisting forces of other kinds, political and social?

These questions gain force when we notice what is perhaps most striking about the moral speeches we have been examining – I mean, how old-fashioned they seem in certain groups. However much they disagreed about moral principles and boundary cases, many Christians agreed for centuries in condemning certain acts. Indeed, there seemed to be a settled moral compact governing sexuality in Christendom, north and south, east and west. But since the 1950s, at least, the compact looks as if it has come undone. Not every-where, to be sure: many denominations or groups within denominations still assert the old condemnations. Some assert them now with proud awareness that they are "defending" positions abandoned by other denominations and groups. Sexual condemnations that once seemed the common property of all Christendom are heralded as the distinctive claim of a particular sect.

The undoing of Christendom's sexual compact is often attributed to another social change – or, rather, to the mythology of a change. I mean the so-called "Sexual Revolution" in Western Europe and North America above the Rio Grande. This "Revolution" is described in various ways and dated differently. For example, some American televangelists delight in telling a story of moral decay that begins in the 1960s with the mass marketing of oral contraceptives and the rise of "hippie counterculture" with its creed of free love. From these lewd beginnings, the story goes, there followed a frenzied increase in sexual immorality – that is, apparently, in the number of sexual sins being committed. Other decriers of decadence would agree about the increase of acts, but would start further back, in the gender dislocations caused by World War II or in the cultural despair after World War I or in the rise of nineteenth-century atheism or nihilism or materialism. There are contrary stories as well, in which the "Sexual Revolution" is, if not quite the dawn of liberation, at least the beginning of a much happier sexual living.[1]

These stories, whether negative or positive, seem to me to offer chiefly the consolations of easy myths. They are more consoling than plausible. Each story presumes that we have reliable ways of determining the number of sexual acts that people perform. They also think it possible to determine one time – a year, a decade, a *fin de siècle* – as the revolutionary moment. Social "revolutions" are more complicated: they are carried out against an existing regime, which may once have fancied itself a revolution and which will certainly survive in many forms under any successor. So far as the "Sexual Revolution" of the 1960s was an increase in the amount of sex, it was prepared long before – and it was not nearly so dramatic as its proponents or opponents suppose.

Other stories, which seem to me more plausible, would tell not of the increase in sexual acts, but rather of changes in sexual speeches and images. Very often we look for explanations of new sexual facts when what we ought to be looking for is an explanation of new words or representations – new admissions of fact or new views on fact. For that matter, some of the most famous changes in sexual mores have to do neither with new acts or new images, but with changed conditions of access and publicity. For example, there has been a sophisticated tradition of literary and artistic

---

[1] See, for example, James B. Nelson, *Body Theology* (Louisville, KY: Westminster/ John Knox, 1992), pp. 15–16, 24–8, where continuing the sexual revolution is made the task of theology.

pornography in European Christendom for at least the last six centuries, but it was largely the well-protected possession of the rich. The recent "explosion" of pornography is in many ways just the wider and more egalitarian distribution of pornography – now brought to its global culmination on the internet (which is, in another sense, just a somewhat larger preserve for the technologically affluent). We should be less concerned to calculate the number of sexual acts being performed than to understand the portrayals of them at various cultural levels – in Hollywood movies and psychiatric treatises, in pulp novels and legislative proposals, in journalism and experimental poetry.

Our wanting to turn to the "Sexual Revolution" to explain new circumstances for Christian teaching on sex is part of a more general glibness in our theological thinking about it. For example, we tend to analyze or evaluate changes in contemporary Christian teaching according to a "liberal"/"conservative" dichotomy. Church "liberals" applaud the new attitudes as an increase in human authenticity. Church "conservatives" decry them as an increase in human disorder and degradation.[2] We hear many such exchanges every day, and we are entitled to be weary of them. We ought rather to wonder whether we don't need to think more clearly, more deeply, about the connection between Christian speeches on sex and their "secular" counterparts.

Let me suggest that the significant change for the Christian ethics of sex was not the "Sexual Revolution," but an earlier reversal in the relation of churches to secular bureaucracies in regard to sexual matters. The Christian churches have negotiated over centuries with many different kinds of governments about who was going to have power to regulate sexual acts, desires, and roles. We have sampled some of those negotiations when considering "unnatural" acts or the making and unmaking of marriages. We need now to conceive the last two centuries as a culminating transfer of power over sex from the Christian churches to agencies of the nation-state.

National and transnational bureaucracies have become ever more efficiently involved in the regulation of citizen-sexuality – in population control, healthy reproduction, or eugenics. The most important thing for us to see is that this enormous sphere of "bio-power," as Foucault called it, is a secular successor to older Christian regimes of sexual surveillance

---

[2] For illustrations of how the dichotomy binds us and for some alternatives, see L. William Countryman, "Finding a Way to Talk: Dealing with Difficult Topics in the Episcopal Church," in *Our Selves, Our Souls and Bodies: Sexuality and the Household of God*, ed. Charles Hefling (Cambridge, MA, and Boston: Cowley Publications, 1996), pp. 3–16.

and marriage control.[3] "Bio-power" replaces many of the traditional church powers, including the Christian speeches about sex. Under Christendom, being a Christian was something like a subject- or citizen-identity. If this meant that government was articulated through Christian language, it also meant that the church and state had to negotiate the allocation of power – and the control of speech with it. Historically, a number of these negoti-ations allowed the churches to continue their regulation of sex. If Christian preachers were expected to be restrained in criticizing war policy, property laws, or ordinary taxation, they were especially invited to castigate sexual sins. With the emergence of regimes of bio-power, this allocation could hardly be tolerated. The resulting reallocation of sex from the church to the bureaucracies of the nation-state has led to a profound loss of authority in Christian speech about sex.

Different churches have lost authority differently, of course, and the reac-tions in particular denominations or national churches require careful ana-lysis. My point is not to replace the simple myth of "sexual revolution" with an even simpler myth of "bio-power." I do want to suggest that the rise of national control over sex is a more important "revolution" in the last century than the "sexual revolution." I also want to argue that the churches would do better to attend to the secularization of sex rather than to its sup-posed decadence. Instead of blaming church members for becoming more sexually immoral, they ought to warn them rather about becoming such docile subjects of the secular bureaucracies for sexual regulation. To make that warning convincingly, the churches would have to reflect more critically on their own role in fostering those bureaucracies as the legacy of Christen-dom. The churches would need to take responsibility for the fantasy of Christendom and the reality of what came afterwards.

The churches find it difficult to speak this historical responsibility candidly. Indeed, the interesting story to be told about the Christian relation to social attitudes on sex since the 1950s is a story of *unacknowledged* accom-modation. The churches have tried to carry on as they had for centuries, prescribing sexual conduct and threatening punishments for deviations. But the old speeches didn't seem to resonate as they had before. The state didn't seem to listen in quite the same way, and Christian believers them-selves didn't seem to respond with the same docility. Believers now expected to get instructions from elsewhere – and precisely from the state or its agencies. Their expectation was not so much a result of the "Sexual Revolution" as its precondition. Also, the churches reacted too often by

[3]   The term appears, for example, in Foucault, *Histoire de la sexualité*, 1:185 (trans. Hurley, pp. 140–1).

trying to accommodate themselves tacitly to the new power over sex. The tacit accommodation never acknowledged the depth of the change in their power-position – in their claim to speak with the voice of authority. It is much easier for preachers to rail against a "Sexual Revolution" than to acknowledge the advent of bio-power and its implication for their customary topics in preaching.

In sketching this story about the recent fate of Christian sexual ethics, I have relied somewhat on notions from Foucault. I would now like to adapt another part of Foucault's history of sexuality to describe the kinds of power that Christian speech once had and then gave up – or gave over. I regard Foucault's history as a parable. I tell it not because I think that it represents all or most of the truth of what really happened, but because it vividly represents a truth about our present situation. So I will not try to "prove" the truth of Foucault's historical claims (whatever proof in history might be). I will use them instead to talk about who we can be as Christian speakers about sex. We have seen the speeches of moral theology specify acts, make rules, and assign roles. We need now to ask how those speeches made authority for themselves by projecting the figures of the speakers behind them. There have been many identities for the Teacher of Christian Sexual Morals – and most of them have been scripted in some relation or another to powers of enforcement, religious or secular. What are those roles now – and what alternatives to them might we find or write?

Negotiating Sexual Regulation

In a 1978 lecture at the University of Tokyo, Foucault presented the "state" of some of the "hypotheses" that structured his project for a history of sexuality as he was then revising it.[4] One of these hypotheses is that Western society, since Augustine at least, has overproduced discourse about sex. A second, which we have already encountered, is that this discourse "very quickly and very early took what can be called a scientific form."[5] Foucault gives content to this hypothesis by contrasting a Western science of sex with an Eastern art of the erotic – a contrast that begs for qualifications and counter-examples. A third hypothesis, and the most pertinent, holds that what was originally distinctive about Christian sexual science was not the content of its prohibitions, but the form of its imposition. "It is then along the way of the mechanisms of power much more than along that of

---

[4]   Foucault, "Sexualité et pouvoir," 3:552–3; compare the translation by Lynch, in *Religion and Culture*, p. 116.
[5]   Foucault, "Sexualité et pouvoir," 3:556 (trans. Lynch, p. 118).

moral ideals or ethical interdicts – it is along the way of the mechanisms of power that one must do the history of sexuality in the Western world after Christianity."[6] The name Foucault gives to this ensemble of mechanisms of power is *le pastorat*, the pastoral or the pastorate.

We can apply Foucault's parable in this way. If what was originally distinctive about Christian teaching on sex was the nature of the power that it exerted over sex, a change in power will make for the deepest sort of change in Christian sexual ethics. More important than the content of rules will be the kind of pastoral power assumed in framing rules. If the power changes significantly, so will the rules – even while their wording remains exactly the same. What matters is the power that speaks and enforces the rules. Foucault has more to say about this power in the lecture. He summarizes the distinctiveness of the original Christian pastoral twice, first in terms of the character of its power, then in terms of its significance or implications. The four characteristics of its power are that it is not territorial; that it is concerned with nurturing its own rather than vanquishing others; that it entails responsibility to the point of self-sacrifice; and that it is exercised over individuals, one by one.[7] The four implications are that the individual is obliged to seek salvation; that seeking is not done alone; that it requires an absolute obedience; and, finally, that there will be a "series of techniques and procedures concerned with truth and the production of truth."[8] But we are now less interested in Foucault's characterization of original pastoral power than in continuing his story about it – the story that is serving as our parable.

Already before the lecture, in *History of Sexuality* 1, Foucault sketched a brief account of Christian pastoral care for sex. He described a series of extensions by which the monastic discipline of chastity was applied to larger and larger groups – to the clergy as a whole; then to all religious, male and female; then to pious laypeople; then to laypeople simply.[9] Foucault then suggested that we can discern the birth of the modern notion of sexuality in the kinds of surveillance practiced within seminaries, religious colleges, and convents since the Counter-Reformation.[10] The sexualities of nineteenth-century psychiatry were pastoral theology bequeathed to other kinds of pastors – to the agents of a new power, of bio-power.

[6]   Foucault, "Sexualité et pouvoir," 3:560 (trans. Lynch, p. 121).
[7]   Foucault, "Sexualité et pouvoir," 3:561–2 (trans. Lynch, pp. 122–3).
[8]   Foucault, "Sexualité et pouvoir," 3:562–4, with the final quotation from 564 (trans. Lynch, pp. 124–5, with the corresponding quotation at 125).
[9]   Foucault, *Histoire de la sexualité*, 1:29 (trans. Hurley, pp. 20–1).
[10] Foucault, *Histoire de la sexualité*, 1:142 (trans. Hurley, pp. 107–8).

I make Foucault's account into a parable by adding this exhortation: The Christian ethicist now needs both to trace the genealogy of secular strategies back into their religious origins and to watch how the secular strategies of bio-power have displaced Christian teaching about sex. It might seem odd to suggest that we look again at the sociopolitical forces driving Christian sexual ethics in a century when Christian ethics looks to have been especially preoccupied by social and political concerns. From the Social Gospel to Liberation Theology, from the "noble experiment" of American Prohibition to the Christian antiwar movements, Christian ethics has been largely if not obsessively concerned with political and social matters – to the detriment, some would claim, of Christian sanctification. But many of the social and political movements have been curiously silent on matters of sex, regarding them as a luxurious concession that the socially committed Christian might just as well do without. Politically active Christianity has often relegated the sexual into the private – which it stigmatized as somehow bourgeois, privileged, dispensable.

Christian sexual ethics should now reexamine the relations between sexual ethics and sexual politics, including its own relation to older regimes of supposedly "Christian" politics. It needs to reexamine the sexual politics of Christendom and their replacement by state bio-power. Then it might begin to think about human sexuality so far as possible outside of the aggressive programs of political regimes. The task seems to me particularly urgent in these years, when many of the major denominations are being pushed to legalize practices or sentiments that have been until now matters of informal or traditional consensus. In just the same way that industrialized societies are increasingly bureaucratic and litigious, so the Christian churches now make everything codified policy. The change is particularly striking – not to say, ironic – in denominations that were founded on principles of local governance and individual discernment.

The parable after Foucault points us in the opposite direction. Rather than fighting furiously with each other over the further codification of sexual sins or rights, we might want to see sin in the exercises of codifying power. These days the most dangerous sins don't seem to come from the pursuit of sexual pleasure, but from the pursuit of power. (For that matter, some sins that were traditionally considered sexual sins – such as rape – now seem to many people violent sins, sins of power in its arrogance or despair.) The parable encourages us to conceive the possibility for rethinking Christian ethics apart from any of the old projects of Christendom or the current project of tacit accommodation to modern state power. If we were able to free Christian ethics somewhat from the visible and invisible needs of regulatory programs, we might conceive the glorious possibility of a

Christian sexual ethics that would not be the ethics of any Christendom. After centuries in which Christian ethics has been enforced as police power, we might rather be grateful for the innocence relative powerlessness affords our discourses. We could stop trying to strike a quiet deal with the successors of Christendom; we could enjoy our dispossession. We might even begin to think of Christian sexual ethics as the salvific teaching of God through the sexual lives of Christians.

Foucault's parable is not the only way of telling the story of the present circumstances of Christian teaching on sex. Nor is it the only story that leads to calls for a new theology. Not a few of the last century's theologians attempted revisions or even revolutions in the ethics of sex. I suggest that some of them, at least, were tripped up by failing to acknowledge plainly enough the transfer of power over sex from churches to states. Indeed, I think that their texts tend to pass over the main rhetorical consequences of the transfer – the need to construct a new kind of authority in Christian teaching on sex. Theologians no longer speak as officers of Christendom; they ought not to speak as delegates of bio-power. Too many church speeches still want to do one or the other. They still want to play the old roles of the Teacher of Christian Sexual Ethics.

Accommodating Contraception – Belatedly

When people think about Christian churches and contraception, they are most likely to think about the Roman Catholic church and its disputes during the last three decades over the ban on "artificial means of contraception." If they are in middle age or beyond it, they may remember the firestorm that broke out in 1968 when Pope Paul VI issued his encyclical *Humanae vitae*. Many expected that the encyclical would permit married Catholics to use condoms and the "pill" in situations where it was morally justified to limit the number of children. The possibility had been urged by Catholic theologians and journalists. It had been raised in the debates and documents of the recently concluded church council, Vatican II. It had even been endorsed by a majority of the Vatican's own commission appointed to study the problem. The commission, interestingly, had originally been appointed by John XXIII to prepare a diplomatic response to UN initiatives in regard to world population.[11] It was a clear case of responding to state initiatives with regard to bio-power.

---

[11] One of the most interesting accounts of the commission's work is based on the memories of a Catholic laywoman invited to serve on it. See Robert McClory, *Turning Point* (New York: Crossroad, 1995).

In 1968, Paul VI did not relax the teaching. He reaffirmed it: "Similarly excluded is every action that, either in anticipation of the conjugal act or in its accomplishment or in the development of its natural consequences, would have as an end or as means, to render procreation impossible."[12] To speak more plainly: no action can be taken before, during, or after intercourse to prevent conception or implantation. The encyclical rules out the "pill" and any IUD, diaphragms and condoms, the "morning-after" pill, and herbal remedies of folklore. The response of the papacy to the initiatives of bio-power was, in this case, a general prohibition that reasserted church authority over sexual matters. Of course, the perfectly general prohibition was amended by the encyclical itself to allow for the use of the "rhythm" method. Amended or not, the prohibition has been ignored in practice by the majority of Catholics of childbearing age around the world. Indeed, some observers think that Paul's ruling inaugurated the stalemate of contemporary Catholicism, in which Catholics decide on their sexual practices with little regard for the pope, his officers, or the local bishop. So that the reaffirmation of churchly power over sex became in fact a discomfiting reminder of how little power the churches actually have over sex.

What is left out of this story is the more interesting and prior history of the Anglican and Protestant churches. There was such widespread expectation that the Roman Catholic position would be changed in large part because the position of the "mainstream" Anglican and Protestant denominations had already changed in recent decades. The same reasons that had led to the reversal of Protestant judgments were expected to correct Catholic teaching as well. In 1920, the official position of the main Anglican and Protestant churches was what it had been since the Reformation: marriages were supposed to produce children, and it was both socially irresponsible and morally sinful to frustrate procreation within a Christian marriage. By 1960, the Anglican Communion and most of the major Protestant denominations had come to teach that contraception was an issue to be decided by the married partners – and that there were a number of acceptable and even compelling reasons for spacing or limiting births. What happened in those 40 years between 1920 and 1960?

---

[12]   Paul VI, *Humanae vitae*, no. 14, as in *Humanae vitae: Encyclical Letter of His Holiness Pope Paul VI on the Regulation of Births*, trans. Marc Calegari (San Francisco: Ignatius Press, 1998), p. 17. The normative text of a papal encyclical is usually the Latin text. Several kinds of evidence indicate that *Humanae vitae* was drafted in Italian. What is more noteworthy, there are at several crucial points important discrepancies between the Italian and Latin versions. Calegari takes both versions into account for his English translation.

The earliest major document to record the change is a resolution of the 1930 Lambeth Conference, the worldwide meeting of bishops of the Anglican Communion. In that conference's Resolution 15, the bishops teach that when there is a "clearly felt moral obligation to limit or avoid parenthood, the method must be decided on Christian principles." The "primary and obvious method is complete abstinence from intercourse," but "where there is a morally sound reason for avoiding" abstinence, "other methods may be used, provided that this is done in the light of the same Christian principles."[13] The statement may be guarded and ambiguous, but it nonetheless marks a clear departure from traditional teaching, which earlier Lambeth Conferences had reaffirmed as recently as 1920.[14] Other statements followed quickly and were more articulate about their reasons. A committee of the US Federal Council of Churches (forerunner of the National Council of Churches) argued in 1931 that births should be spaced or limited for the health of the mother or child, for the stability of the family, and for strengthening the bond between the parents. It further acknowledged the possibility of "overpopulation." Though this report was not endorsed by the whole Council, a number of the main Protestant bodies issued individual statements affirming its reasoning.[15] They asserted both that Christian couples had the right to regulate the number of their children and that they could do so using new medical methods.

Official Protestant statements from the 1930s up through the 1950s repeat similar arguments in favor of contraceptive intent and the use of artificial means to attain it. First, they share a growing recognition that human overpopulation raises acute moral issues of its own. Children should not be born for starvation, and families should not be formed only to be torn apart by harsh economic necessities. Second, the statements agree in appealing to ideals of health – the health of the child, the mother, the family as a whole. Advances in medicine have made contraception more reliable. Christians should use these advances just as they would use other medical advances for morally good ends. Third, mere procreation is spoken of less and less as the highest purpose for Christian marriage. It is balanced against the claims of intimacy between parents and adequate care of the children.

[13] Lambeth Conference (1930), *Encyclical Letter from the Bishops with Resolutions and Reports* (London: SPCK, and New York: Macmillan, 1930), pp. 43–4.
[14] See the analysis by Harmon L. Smith, "Contraception and Natural Law: A Half-Century of Anglican Moral Reflection," in *The Anglican Moral Choice*, ed. Paul Elmen (Wilton, CT: Morehouse-Barlow, 1983), pp. 181–200, p. 185.
[15] Richard M. Fagley, *The Population Explosion and Christian Responsibility* (New York: Oxford University Press, 1960), pp. 195–6.

Fourth, finally, some denominational statements assert distinct moral values in sexual relations, such as freedom or spontaneity. So far as artificial means of contraception increase those values within legitimate sexual relations, they are good.

A short step separates this fourth reason from the start of a more general reform of sexual teachings within Christendom. Effective contraception separates sexual pleasure from reproduction for heterosexuals in a way that biology has always separated it for homosexuals. Contraception allows other-sex couples to behave as if they were same-sex couples. It leads them to ask whether the Christian account of sex as inevitably reproductive is adequate to sex that need not be reproductive. It stops the expected trans-formation of Wife and Husband into Mother and Father.

Protestant denominations changed their teaching on contraception in response to changing social views and to one another. Their new statements on contraception still seem to me to suffer from tacit accommodation to social and medical changes. They react to social and medical changes; they do not lead them. As Richard Fagley writes, "The struggle of the 'birth control' movement to establish itself was conducted . . . without much benefit of clergy of any description."[16] Once the movement did succeed, it was belatedly endorsed by a growing number of Anglican and Protestant bodies – and endorsed de facto by Catholic laity. The tacit belatedness of Christian ethics with regard to contemporary social and political facts may suggest another sort of legacy from Christendom. Centuries of negotiation with various secular regimes may have done much for Christian life in other ways, but they have not done much for candid admissions of powerlessness.

It would be more helpful for theologians to admit that changes in the teaching on contraception have opened up the oldest and most fundamental questions about Christianity and sex. Some theologians have admitted it; indeed, they have prepared for it by rethinking sexual relations. Others, responding to these proposals for fundamental change, have sought to discover new foundations for old teachings. More frequently, especially in official documents, we find a wish to forget the change. It is so much easier to pretend that we are not facing any discontinuity in Christian moral tradition, because the alternative would be immensely unsettling. It would require us to recognize that the shift on teachings about contraception is a sign that Christian moral theology can no longer win acceptance just because it is the legislative speech of Christendom. It must now persuade on other grounds, in its own voice. It cannot just rehearse its old scripts of power.

[16] Fagley, *Population Explosion*, p. 193.

To accept that Christian moral theology is no longer privileged speech about sexual matters is to accept that it must find new rhetoric. But here too we can find odd repetitions, because some of the most interesting attempts to make new forms of speech can end up falling back into the old scripts in unexpected ways.

"Revolutionizing" Christian Ethics

In the twentieth century, Christian writers produced major works about sex. To catalogue even the most important would fill many pages. To assess them would take many more – if it could be done at all from our present vantage point. Another century may be needed before we have any interesting judgments about what the twentieth century has meant for Christian sexual ethics. Karl Barth's famous (or infamous) analysis of the man–woman relation in *Church Dogmatics* once seemed to some readers a profound theological reflection on sexual matters.[17] It now seems to other readers a strikingly unreflective theological mystification of European gender roles.[18] How will it appear in another hundred years? Similar questions can be asked of other major books from the twentieth century. Anders Nygren's *Agape and Eros* once set the terms for much of the Protestant debate about sex.[19] These days the dichotomy in its title seems distressingly simplistic. Among Roman Catholics, Bernard Häring's *Law of Christ* used to be singled out as a breakthrough in moral theology. Its discussion of sexual matters can now appear embarrassingly legalistic – for example, in spending pages on a woman's exact degree of culpability in heterosexual *coitus interruptus*.[20]

One safe judgment about Christian sex toward the end of the twentieth century is that it began to admit new voices: women's voices, lesbian and gay voices, voices from outside of Europe and North America above the

---

[17]   See especially Karl Barth, *Kirchliche Dogmatik (Church Dogmatics)*, III/2, sect. 45, no. 3 (Zurich: Evangelischer Verlag, 1948), pp. 344–91; trans. Harold Knight, G. W. Bromiley, J. K. S. Reid, and R. H. Fuller (Edinburgh: T. & T. Clark, 1960), pp. 285–324.

[18]   For a generous critique of Barth's views on gender, see Eugene F. Rogers, Jr., *Sexuality and the Christian Body: Their Way into the Triune God* (Oxford: Blackwell, 1999), pp. 180–91.

[19]   For an abbreviated introduction to the book and the debate after it, see Anne Bathurst Gilson, *Eros Breaking Free: Interpreting Sexual Theo-Ethics* (Cleveland, OH: Pilgrim Press, 1995), pp. 16–36.

[20]   Bernard Häring, *The Law of Christ: Moral Theology for Priests and Laity*, vol. 3: *Special Moral Theology: Man's Assent to the All-embracing Majesty of God's Love*, trans. Edwin R. Kaiser (Westminster, MD: New Press, 1966), pp. 357–60.

Rio Grande. These voices had long been excluded from authoritative theological speech. Their breaking into the male, Euro-centric, and presumptively heterosexual discourse of sexual ethics has had profound effects, which we are just beginning to appreciate. The appearance of feminist theology, for example, has provoked continuing reconsideration of the oldest assumptions in the description and judgment of sexual matters. A string of provocative works has condemned some topics to embarrassed silence as it retrieved or constructed others.[21] These works have been so influential that it can sometimes be hard to remember the bizarre things theologians permitted themselves to say about women before women were allowed to be theologians. Something equally new in the history of Christian ethics is the sound of honestly lesbian and gay voices. As we saw in the discussion of unnatural acts, it is nothing new for "sodomites" to be compelled to speak in front of the church. They have long been compelled to confess their practices before repenting them. It *is* new for those who desire members of their own sex to be allowed to speak as Christians in good standing and even as Christians with something positive to teach about sexual ethics.[22]

There is no way to summarize these new speeches. There is as yet no way to judge what they will mean for the future of Christian ethics. What

---

[21] I think, for example, of the first edition of Mary Daly's *The Church and the Second Sex* (New York: Harper & Row, 1968) or her *Beyond God the Father* (Boston: Beacon Press, 1973); of Rosemary Radford Ruether's *New Woman, New Earth: Sexist Ideologies and Human Liberation* (New York: Harper & Row, 1975), and her *Sexism and God-Talk: Toward a Feminist Theology* (Boston: Beacon Press, 1983); of Phyllis Trible's *God and the Rhetoric of Sexuality* (Philadelphia: Fortress Press, 1978); of Sallie McFague's *Metaphorical Theology: Models of God in Religious Language* (Philadelphia: Fortress Press, 1982); of Elizabeth Schüssler Fiorenza's *In Memory of Her: A Feminist Theological Reconstruction of Christian Origins* (New York: Crossroad, 1983); of Beverly Wildung Harrison's *Making the Connections: Essays in Feminist Social Ethics*, ed. Carol S. Robb (Boston: Beacon Press, 1985), and so on into the extraordinary and still growing library.

[22] Here some of the early works would be John J. McNeill, "The Male Christian Homosexual," *Homiletic and Pastoral Review* 70 (1970): 667–77, 747–58, 828–36, and his *The Church and the Homosexual* (Kansas City, MO: Sheed, Andrews, & McMeel, 1976); Charles E. Curran, "Homosexuality and Moral Theology: Methodological and Substantive Considerations," *The Thomist* 35 (1971): 447–81, and his *Catholic Moral Theology in Dialogue* (Notre Dame, IN: Fides, 1972), esp. pp. 184–219; the essays collected by Sally Gearhart and Bill Johnson in *Loving Women/Loving Men* (San Francisco: Glide Publications, 1974); Margaret Farley, "An Ethic for Same-Sex Relations," in *A Challenge to Love: Gay and Lesbian Catholics in the Church*, ed. Robert Nugent (New York: Crossroad, 1983), pp. 93–106; and so on. For lesbigay theology, as for feminist theology, one of the principal tasks has also been to reexamine church history.

we need to notice is that the introduction of new voices into Christian ethics has curiously coincided with something like a loss of "voice" in Christian ethics.[23] I don't mean to suggest the cynical conclusion that marginalized voices are now allowed into theology just because theology as a whole is less valued socially. I do mean that the multiplication of voices has been encouraged in part by the disruption of speaking roles in Christian ethics – the disruption produced by the unacknowledged transfer of power over sex from church to state.

At the end of this chapter, I will try to take account of the ways in which these formerly excluded voices have wanted to find a new authority for Christian moral speaking. At the moment I want to warn of the danger of repetition in individual attempts to speak a revolutionary Christian ethics without adverting to the extent of bio-power, the degree of state control. My first example comes from the application of Protestant "situation ethics" to sex, my second from a Catholic draft of new criteria for judging sexual relations. Both seem to me to show how easy it is even for revolutionary proposals to fall back into the old roles of Christian teaching, roles that assume at least the sharing of power between church and state.

From the late 1950s on, one of the most "revolutionary" voices in Protestant sexual ethics was that of Joseph Fletcher. The case of contraception figured prominently in his *Situation Ethics: The New Morality* (1966), counted by many a milestone either in the reform or decadence of Christian ethics.[24] In 1967, Fletcher collected under the title *Moral Responsibility: Situation Ethics at Work* a number of related articles, including four on sexual topics. One of these articles, "Ethics and Unmarried Sex," offers two principles that he considers common to both "theistic" and "humanistic" "ethical orientations."[25] The first principle asserts that "no sexual act is ethical if it hurts or exploits others. This is the difference between lust and love: lust treats a sexual partner as an object, love as a subject" (p. 138). The second principle belongs to "situation ethics – making a moral decision hangs on the particular case. How, here and now, can I act with the most certain concern for the happiness and welfare of those involved – myself

---

[23]   I borrow the controlling image and some of the description from Jeffrey Stout, *Ethics after Babel: The Languages of Morals and their Discontents* (Boston: Beacon Press, 1988), pp. 163–88.

[24]   Joseph Fletcher, *Situation Ethics: The New Morality* (Philadelphia: Westminster Press, 1966).

[25]   Joseph Fletcher, *Moral Responsibility: Situation Ethics at Work* (Philadelphia: Westminster Press, 1967), p. 137. Until otherwise indicated, I will cite the pages of this book parenthetically.

and others?" (ibid.). The two principles might seem to authorize almost any sexual behavior. Fletcher insists that they do not. To the question, Should Christians approve premarital sex?, he gives "an equivocal answer, 'Yes and no – depending on each particular situation'" (p. 137). Fletcher then seems to endorse what he takes as agreed among all Christians: "the *ideal* sexually is the combination of marriage and sex" (p. 138). He adds immediately: "But the ideal gives no reason to demand that others should adopt that ideal or to try to impose it by law, nor is it even any reason to absolutize the ideal in practice for all Christians in all situations" (ibid.).

Grant for the moment Fletcher's remark about the limits on the law. He takes it to be no different from the principles in the Wolfenden Report (released in 1957) that led to the reform of English criminal law on sexual offenses. What are the situations in which premarital sex is ethical for *Christians*? Fletcher replies: Situations in which sex does not harm or exploit the partner, and in which it enacts the most certain concern for the happiness and welfare of those performing it. And those situations are? Fletcher refuses to answer this question on his own deepest principles. He has argued at length that lawlike rules are intrinsically defective as moral guides, because their coercive generality destroys that free, personal respons-ibility at the center of morality, whether "theistic" or "humanistic." The force of Fletcher's teaching on sex outside of marriage is not in providing detailed guidance for making decisions in particular cases. The force is in the denial that there can be such guidance – and especially that there can be the perfectly general negative guidance of a prohibition against extramarital sex.

Defenders of "traditional" Christian prohibitions often argue that any concession will open the floodgates. Fletcher's brief remark may show that they are right – though not in the way they expect. By the standards of the present, Fletcher's allowances for sexual relations outside of marriage might seem rather tame. Indeed, it can be striking how traditional his questions and answers are. He is, after all, talking about "premarital" inter-course – that is, intercourse between one woman and one man on the way to their being married. He allows this much while still affirming married sex as the Christian ideal. And so on. Still "traditional" critics may be right to suspect that allowing even a limited exception will undo much of the traditional morality – and that Fletcher intends to undo it. The force of such a traditional morality depended on its presenting itself as an exception-less law. To admit even one exception is to undo that kind of law. So far as the old sexual morality consisted of a number of such laws, admitting one exception means throwing doubt into that whole. Fletcher sees that this is good evidence that the old morality can't have been right.

The urgent thing now is not to adjudicate the controversy between Fletcher and his critics. It is rather to ask what authority Fletcher himself claims for his speech. He rejects the authority of the exceptionless law – in favor of what? Well-formed conscience? Mature ethical reasoning? Some other part of the common agreement between "theistic" and "humanistic" morality? But if Christian ethics speaks mainly out of that agreement, what special authority does Fletcher have to speak as a Christian ethicist about such matters? In proposing a revolution in the principles of Christian ethics, Fletcher presupposes the continuing, public pertinence of Christian ethics to sexual matters. He presupposes that theology has its own "voice" and that its voice will be sought out in public debates. But Fletcher speaks after Christendom, after the transfer of most power over sex into the state's bureaucratic hands. Doesn't his presumption of authority seem an anachronistic repetition?

Another and perhaps more obvious sort of repetition can be found in revolutionary Catholic works. A decade after the publication of the essays by Fletcher from which I've been quoting, a group of Catholic theologians attempted to offer a detailed rationale for overturning the traditional teachings. In 1972, the Catholic Theological Society of America (CTSA) established a committee to report on recent trends in the moral theology about sex. It asked the committee to provide "some helpful and illuminating guidelines in the present confusion."[26] The confusion was caused not just by the "Sexual Revolution" or other social changes, but by the widespread dissent within the Catholic church from *Humanae vitae* and other official teachings on sex. The CTSA's committee consisted of five persons, four men and one woman, of whom three were priests or members of religious orders.[27] The committee's draft report went through several stages of review and revision. In the end, it proved too much for the CTSA itself, which voted to "receive" and publish it without endorsement. The Society's hesitation was justified. Once published, the volume was condemned by various bishops and Catholic agencies. So the volume entitled *Human Sexuality* can hardly be considered official teaching. It can be considered – it is – an accurate representation of the more progressive thinking on sexual morality by Catholic academic theologians in Europe and English-speaking North America.

---

[26] Anthony Kosnick, William Carroll, Agnes Cunningham, Ronald Modras, and James Schulte, *Human Sexuality: New Directions in American Catholic Thought, A Study Commissioned by the Catholic Theological Society of America* (New York, Paramus, and Toronto: Paulist Press, 1977), p. ix, which reproduces a statement by the Board of Directors of the CTSA.

[27] Kosnick et al., *Human Sexuality*, pp. 321–2.

I want to look at only one part of this large volume. It is the point at which the committee tries to set down criteria for evaluating sexual activities. The criteria are "values that are conducive to creative growth and integration of the human person."[28] According to the committee, human sexual acts should be:

1 "Self-liberating," hence "neither fearful nor anxious but rather genuinely expressive of one's authentic self."

2 "Other enriching," expressing "a generous interest and concern for the well-being of the other. It is sensitive, considerate, thoughtful, compassionate, understanding, and supportive. It forgives and heals and constantly calls forth the best from the other without being demeaning or domineering." A "wholesome sexuality must contribute positively to the growth process of the other."

3 "Honest," expressing "openly and candidly and as truthfully as possible the depth of the relationship that exists between people. It avoids pretense, evasion, and deception in every form as a betrayal of the mutual trust."

4 "Faithful," "characterized by a consistent pattern of interest and concern" that "facilitates the development of stable relationships."

5 "Socially responsible," reflecting "the relationship and responsibility of the individuals to the larger community (family, nation, world)."

6 "Life-serving," respecting "the intimate relationship between the 'creative' and 'integrative' aspects." Though the language echoes Paul VI in *Humanae vitae*, this value is apparently not restricted to procreative couplings, since "every life style provides means for giving expression to this life-serving quality."

7 "Joyous," giving witness "to exuberant appreciation of the gift of life and mystery of love. It must never become a mere passive submission to duty or a heartless conformity to expectation. The importance of the erotic element, that is, instinctual desire for pleasure and gratification deserves to be affirmed and encouraged."

The CTSA report is to be praised for its historical range, its analytical detail, and its generous attempt to incorporate or at least engage traditional formulations. It did not convince Vatican authorities, but it did succeed in representing the leading edge of Catholic moral theology at the time it was written. Indeed, it may represent the leading edge of Catholic moral theology today, because there has been so little room left by church

---

[28] Kosnick et al., *Human Sexuality*, p. 92. The criteria that follow are found on pp. 92–5 of the same volume.

officials for any advance since the 1970s. Yet the report has its problems. One set of them concerns the realism of the list of values. It is a general feature of Christian ethics that it uses the indicative when it ought to use the hortatory. Ethicists will write: "Sex is . . . ," when they really mean "Sex should be . . . ," or "If only sex were . . . ," or "Life would be so much simpler if only sex might be . . . ." The CTSA report is not free from this wishful rhetoric. Indeed, far from being too lenient, its list of "values" may be unrealistically strict. How many sexual interludes in human history could realistically be described as "genuinely expressive of one's authentic self," as "sensitive, considerate, thoughtful, compassionate, understanding, and supportive," as expressing "openly and candidly and as truthfully as possible the depth of the relationship," as avoiding "pretense, evasion, and deception in every form," as "characterized by a consistent pattern of interest and concern," as reflecting "the relationship and responsibility of the individuals to the larger community (family, nation, world)," as respecting "the intimate relationship between the 'creative' and 'integrative' aspects," and as giving witness "to exuberant appreciation of the gift of life and mystery of love"? That seems rather a tall order, to put it mildly. In moments of erotic desire one's thoughts are otherwise engaged (to paraphrase Jonathan Swift) — and yet sex without erotic desire violates value number 7. Taken literally, the combination of these criteria would have the unintended effect of eliminating moral sex — or leaving it as tiny a space as it had in traditional Catholic theology.

More interesting than problems in the report's criteria are troubles in its teaching voice. The CTSA document is decidedly a report — the report of a committee of (mostly clerical or religious) theologians appointed by the recognized national society. The authority of the report is an authority that derives from recognized roles in official Catholic theology. If this particular discourse of authority was quashed by a higher power, its claim for a hearing nonetheless refers to those structures of power. Moreover, the form of the report is entirely traditional. Even its list of criteria, however innovative their content, looks rather like a casuist's list of criteria for evaluating cases. Whatever is truly revolutionary in the report is troubled by so many repetitions of older forms of power.

Repetitions, I have been calling them: the repetitions of Christian speeches that were elaborated within Christendom, that are rehearsed now after Christendom. They find their matches in the speech of bio-power, which itself still uses Christian sexual categories, judgments, justifications. These operate within even the blandest "descriptive" language, the merest statement of "facts." Terms for sex in European languages are still so informed by the categories of Christendom that Christian theology is still curiously implicated in the works of bio-power – implicated and yet impotent. Theologians repeat the old rhetorics of teaching power, even tacitly accommodating themselves to the edicts of bio-power. Those edicts echo the old languages of Christian theology, but without any theological content. The rhetoric of power without power; the scraps of religious teaching without religious pedagogy. A cycle of speeches from which there often seems to be little hope of escape.

Hope comes in taking responsibility for speech. One obligation of any Christian teaching about sexual matters is to take up a double responsibility with regard to the cycles of speech about sex. Theology needs to tell where the inherited categories have come from and how far they have been deformed in being "secularized." Then it needs to admit that it has lost authority over those terms. It needs to make a good act of confession, though not of the sort that theologians often undertake.

Being Responsible for Christian Speeches

How can a Christian ethicist take responsibility for the bodies of Christian speech already spoken about sex, the ones we have sampled and the thousands more? For the twisting arguments, ugly condemnations, mocking caricatures – for summary judgments that issued in violent punishments? There are personal issues here: How far are we as individuals implicated in the crimes of our Christian predecessors? How far do we endorse their crimes in affirming creeds or praying liturgies that were also theirs? But our present inquiry poses other, more focused questions: What can a Christian ethicist do to engage earlier speeches so that they help rather than hinder the attempt to speak Christian truths about sex in the present? It is much easier to proclaim a revolution than to make one. So it is much easier to say that we are reforming Christian ethics than actually to escape from the grip of the old Christian speeches about sex.

As we have seen, two of the earlier discourses are particularly weighty. One looks like an argument about sexual behavior on the basis of claims about nature. The other is a disgusted shaming of anyone who speaks favorably of sexual pleasure – or who savors it in silence. We have encountered both kinds of discourse many times already in the texts we have sampled. Now I can suggest why they are not so easy to escape – why they seem to be reinvigorated with every generation of Christian discourse, including our own attempts to be revolutionary.

"Arguments" from nature are often thought of as Catholic arguments, but they are not only Catholic. Natural law arguments about sex have figured historically in Anglican and Protestant discussions, and at present they seem to be more popular than ever. But the natural "arguments" are in fact quite peculiar. Take the most basic case, the claim that voluntary ejaculations or orgasms are to be restricted to marriage. Even on its face, the claim seems confusing. It is contradicted by human physiology, at least so far as our medical or biological sciences describe it to us. Men experience spontaneous ejaculations from puberty on. Indeed, for many men the onset of puberty is marked by a spontaneous ejaculation. Mature men and women can be stimulated to orgasm by non-sexual physical activities. So it is odd to claim that it is an abuse of the nature of human sex to provoke orgasms outside of a permanent, monogamous union open to reproduction. On our most disciplined scientific accounts, our sexed bodies don't seem to work that way.

Of course, in Christian moral theology it is always possible to counter a scientific fact with the reminder that some or many features of the present cosmic order are the results of original sin. Many theologians have argued that spontaneous ejaculations or orgasms were not part of God's original plan. They began to occur only because desire ran riot through our fallen bodies. If human beings now regularly experience such ejaculations or orgasms, that is because human beings are now fallen. It is certainly possible to make this critique of nature as it appears to contemporary science, but only if one is willing to pay a price. The critique is forced to hypothesize unfallen bodies so very different from our present bodies that we are no longer able to make any inferences from our present condition to God's original intention. If God's intentions for human nature are to be inferred only from what we hypothesize about Adam and Eve in Eden, we will not be able to reason about those intentions very convincingly. Nor can we invoke scientific evidence on one page of theological argument and then reject it out of hand for the next. If our medicine and biology reveal nothing theologically significant about sex, then we shouldn't trust them in other cases either – say, in constructing arguments about abortion or alcoholism or insanity. To do otherwise produces a kind of dissonance, of doublespeak, that makes the speaker into that particularly modern tyrant, the state ideologue.

If we begin to suspect that a Christian church's teaching on sexuality is deliberately self-contradictory in the way ideology is, we ought to hesitate before responding to it. Whether in churches or other institutions, ideological discourse is immune to logical refutation because it is already self-contradictory. If you cut off one argument, a contrary argument will spring into its place. Ideology is always ready to mobilize entirely new reasons, because its purpose is precisely to defuse its opponents by engaging them in an endless and essentially wasteful discourse. Responding to ideological discourse requires a rule, not just of suspicion, but of inversion: we should attend not to what the discourse says, but to how it operates.

This procedure must be adopted with some care by the critical Christian ethicist who wants to reform or "revolutionize" a large number of earlier theological "arguments" about sexual acts. One can waste several lifetimes identifying their logical fallacies, their equivocations in central terms, their sleights of hand. To what end? It is not at all clear that the arguments can be successfully refuted, since they are not really arguments to begin with. Nor is it clear that many people who advance those arguments would change their minds if the arguments were refuted, since they do not seem to hold their convictions in view of the arguments. At the same time, the Christian ethicist cannot simply pretend that those earlier arguments vanish. The arguments have to be taken apart – not as devices of reason, but as instruments of power.

I admit that the inverted reading of theological ideologies is risky. I worry, for example, whenever we begin to treat all religious discourse as self-evidently pernicious. In fact, religious discourses have served at many times to revolutionize the possibilities for human living. Particular forms of religious community have served to protect the position of the marginal while religious institutions, despite themselves, have served as havens for those with alternate experiences of sexuality. So the Christian ethicist who wants to "revolutionize" teachings about sex has to assume a sequence of attitudes with respect to the meaning-dissonant arguments defending those teachings. On the one hand, she cannot be mesmerized by them into wasting her life on attempts at refuting them. On the other hand, she cannot ignore them altogether. They may contain some truth deep within. They certainly contain the record of the long play of power over Christian speeches about sex.

They also contain a last and fatal trap. Ideological speech is designed to convert its opponents into ideologues. It does this by wasting language to the point that an opponent despairs of speaking – except by shouting back. Faced with the ideology that speaks (for the moment) in natural law arguments, the Christian ethicist has to respond without descending into the speech of ideology, without putting on the role of the Theological Ideologue. This is a particularly powerful role in the present because a few of the twentieth century's bloodiest ideologies borrowed the rhetoric and the scripts of the Christian theologian. It is all too easy, then, for the revolutionary theologian to slip over into the role of new Ideologue when confronted by ideology.

Another sort of trap appears in the second category of Christian speech singled out above, the vivid discourses of shame. While the nature arguments work by entrapping the resistant reader in an endless and deforming effort at refutation, the speeches of shame are always misdirecting her. Christian preaching about shame commands an enormous arsenal of rhetorical devices. The most subtle of these infuse shame into the very categories for describing sex. Indeed, most of our basic words for sexual activities carry the charge of Christian shaming. Who can speak words such as "adultery," "fornication," "masturbation," and "sodomy" without feeling that charge? You feel it even when you disagree with the churches' valuation of those acts.

Theological shame has corrupted or determined the language of sex in these fundamental ways. It has subjected sexual utterances to a ruthless hermeneutic of suspicion, and then it has suspected sexual motivation in every kind of utterance. These categories cannot easily be made pristine. It is not possible to forget that suspicion, to return to a time when our language and thoughts, or dreams and desires, had not been subjected to relentless interrogation for any sexual sin lurking in them. We are always being directed to look for shame in sex because our language itself codes shame into it. Not only our language: those of us raised in Christian or post-Christian societies are likely to have been raised within family systems affected by theological shames. We can hear in Christian condemnations not just the voice of the church, but the voice of our parents. In responding to Christian arguments about shame, the Christian ethicist can be talking back not only to Pastor or Pope, but to Mother and Father. The role for the person who talks back to parents is the role of the Child. The revolutionary moral theologian is always at risk of lisping the scripts of the naughty Child.

Christianity is certainly not the only religion – the only moral code, the only system of taboos – to infuse sexual terms with shame. But Christianity is partly responsible for the particular shames felt by many members of the cultures that used to be Christendom. Those shames are written into our laws and our daily languages. How is the Christian ethicist who wants to think sex anew, apart from and even against Christendom, to take responsibility for this infusion of shame into our most common sexual categories? By a severe discipline of theological language – for which there is ample authority in the most canonical traditions of Christian theology. They are the demands of what is traditionally called "negative theology."

I can say this more generally – and perhaps more agreeably. Whether we consider ourselves revolutionaries or reactionaries, we need to take responsibility for Christian speech about sexual morality. Having shown the play of sexual teachings in the complex history of Christian society, in the unfolding of Christendom, we ought not to want to contribute just one more speech of the approved kinds to that play. Yet as soon as we want to say something different, we find ourselves being offered already approved scripts. Do you want to reject churchly ideology? Speak as a better Ideologue. Do you want to resist shame? Speak as the Child. We need to think our way into more original ways of speaking anew about sex. We can do this, curiously enough, by attending to potentialities in Christian theology that have never been actualized for ethics. I mean just the demands of negative theology.

Two of the oldest principles in Christian theology are that God teaches humankind progressively, in stages of "law"-giving, and that Christian moral teaching itself has levels or stages of disclosure. The first principle is seen most clearly in the succession of "Old" and "New" Testaments, but also in the sequence of Old Testament covenants. It has been developed theologically in accounts of salvation history and the various meanings of "law." The second principle is seen in Jesus' teaching through parables, in the Gospel narrators' talk of secrets or mysteries, in Paul's notions about what is suitable for "infants" in the faith. It has been developed as the ideal of "negative" or "apophatic" theology, in models of spiritual ascent or development.

I combine these principles in an unusual way when it comes to thinking about new roles for speaking Christian sexual ethics – roles that might discover new grounds for conviction apart from bio-power. I combine the principles as a test for our speaking. Where do *we* stand as a community before God's progressive teaching about sex? Where do *I* stand in God's teaching me, in the disclosure of moral truths within my history? What, then, are my responsibilities when it comes to speaking about these things to others?

Before we can engage in responsible moral teaching, we have to wait on what God teaches. God teaches Christian communities about moral matters in any number of ways, but perhaps especially through the holy lives of their members. It is only very recently that Christian communities have permitted members to live their sexualities openly, to show God at work in their sexual lives. For example, it is only very recently that lesbian or gay Christians have been able to speak candidly and at length even with one another about the realities of their lives. We have barely begun to see what freely lived lesbigay lives look like. We have hardly begun to experiment with these lives in genuine Christian freedom. The same could be said about other forms of human sexuality or other human sexual practices. How long has it been, for example, that Christians were willing to talk frankly about the sexual relations of heterosexuals who, for one reason or another, could not get married? We need much more time to see what God is teaching in the sexual lives of Christian believers. Everything we say at present will be anticipatory, fragmentary, hypothetical. It needs to labeled as such. We should also distinguish this very specific historical condition from the general state of pilgrimage in Christian life. Christians are always on the road, but we are much nearer the beginning of the road that leads to persuasive sexual theology. For that matter, we are probably just learning to crawl along it, not yet having learned to walk.

Just here we can usefully adapt some suggestions of negative theology to speech about sexual ethics. In its severe control over our assumptions in speaking about divine revelation, it does not rule out inventive language. On the contrary, it has authorized some of the most experimental Christian writing, writing in beautiful language loosed from the false restraint of literalism or "accuracy." It has encouraged a diversity of genres, from the critical or analytic to the liturgical and lyrical. Most importantly, it has freed theological language from the smallness of human purposes – of human regimes – for the possibilities of transcendence. We need new roles for speaking Christian sexual ethics. We thus also need new genres for our speaking. I imagine that they will be less like the single-voice genres of legal code or verdict and more like the polyphony of complex narratives or lyrics written over a lifetime. Audre Lorde, that great teacher of the erotic, once wrote: "where language does not yet exist, it is our poetry which helps us to fashion it. Poetry is not only dream and vision; it is the skeleton architecture of our lives."[29] She says something very much like what I understand by negative theology – especially in relation to the erotic.

In the next chapter, my last, I will explore some reformulations of Christian speech about sexuality. As you read them, remember that the reformulations in no way proclaim a "revolution" in theological speech. We aren't ready for one. We may just be ready to begin describing the truly revolutionary time when a happy "attack" upon Christendom has finally freed theological ethics from the need to be a handbook for the police. For now, the sexual revolution has yet to take place.

---

[29] Audre Lorde, "Poetry Is Not a Luxury," reprinted in *Sister Outsider: Essays and Speeches* (Freedom, CA: The Crossing Press, 1984), pp. 36–9, at pp. 37–8.

Chapter 7

Redeeming Pleasures

Nietzsche writes: "Christianity gave Eros poison to drink – he didn't die from it, but he did degenerate, into a vice."[1] Nietzsche means to recall many things, beginning with the war between Christianity and the pagan gods or the contrast between the divine Eros of antiquity and the sordid, "degenerate," Christian sin of lust. But Nietzsche also means to recapitulate the ancient accusations that Christianity had conducted a barbarous and fanatical campaign against erotic pleasure itself.

We have seen dozens of passages in which Christian authors condemn erotic pleasure with one degree of severity or another. What do Christian authors really condemn in erotic pleasure? What do they argue against it exactly and on which particular principles? Do their principles still deserve support? We have also noticed dozens of passages in which arguments against pleasure mingle with arguments for procreation and child rearing or against pollution and uncleanness. What is the relation of the arguments against pleasure to these other arguments? Where does the language of pleasure stand in the group of languages that Christianity has used to describe and condemn certain sexual desires, acts, or relations – or states, statuses, and identities?

The questions are gathered for me in the exasperated remark I usually hear in class after a semester with early and medieval texts: "What is it about Christianity and sex anyway?" Dozens of replies have been offered to this challenge – scriptural, theological, historical, psychological, anthropological. We have encountered some of the replies in the course of our readings. It would not be difficult to find many more. Still I suggest that

[1] Friedrich Nietzsche, *Jenseits von Gut und Böse (Beyond Good and Evil)*, no. 168, in *Sämtliche Werke: Kritische Studienausgabe*, ed. Giorgio Colli and Mazzino Montinari, vol. 5 (2nd ed., Munich: DTV, and Berlin and New York: de Gruyter, 1988), p. 102.

we might make more progress with Christianity's negative judgment on sex if we took it not as a historical puzzle, but as a rhetorical challenge. If we wanted to find elements for encouraging positive accounts of sex in Christian speeches, where would we look? What alternate topics or roles does Christian rhetoric already offer us for discovering how to say more persuasive things about sexual pleasure?

The challenge is not a small one. Often enough in Christian writing, even those who are disposed to take a "liberal" or encouraging view of sexual life try to step around the question of its pleasure. They praise its fruitfulness or its capacity for generating intimacy. They commend its generosity or its joy. They argue that the prosecution of many sexual "perversions" or "deviations" is in fact an unjust infringement of human rights of privacy and self-determination. These appeals are good things, but they bring us face to face with what has proved so problematic for Christian moral teaching in regard to sex. They will not get at the center of the old quarrel between Christianity and Eros.

I would say the same for discourses about the complementarity of the kinds of love – say, the connection between eros and agape. Any Christian teaching about how to live will have to be brought back in the end to Jesus' great commandment to love God and our neighbors as ourselves. To begin an ethical discussion about erotic love by translating it immediately into the terms of (what is counted) another love is to miss the most aggravated questions. I am not assuming, of course, that eros and agape are intrinsically opposed. I do conclude that the relation of agape to eros is anciently contested in Christian thought and practice. Christian theologians have struggled most with sexual activities as the site of intense physical pleasures. If we are to sketch alternate Christian speeches about sex, we have to begin by talking about those pleasures.

Pleasures and not procreation. As we have seen, Christian theologians learned early on that they could use the principle that sex is for procreation in a number of ways, though never alone. Still that principle is neither the original nor most powerful principle in Christian discourses about sex. I argued above that many Christian judgments about sex were formed first on other bases and then translated into discourses about procreation. To say that it is better to marry than to burn with vain desire is not, after all, quite the same as saying that God gave us sex for procreation inside marriage – though the two principles may yield very similar judgments on a number of sexual situations. We have been led to speak as if Christian reasoning about sex were mainly reasoning from procreation. In fact, it has mostly been reasoning about something else, such as purity or pleasure. The suspicion of an impure pleasure is the most radical and comprehensive principle in Christian sexual ethics, the one with the greatest power to exclude acts, desires, and dispositions. We will be able to look at that principle only if we think about pleasure apart from procreation.

I will consider Christian topics about pleasure in several ways. First, I will take the main topics of Christian condemnation and suggest how they might be reversed, how they might be turned from producing condemnation of pleasure to producing illumination of pleasure. Then, second, I will turn elsewhere in Christian discourse to find new topics for generating speech about pleasure, that is, for soliciting the performance of Christian roles that include erotic pleasure as something other than sin.

Calumnies against Pleasure

Our cultural traditions have spoken so many complaints against erotic pleasure that it is difficult to know where to begin in responding to them. The complaints come not just from Christian theologians, of course. Pleasure has been denigrated by any number of ancient and modern philosophers, not to say by generations of legislators, physicians, schoolteachers, and parents. Christian theologians have borrowed from these other discourses and contributed to them, in a bewildering variety of ways. I want now to suggest that many of the traditional complaints are calumnies, and I will do so by displaying some of their topics – that is, their argumentative curiosities.

A first calumny about erotic pleasure that we hear in Christian authors from early on is that it is self-evidently "unclean" and therefore "disgusting." The claim is difficult for many modern ears, Christian or not. In the same way that sex has been transferred from church to state, bodily "purity" has been transferred from religion to medicine. Much work is required to recover a sense of the term other than the hygienic. On contemporary medical accounts, there can be issues of hygiene in sexual acts, but not more so than in personal grooming or the preparation and consumption of food. If modern Christians do not fixate on hygiene generally, they should not do so in the case of sex. Many people dismiss as superstitious those Christians who regarded certain substances (such as semen or menstrual blood) as so intrinsically unclean that they prevented one from properly receiving the Eucharist or other sacraments.

Of course, these "superstitious" Christians held such views not for hygienic reasons, but for what they thought were theological ones. Their beliefs raise more difficult questions for us. What, then, can canonical writers mean when they cry out that sexual acts and the pleasure produced by them are "unclean" or "impure"? What have Christian traditions meant, more generally, by naming sexual sins "sins against purity"? We might indeed find ways of translating theological metaphors of "impurity" into other metaphors. But then we would still face more difficult questions about the wisdom of using these metaphors. Many New Testament texts are firm in their refusal of what they take to be rabbinic notions of purity and impurity. They present or understand Jesus' ministry as a deliberate violation of various scruples about ritual cleanliness. Is it wise, then, for Christian moralists to reintroduce such notions, even metaphorically? Doesn't this risk reanimating pre-Christian notions that were supposed to have been abandoned with the advent of the Gospel?

It is tempting, of course, to treat Christian discourses of "impurity" not as theological arguments, but as personal confessions of a failure to think a way through to new metaphors. The failure is easy enough to understand, both institutionally and psychologically. For example, languages of "impurity" or "uncleanness" remain powerful rhetorics in child rearing. When a Christian theologian continues to use them, we may suspect that we are told most not about the Gospel, but about the speaker – about the speaker's unexamined loathing, anxieties, or preoccupations. We may suspect that the person who says, "Sex is dirty" suffers from particular spiritual difficulties. These psychologizing suspicions are tempting, but also perhaps not wise. In our prevailing cultures, almost any locution can be treated as the stuff of therapy. "Therapy" is too often a euphemism for social management. If we want to resist handing theological argument as a whole over to the "care," that is, the control, of one or another bureaucracy, we ought to be careful when invoking therapeutic models – even against theological speeches that offend us.

Better to note that little or nothing can be said in reply to a claim that sex is self-evidently "unclean" and "disgusting." If these words are not being used as terms for sanitation, we have no common conventions for understanding them as metaphors. Indeed, and especially when faced with a term like "disgusting," we have no way of hearing it except as an expression of personal taste. Our contemporary cultures are famously lacking in protocols for discussing expressions of taste. So the Christian writer who wants to describe sex in terms of impurity must construct some meaning for those terms or else expect no reply.

A second calumny that calls for sharp theological analysis is the assertion that erotic pleasure is original sin, implicated in the Fall as both cause and effect. Here the claim has several consequences. On the one hand, it pushes any further discussion about well-ordered sex into the realm of extravagant hypotheses. On the other hand, it associates sex with the demonic. Hypotheses about sex in Eden have their theological uses, but most often they seem to be sterile exercises in the logic of reversal. Hypothesized Edenic bodies turn out to be so very different from our present bodies that we are no longer able to reason about them convincingly. We don't know what to say. It may be that our present experience of sexual desire is very different from what it was created to be. But what evidence do we have, then, for what was intended – except perhaps the rule that we should be exactly the opposite of what we are now? Consider, for example, the theological claim that our sexual desire was completely under our control before the Fall. The claim has implied to some theologians, for instance, that males were originally intended to have erections only voluntarily, and that the intensity of sexual pleasure for both males and females was supposed never to blur rational processes. To others it has implied that unfallen men and women would have copulated only for the end of procreation and achieved this end every time.

To speculate about an Edenic or angelic existence is not just to go beyond scriptural evidence, it is to turn the conversation back toward rupture. Theologians have written at length about the properties of resurrected bodies, their abilities to pass through solid objects or to travel instantly across vast distances. You may find these pages interesting as examples of speculative fiction (or of patristic and medieval science fiction), but you cannot offer them as examples of compelling theological analysis of the human condition. They are about a kind of life other than what we mean by "human life." The same judgment applies to theologians' theories about pleasureless erections on command. These theories are not about the bodies we know how to describe. If some Christians claim to have attained such a condition of physical otherness, we may applaud them, but we might also note that their attainment comes at the cost of a body-breaking effort – and that they leave us without much to say or to infer.

The other side of the argument from Eden is the claim that fallen sex is somehow intrinsically demonic. The claim takes a variety of forms. In theologians of the patristic period, it can be the claim that the debauched sexual practices of paganism were likened to pagan idolatry, itself understood as demon-worship.[2] In medieval moralists, the claim can become the notion that sex is the special weapon of demonic temptation or that sexual sin makes one the prey of demons. In contemporary writing, inside Christian theology and outside of it, you can still find the claim that human sexuality is somehow particularly "dark" or "violent" or "inhuman." Sex is seen as the path to

---

[2] Compare this with Blenkinsopp's characterization of "the fatal fascination which the orgiastic practices of Canaan exercised on the Hebrew"; see Joseph Blenkinsopp, *Sexuality and the Christian Tradition* (Dayton, OH: Pflaum Press, 1969), pp. 65–6.

a night-world in which the rational, productive arrangements of human society are dissolved in horror. The orgy, imagined as the eruption of dark forces, becomes the symbol of the destructive power of sex.

How to evaluate these claims? I don't know how to judge allegations that human sex as we know it is the particular province of demons. I am not even sure how to judge the (secularized) claim that sex is particularly threatening to human society. Certainly sexual feelings or actions can disrupt or destroy social arrangements. The same is true of greed, ambition, sloth, arrogance, and other of the major vices. How is one to rank the evil produced by these vices? Does it make much sense to argue, for example, that the worst of the twentieth century's crimes were due more to lust than to the mania of power or the dissolution of responsibility in absolute obedience? Of course, there are theories, both theological and sexual, in which the other vices and most of human action are reduced to erotic motives, but those theories are the ones I am here putting into question.

Severe deformations of human character may often or always involve deformation of sexual life. Again, those who are troubled by the erotic may struggle to partition it off – and then discover how easy it is to put whatever else they mean to segregate behind the same partitions. I am not denying that sexual faculties or energies can be implicated in any number of psychological or spiritual monstrosities. I do deny that sexual energy is uniquely or principally to blame for what is monstrous in human life. We should wish that things were so simple.

When we link the erotic to the demonic, when we fret over the destructiveness of sex, when we prophesy the disasters that follow from it, we must ask ourselves (once again) whether we aren't projecting onto sex fears that would be more difficult or dangerous to confront elsewhere. It is easy for Christians to make a scapegoat of sex, because it has so few theological defenders. We might also admit that we have an abundance of reasons for wanting to make sex "dark," "violent," or "inhuman." For example, to describe sex in such terms may give it a narcotic interest, investing it with mysterious drama. More dramatic sex is not only attractive to some, it also authorizes them (or their opponents) to surround sexual activity with ever more elaborate ritual (or ever more intrusive police machinery). In short, "dark" sex can be useful to many purposes, including theological ones. That is a remark about the purposes and not about sex before it is useful to them.

A third sort of theological calumny against pleasure comes from notions of human distinctiveness or superiority. At its most general level, the accusation moves from distinctiveness to superiority. If humans share with other animals the need for copulation in order to reproduce, then copulation must be something inferior, ignoble. Whatever we share with animals is regarded as a source of embarrassment. This prejudice is often played out as an argument against sexual pleasure so far as it interferes with reason. Analogously hierarchical arguments can also be made from alleged differences among kinds or classes of human beings. The implicit claim in all of them is that better people – higher, nobler, finer people – hold themselves back from physical pleasure. Whenever sexual sin is called "base" or "ignominious" or "disgraceful," it is condemned by implicit reference to a system of rank. Now Nietzsche argues at length in the *Genealogy of Morals* that the origin of terms for moral valuation lies in the tastes of an aristocracy. He is perfectly content, then, to propose aristocratic valuations of his own. Christian theologians cannot appear so easily contented. So they have tried to move further along, endorsing numberless hierarchies of creation, in which the body seems somehow always to end up on the bottom, while the mind, especially pure mind, inevitably rises to the top.

Two objections can be raised against these hierarchies of material and immaterial. First, when you assert that bodies are "lower" in the created hierarchy, you are not thereby authorized to speak calumnies against bodies or their pleasures. It may be that in some conceptions of hierarchy – say, in some Neoplatonic hierarchies – it is perfectly appropriate to denigrate the lower members by contrast with the higher. But a Christian hierarchy supposes the direct and unmediated activity of God at every point in creation. Every level of the hierarchy has been willed by God and blessed by God. So even if one endorses a strongly hierarchical notion of the created order, with mind on top and body on bottom, it does not follow that you can speak ill of bodies – unless you mean to contradict the divine wisdom.

The second objection is much simpler. Every hierarchical argument against bodily pleasure supposes that it makes sense to describe some pleasures as bodily and others as not bodily. Is our experience of pleasure so easily divided? Aren't erotic pleasures mental and mental pleasures – the pleasure of solving an equation, say – often erotic? I suspect that the confidence in being able to segregate bodily from intellectual pleasures comes either from bad ontology or from the sense that pleasures come prepackaged in morally distinct brands.

A fourth calumny against pleasure, and the last I will consider, is in some ways the most subtle. It is an accusation that pleasure, so far as it is powerfully selfish, blocks access to the level of the truly moral. The block can be psychological. A longstanding dispute in Greek philosophy circles around the question, whether some are so unable to resist pleasures that they have to be counted as morally defective, as incapable of being moral agents. The block can also be conceptual or logical. Much of moral theology or philosophy since Kant seems to regard pleasure as a sub-moral motivation.

Here again we meet a complex theologico-philosophical argument that would require much effort to rebut. Let me begin a reply just by making the sort of simple counter-suggestion I have been using for all of the calumnies. The claim that pleasure falls below the level of moral motivation seems to me to assume either very reductive experiences of pleasure or ridiculously high standards of altruistic motivation. Rational duty can be a perfectly selfish motive, as it can bring any number of pleasurable rewards. Moreover, as the twentieth century showed with dreadful clarity, claims to be acting out of rational duty can cover unthinkable crimes. We also have many experiences of ways in which experiences of pleasure lead to acts of kindness, generosity, even reconciliation. The day of festival is a day of healing. So the accusation that pleasure cannot be taken seriously as a moral motive seems to me both untrue and dangerous.

Much more could be said about each of these classes of arguments. Much more should be said, but not here. I end instead by noting a rhetorical feature that all the calumnies share. When arguments like these appear in Christian theological writing, they almost always speak of bodily pleasure with contempt. The rhetorical tone may suggest to us that the discourses in condemnation are in fact acts of ingratitude against divine creation.

Here a philosophical teaching may be of help. When Aristotle comes to describe pleasure in the *Ethics*, he speaks of it as a concomitant of proper operation. When things work well – when bodies do what they are structured to do – bodily pleasure blossoms in the operation itself. For Christians, this definition can be made much stronger, because there is a much stronger sense of the original structuring of creation. Pleasure ought to be understood as the sign of approach to the original created order. It is something like the residue of the good of creation – the echo of God's original judgment that the world was good. If the world had to be won back to its creator by suffering and death, by a cross, the full graciousness of that act can be seen only in acknowledging its full horror – in confessing again that the world was not made for suffering and death.

It will be objected immediately that human beings take pleasure in all sorts of things that cannot be willed by God. People take pleasure in killing one another or in impoverishing one another. Pleasure cannot, then, be any kind of guide to the original order of creation. This is a serious objection, but also a misleading one. First, it forgets that moral reasoning almost always supposes multiple layers of description for moral motivation or judgment, some more superficial than others. It is also true, for example, that people will name very different things as their ultimate goals, but this has not prevented centuries of moral theology from asserting that all human beings are ordered by creation to a single end – life with God. So, too, a claim on behalf of pleasure as a trace of creation could interpret and rewrite individual testimonies about pleasure in any number of ways. People may say that they kill "for pleasure." They may not know more accurate descriptions of what is happening inside of them. Or we may not yet have a rich enough pleasure-language in theology for writing more accurate descriptions.

Second, the objection allows the negative cases of pleasure to occlude the positive ones. This is another way in which Christian considerations of pleasure deviate from typical patterns of Christian moral reasoning. It seems true, for example, that many and perhaps most husbands in contemporary American marriages commit at least one act of adultery. Christian theologians do not typically infer from this that monogamy ought to be abandoned as an ideal. Similarly, if many or most people have experiences of pleasure from sin, we are not authorized to conclude that pleasure is intrinsically evil or completely untrustworthy as a moral indication of the original created order. We might insist on original pleasure all the more as an ideal for Christian living.

The third thing to be said in defense of the moral significance of pleasure is that the capacity for pleasure may be more important than the occasion for particular pleasures. It may be, for example, that someone takes pleasure selfishly and incompletely in acts that destroy others. The most interesting moral fact about this person may not be the destructive character of the particular pleasures, but the remaining trace of an original capacity for pleasure itself. The trace might point backwards toward the original capacity for the astonished, generous openness to the goodness of creation that full pleasure requires.

In offering these reasons, I have been speaking of bodily pleasure in relation to creation and resisting the all-too-familiar assumption that the moral worth of pleasure was undone or cancelled by the Fall. Christian moral reflection does not stop with the Fall. On the contrary, it starts with the assumption that we have been redeemed from the Fall. So we must ask, how might we speak of pleasure on this side of redemption?

Redeemed Pleasure or the Intimacy of Prayer

How much has Christian theology helped to make a speech adequate to consideration of erotic pleasure? Christian theologians have richly supplied us with the language of invective and stigma in regard to sex. They have minutely classified types of sexual acts, ideas, and desires in order to condemn them. And so on. But have they helped us to talk seriously about sexual pleasure? The question might be generalized as an accusation. So far as Christian judgments or prejudgments have determined much of the history of European and American culture, they have deprived us for long periods even of secular speeches about sex that were not condemned as pornography or permitted only because they served the purposes of medicine or law. Until quite recently, we haven't had many models for what a helpful discourse about sex might be. There have been the meager and rather chilly "marriage manuals," the privately circulated pages of pornography, the highly technical discourses of psychiatry or gynecology or criminal law. Of course, the poverty of European models for writing richly about sex is itself a legacy of Christendom.

Imagine an alternate history of Christian literature. In this imagined history, an early commitment both to God's goodness in creation and to the transfiguration of human bodies promised by the Lord's resurrection would lead to the cultivation of erotic genres. Theologians would regard a rich and detailed language of sexual love as an index of their fidelity to God's incarnation. From this patristic period, we would inherit exhortations to sexual discovery, rules for conducting it, and public letters of sexual encouragement or advice. From this Scholastic period, we would still have a vast Christian compendium of sexual arts, which we would count as one of the most authoritative works in moral theology, meriting generations of commentary. Our contemporary theological schools would vie in providing interesting departures from it.

This imagined history is not entirely fantastic. There are and have long been genres and topics through which theologians celebrate erotic pleasure. The languages for describing mystical experiences are famously erotic. They are authorized to be so by linked examples in the Christian Bible. On the one hand, both Jewish and Christian writers use the imagery of erotic relations to describe the relations of human beings to God. For the prophets, Israel is often God's bride – and in Hosea, God's prostitute-bride. For Paul, in turn, the Christian community is the bride of Christ. From these explicit images, Christian readers were led to interpret the fiercely erotic lyrics of the Song of Songs (or Canticle of Canticles) as an allegory of the soul's passionate union with God in prayer. That Old Testament book called forth masterworks by Christian mystics such as Bernard of Clairvaux and John of the Cross. Theologians who didn't comment on it were reported to have done so. Thomas Aquinas, prevented from writing by a vision of his own, confined by his last illness to the Cistercian house of Fossanova, was asked by the monks to give them a commentary on the Song of Songs. Perhaps he broke his authorial silence to do so – though no copy has survived.

Among Christian theologians, the highly erotic language of mysticism has often been excused or dismissed. They have said that it was only meta-phorical or traditional or scriptural, or they have counted it as excessive (mysticism itself being suspected of excess), or they have set it aside as something less than real theology. These excuses or dismissals fail to ask the most obvious question: Why should mystics use *erotic* language to describe their most privileged relations with God? Is it because only erotic language carries the intensity or importance or intimacy of mystical experience? Or it is perhaps that only language about erotic pleasure can hint at the pleasure of union with God?

We should register the implications in these questions before we try to explain them away. They may imply that the erotic has a much larger role in our spiritual life than we ordinarily admit. For example, mystical expe-rience can produce sexual arousal. This is not a discovery of secular psy-choanalysis, but the experience of the most approved spiritual writers. The disconcerting fact should suggest something more interesting still. Mystical experience marks a return of bodily pleasure – which was supposed to have been left behind in the long ascent from purgation through illumination to union. Official saints are presumed to have acquired sexual purity early on in their journeys toward God. Indeed, we have heard from some spiritual authors that the absence of even involuntary arousal is an index of one's spiritual progress. But then, meeting God, the mystics are overwhelmed with what is in some cases marked by the physiological effects of sexual intercourse and described in all cases with the imagery of that intercourse. Mystical experience seems not so much an allegory of the erotic as its return.

The erotic returns in less extreme cases than mystical vision. Our ordinary language for describing the unions of prayer is astonishingly like our language for the sexual unions of bodies. If an hour of contemplative prayer does not produce orgasms in most believers, it can produce "inner warmth" and "closeness" and "deep relaxation." It can lead ordinary believers to speak in the effusive and unguarded language of physical connection, physical passion. Is this language allegory? Is it only an analogy between sex and prayer? Why, then, do we return to just this language when we want to talk about prayer?

I suggest that we set aside explanations in terms of allegory in order to consider a more direct connection between consolation in prayer and erotic pleasure. But let me first distinguish my suggestion from two alternatives. Some might concede that any experience of pleasure is going to have sexual side effects in us so long as we are embodied. Others might suggest that the religious is just the erotic "sublimated" – concealed or transmuted. I am suggesting instead that our union with God in prayer is the fulfillment of our capacity for erotic pleasure. It is what our erotic capacity prepares us for, what it is given for. We use erotic imagery quite appropriately to describe forms of prayer because our ordinary experience of the erotic is on the way to the experience of union with God. If this suggestion has any plausibility, then we can reverse the movement from eros to prayer. When Paul compares the church's relation to Christ with the relations of wife and husband, he means to teach both about the church and about marriage. The one is the completion of the other. So too with sex and prayer. We can borrow the language of sex to describe prayer, but then we can also borrow what we learn about prayer to guide our sexual relations.

We learn in prayer, for example, that there are inevitable fluctuations in our sense of intimacy. The sense of consolation in prayer varies, withdraws. Indeed, one can be led into a long desolation – the "dark night of the soul," people often call it, after John of the Cross. They fail to remember that the dark night is not for him so much the desolation as the nameless, inarticulate learning to see God as "nothing" in that darkness. The highest moment of mystical union is a nocturnal encounter with the beloved who in that moment eludes our expectations. So the first lesson from John, the easier one, is that we expect of our erotic relations that the pleasure in them will wax and wane. We might begin to look not for a steady supply of the pleasures we have known, but for new and unexpected pleasures. We might learn to think of erotic pleasure as what is present in both consolation and desolation, in the familiar genital acts and in unfamiliar disclosures through sensation. The second, more difficult lesson is that our lover cannot be possessed by us or integrated into us without being lost to us as lover. As soon as the lover is claimed as fully known, we have lost the lover and the lover's gift of pleasure.

The Christian experience of prayer can give us not only an old and elaborate theological language for describing pleasure, but also any number of counsels about how to grow in erotic life. Some of the teachings will show us how to nurture or recover our capacity for erotic pleasure. Others will show us how pleasure can heal our pain. Others still may suggest that pleasure corrects what is selfish and even violent in our inward lives. Indeed, I think that we can find help from our teachings on prayer for a variety of difficulties in sexual ethics. By "difficulties" I don't mean the sorts of sexual limit cases with which some moralists tease themselves. I mean something more like difficult motives. I think particularly of the motives of selfishness and sadomasochism.

Selfishness, first. In many ways, intense private prayer resembles masturbation. To human eyes, it is performed by oneself, often in hiding, and it can result in extraordinary pleasures. Even when its pleasures are not extraordinary, prayer offers comfort or consolation, takes one out of painful or oppressive situations, gives one a sense of self in the midst of the world. But private prayer and masturbation are usually assigned exactly opposite moral evaluations. One of the reasons for this is that masturbation is supposed to make those who practice it more selfish. Sexual pleasure is devalued generally for the same reason: it makes people more self-centered, less generous, less involved in community. Without admitting that any of these claims is true, I want to pose a different question. Why don't we make the same accusations of private prayer? The obvious answer would be that prayer is conversation with someone else – with God, and so prayer persisted in will correct selfishness. Of course people are drawn to prayer with selfish motives – they pray to be given things or, at least, to be afforded spiritual pleasures and consolations. But if they persist in prayer, they often find that they are led out of this selfish insistence into a generous intimacy with God and with others.

Why couldn't we say the same of sexual "selfishness," in all its forms, solitary or not? Of course people will begin performing sexual acts for themselves, but if they will persist in them, they can be led out of selfish pleasure into a more generous sense of intimacy. If this fails to happen now for many Christians, it may be because they have been taught to segregate and silence their sexual experiences. They are never allowed to grow up sexually. So they continue in masturbation when they know richer possibilities are open to them – or they impoverish those possibilities by greedily reducing them to a kind of masturbation with another person. Precisely the same thing happens to people who segregate and silence their inward conversation with God. It remains, not prayer, but a theater of private petition.

Another set of difficult motives cluster around what we call sadomasochism. Indeed, sadomasochistic acts seem to pose a decisive challenge even for "liberal" Christian ethics of sex.[3] How could a Christian theologian condemn them without seeming to deny what modern psychology knows of sexuality – and, indeed, of religious institutions and behaviors? But how could a theologian possibly approve them without abandoning fundamental Gospel precepts? Now the dilemma seems to me misleading on several accounts. It implies, for example, that sadistic elements are not present in most sexual acts, as it ignores the ways in which socially enforced notions of the feminine are intrinsically masochistic. But here I mean to respond to the dilemma by noticing that it takes us back into Christian discourses of prayer.

[3] See, for example, Christine E. Gudorf, *Body, Sex, and Pleasure: Reconstructing Christian Sexual Ethics* (Cleveland, OH: The Pilgrim Press, 1994), pp. 143, 148.

Many Christian traditions have prescribed austerities of various kinds to those who want to pursue God in prayer. Some of the austerities have exactly resembled the rituals of sadomasochistic sex. Flagellation, bondage, and cutting or piercing have all been practices of Christian asceticism. Other Christians have rejected these practices as extreme, while approving such milder practices as confinement, exposure to the elements, and fasting. Those who would reject outward physical expressions of "mortification" altogether have still typically recommended spiritual mortification – that is, the sometimes violent forcing of emotion or concentration in an effort at more complete openness, of surrender to the divine. Indeed, all of the practices of Christian self-punishment are justified as means toward intimacy with God – on the other side of our pride and self-will. But that is exactly the sort of self-description given by those who engage in sadomasochistic sexual rituals. For them too, pain or subjection is used as a way beyond ordinary consciousness – a way to reach the point where the apparent relations of dominance and subjection are dissolved in mutuality, intimacy.

When we realize this agreement between the narratives of Christian asceticism and the narratives of sexual "S&M," we may react in several ways. We might conclude that we have allowed our human experience of domination and submission to distort our descriptions of prayer. We would then call for a thorough rewriting of our discourses about prayer in order to rid them of the distortion. Or we might conclude that the agreement between religious asceticism and S&M shows how inevitably we construe all intimacy in relation to power and the possibility for subversion. Or we might be led to wonder whether the main spiritual lesson to be learned in all of human life is the presence of God in and under affliction. Pursuing any of these alternatives, we will find ourselves learning that sexual sadomasochism lies closer to many of our "purely religious" experiences than we might have supposed.

Selfishness and sadomasochism are only two places where the discourses of prayer and of sexual morality intersect in unexpected ways. There are others. My aim is not to catalogue them all, but to suggest from these two that we already have to hand a Christian discourse of bodily pleasure – if only we know where to look for it. In the Christian records of private prayer, we see a striking variety of erotic responses to intimacy with God. The responses express themselves in passionate address, in nostalgic narrative, in breathless hymns and lyrics. Our intimate encounters with God through prayer are erotic because they are the pleasurable intimacies of creatures with bodies. So the Christian teaching about prayer is already the Christian *ars amatoria*. It is the Christian discourse of the erotic – and not only with regard to the divine. From it, we can learn not only to deny the calumnies against bodily pleasure, but how far pleasure can direct us as a moral teacher. We can learn how the discourse of personal prayer opens out into community – our languages of and about public worship or liturgy.

For the liturgical churches, the event of worship is evidently full of physical pleasures. Indeed, the Eastern churches describe the event as a kind of anticipation of heaven – as the transformation of an earthly place and time into a splendid glimpse of beatitude. The glimpse is not only visual. Good liturgy delights all the senses, sometimes too much. An excessive devotion to liturgy was often considered a sign of voluptuousness, when it was not a symptom of sexual deviance. Oscar Wilde's Dorian Gray "had a special passion . . . for ecclesiastical vestments, as indeed he had for everything connected with the service of the Church. In the long cedar chests that lined the west gallery of his house, he had stored away many rare and beautiful specimens of what is really the raiment of the Bride of Christ."[4] Des Esseintes, the protagonist of Huysmans's *Against the Grain* and one of Dorian's inspirations, decorates his retreat at Fontenay with choice vestments. The ceiling tondo shows angels from the fabric of a cope "embroidered by the weavers' confraternity in Cologne"; the curtains are made of priests' stoles; and the fireplace screen is cut from the "sumptuous stuff of a Florentine dalmatic."[5] These examples of excess can remind us how physically pleasurable Christian liturgy has been and in how many ways.

Churches that reject these "high" liturgies fill their worship with other beauties. Some have cultivated music – the rush of voices singing alone or together, with instruments or without them, in complex polyphony or straight tone. Hymnody has so many pleasures – and they are pleasures of the body. Even the most austere forms of Christian worship – the ones that reject vestments, artworks, music – still cultivate the beauty of the word. The sonority of Scripture proclaimed, of the exquisitely rhetorical sermon, of the inspired prayer. The silence of a Quaker meeting is broken by voices moved to speak by God.

In these frustratingly brief remarks, I mean to point out some of the many places in which Christian discourses offer topics for speaking about bodily pleasures. New speeches about Christian sexual ethics could well begin from them. These topics are only a beginning, of course. I don't mean to suggest that all bodily pleasure is identical, that there are no morally significant

---

[4]   Oscar Wilde, *The Picture of Dorian Gray*, in *The Complete Works of Oscar Wilde* (New York: Barnes & Noble, 1994), p. 110.

[5]   J. K. Huysmans, *À rebours*, ed. Marc Fumaroli (2nd ed., Paris: Gallimard, 1977), pp. 94–5.

differences between hymn singing and sexual intercourse. Of course there are. My point is rather that we have well-developed speeches in Christianity through which physical pleasures are both approved and elicited. We ought to consult those speeches, and not the calumnies of moral theology, if we are to speak convincingly about sexual pleasure.

We might even find models for speech about pleasure within Christian ethics itself if we looked not to the content of its condemnations, but to the forms of its persuasion. The power of the word is not confined in Christianity to private prayer or public worship. It sometimes extends to moral theology. The extension is obvious when moral theology borrows the forms of Christian preaching. Even when it describes ugly things, powerful preaching is beautiful. It uses the beauty as an instrument of persuasion. So too with moral theology: the speeches we have sampled from the libraries of Christian discourse have employed a remarkable range of rhetorical devices, have relied on innumerable rhetorical beauties. The presumption in much of this discourse has been that beautiful speech can exert a kind of control over the beauty of bodies. The beauties of words have been relied on to curtail our pleasure in the beauties of sexual bodies. But the beauties of words are, in their effects, often enough physical beauties too. The gap between word and flesh is for Christian theology always a gap to be closed. So the rhetorical art of Christian moral theology may well rub up against the art of the erotic. It may, in its form, offer a model for a more persuasive content.

Pleasurable Identities

Imagining a new Christian teaching about sex cannot stop, of course, with new terms, topics, metaphors, rhetorical tropes. It cannot stop just with pleasure. The main work of Christian speech about sex has been the projection of identities constructed around sex – identities of salvation and damnation. So, too, the main work of any new theology of sex would be to project alternate identities in which the capacity for erotic pleasure was integrated rather than rejected. In projecting these identities, it would rely on the deepest Christian teachings – and the most distinctive Christian devices for change.

As we have seen, Christian pastoral care is not just words – and certainly not just didactic words. We may think of ritual actions (the sacraments or sacramentals, liturgical and paraliturgical rites) or places (the confessional, the pulpit, the churchyard, the town square) or punishments (fasting, flogging, exile, execution). So theological scripts for sexual identities are not presented just in descriptive or prescriptive words. In late medieval or early modern Catholicism, for example, sexual identities were of course projected in moral teaching – but not only in moral teaching. Catholic moral discourses are reinforced by liturgy or sacrament and by fundamental doctrine. I note this not just to say that words about identity were part of a larger set of cultural practices, but to stress that those practices displayed or enacted distinctive notions about what identities were and how they could be assumed. In Latin liturgy, there are multiple substitutions of identity: at the Mass, a priest becomes Christ, but also Christ's spouse; a nun at her veiling becomes the virgin martyr Agnes, but also Christ's bride. In baptism, the new believer puts on Christ; in the Eucharist, she or he consumes Christ as bread and wine in order to be united with Christ; and so on. In Christian doctrine, the central claim of vicarious atonement requires multiple exchanges of identity. I suggest that the successful projection of sexual identities in Christian pastoral practice depends on the substitution of gendered roles performed in Christian preaching and praying, ritual or sacrament, and moral and dogmatic theology.

You can draw historical conclusions from this claim. You can see, for example, that Christianity has bequeathed to its successors certain conceptions of what an identity is and how it can be managed. But you would do better to take the claim as a suggestion of where to look for the source and goal of new Christian speeches about sex. The development of a new Christian theology of sexual life will not be just the expounding of topics or principles. It will be the projection of new roles in a series of dynamic relations between scripts and their performances. There are many Christian resources for projecting different roles, roles in which the erotic figures not as a deformity, but as an adornment.

On my reading of Foucault as parable, Christian theology was distinguished not so much by its precepts as by the form of its pastoral power. The pastoral power was bequeathed to the modern state as a means of regulating bodies, their pleasures and fertilities. I added to the parable a particular emphasis on the projection of roles in the Christian pastoral power over sex. We have followed a long line of varying roles from the canonical New Testament down to the last generations of Christendom and then watched those roles or motifs from them pass from the churches into the secular bureaucracies. The bureaucracies learned from Christian pastoral care how to construct and maintain bureaucracies for policing identities. What they could not learn, because they did not believe, was the power to exchange identities – to save persons by exchanging identities. That power resides still, as promise and as eschatological hope, in the churches.

We might suspect that Christianity used its power over sexual identities very badly. It projected and enforced a series of dichotomized identities: Virgin Martyr against Lascivious Widow, Angelic Monk against Sodomitic Prelate, and so on. It then insisted on the fragility or fixity of these identities. All the emphasis fell on the dangers to the saintly states and the cursed persistence of the damned ones. But we can imagine a different use of the rhetorical resources of Christian speech in regard to sexual identities. We can imagine a moral theology that would reverse many of the rhetorical choices in earlier theologies of sex. It would emphasize, not dichotomies, but the drawing of all created goods toward Christ, the transfigurative union in Christ of apparent opposites. It would describe, not the sinful fixity of sex-identities, but the graced capacity for learning, transformation, even exchange. Its scripts would not be fearful comedies or dreadful tragedies of endless reiteration, but invitations to variations that we would remember and redo.

Most of all, we might want to imagine a moral theology that would recover the extraordinary power of Christian narrative, the power to put the scripts of identities into cosmic tales of creation and redemption, procession and return. Having given some of its categories and devices to the new bureaucracies of bio-power, Christian theology might now reply to those bureaucracies with other powers that it did not and could not give over. Revelation teaches in ways that bureaucracy cannot. That is the best hope for Christian speeches about sex.

Epilogue: Sex and Schism

At present Christian churches are badly divided over questions of sexual ethics, particularly homosexuality. Homosexual issues are by no means the only ones, but they seem right now to condense the whole range of sexual issues most divisively. Individual congregations quarrel loudly over whether to accept lesbians or gays as members or ministers, or whether to endorse same-sex unions. "Affirming" or "welcoming" congregations align themselves against others that judge it inappropriate to take such a stand. Some churches distance themselves from their denominational leadership; others are expelled by regional or national authorities. Right now, the divisions do not seem to be healing. They threaten to become worse. Some Protestant denominations now face the real possibility of schism over the ordination of "practicing homosexuals" or the blessing of same-sex unions. "Shadow" denominations are springing up within them and taking on many of the usual denominational functions, such as issuing creeds, coordinating missions, or publishing education materials. There are fears that the US National Council of Churches will split over the same issues. If the Roman Catholic hierarchy publicly refuses to reconsider its teaching on them, its members acknowledge privately a steady loss of parishioners who want a more welcoming church – and the dilemma of a priesthood that already contains many gay men.

How can issues of sexual ethics prove so divisive? After our introduction to the topics in Christian discourses about sex, the question ought rather to be: When have they not? Christians have always disputed about sexual ethics. Indeed, they have often translated their other disagreements into disputes about sex. The boundary between orthodoxy and heresy has typically also been a line between holy and unholy sex. Christians on both sides of the boundary have accused those on the other side of excess in what they thought and what they did – an excess of pleasure or of opposition to pleasure, an excess of sex or of its denial. For Christians to cite sexual issues as grounds for separating from one another is nothing new. It is just what we should expect from the library of Christian speeches.

We can balance that pessimistic expectation with a more hopeful one, taken just as plausibly from the library. Christian churches have shown themselves capable of remarkable adaptations on a range of ethical issues, even issues involving sex and gender. The "conservative" association of Christianity with "family values" is itself one result of a remarkable change over centuries in the valuation of virginity. There have been much more rapid changes. We have traced the quick reversal of Protestant views on artificial contraception since the 1920s. We could have traced similar changes in Christian views about divorce or cohabitation. We might even concede how much the boundaries of the debate over homosexuality have shifted since the 1970s. Who would have imagined, two decades ago, that an introduction to the Christian ethics of sex would be written by an "unrepentant homosexual"? For that matter, who would have imagined that church blessings for lesbian or gay unions would be a matter for debate? Or that gays and lesbians would be serving proudly in the churches of many denominations with the full support of their congregations?

It would once have been astonishing to see women at the altar or in the pulpit; to find Catholics, Protestants, and Eastern Orthodox teaching together on seminary faculties; to assert that Christians of different denominations could live peaceably together under a single civil government. One benefit of remembering old church controversies is to be reminded how many of them have been surpassed.

I would not understate the pains of our present divisions – or the threats of rupture we face in overcoming them. Churches will undergo this trial differently. At the middle of the nineteenth century, American churches faced a similar crisis in regard to traditional teachings on slavery. Denominations divided in fact and in law. Faith was shaken or broken. Abominable things were said from the pulpit and in books of theology. Yet today even the churches founded by slave-holders teach that slavery is immoral, however much they might still be implicated in the racial and economic consequences of that slavery. It may be, a hundred years on, that something similar will have happened with our most hotly debated issues in sexual ethics.

In the meantime, in our present, Christian ethics should be preparing speeches for that more hopeful future. It should also be healing the wounds inflicted by the ongoing debates – indeed, by their very intensity. So long as we permit sexual ethics to be the main battlefield on which we fight out the tensions of our lives together as Christians, we prevent ourselves from integrating our sexuality into our selves. In many times and places, sexual behavior was treated as the sum total of morality. A woman who transgressed sexual boundaries was an "immoral woman," simply speaking, and laws regulating sex were laws for preserving "public morals." Many churches endorsed this equation of sexual morality with morality as such. We risk going further in our debates: we have begun to equate "orthodox" views about sex with the whole of orthodoxy. To make sexual rules or roles the most important thing in Christianity not only distorts our efforts to live integral lives, it utterly undoes any sense of the hierarchy of the truths proclaimed as the Gospel. I mean, of course, as we proclaim the Gospel now.

In the course of the readings here, I have often pretended that texts were living voices speaking to us from various points in the past. I spoke of listening to those voices, of understanding them well enough to engage their rhetorical programs. For Christian belief, those voices live indeed in theology and liturgy, in the communion of saints. The voices are caught up in the most powerful voices of revelation, which speak across times and powers. But it is also true that texts only have fleshly voices when we let them speak through ours – when we give them our attention in the present. The divisive questions with which we have been engaged are not principally questions about Christian theologies past. They are questions for Christian theologies in the present. The answers to them – so far as they find answers – can only be given in the present, which is to say, in the future. Christian topics in the ethics of sex retain the power they ought to have just so long as they enable us to discover things to say. They show themselves in what we will say next.

Works Cited

Abelove, Henry. "The Sexual Politics of Early Wesleyan Methodism." In *Disciplines of Faith: Studies in Religion, Politics, and Patriarchy*, ed. Jim Obelkevich, Lyndal Roper, and Raphael Samuel, pp. 86–99. London and New York: Routledge & Kegan Paul, 1987.

Ambrose. *De virginibus*. Migne *PL* 16:197–244.

——. *Some Principal Works of Ambrose*. Trans. H. de Romestin. Nicene and Post-Nicene Fathers, ser. 2, vol. 10. Reprint, Peabody, MA: Hendrickson, 1995.

Anonymous. *Onania, or the Heinous Sin of Self-Pollution, with A Supplement to the Onania*. Ed. Randolph Trumbach. New York and London: Garland, 1986.

Antoninus of Florence. *Summa theologica* (*Sancti Antonini Archiepiscopi Florentini Ordinis Praedicatorum Summa Theologica*). Verona: Typographia Seminarii, Augustinus Carattonius, 1740. Reprint, Graz, 1959.

Arndt, William F., and F. Wilbur Gingrich, eds. *A Greek-English Lexicon of the New Testament and Other Early Christian Literature*. Chicago: University of Chicago Press, 1957.

Athenagoras. *Supplicatio pro Christianis*. In *Zwei griechische Apologeten*, ed. Johannes Geffcken, pp. 120–54. Leipzig and Berlin, Teubner, 1907. Reprint, Hildesheim and New York: Georg Olms, 1970.

Augustine. *Confessiones*. Ed. M. Skutella. Rev. L. Verheijen. Corpus Christianorum Series Latina, vol. 27. Turnhout: Brepols, 1981.

——. *Confessions*. Trans. Henry Chadwick. Oxford: Oxford University Press, 1992.

——. *De bono coniugali*. Ed. Josephus Zycha. Corpus Scriptorum Ecclesiasticorum Latinorum, vol. 41. Vienna: F. Tempsky, 1900.

——. *De civitate Dei*. Corpus Christianorum Series Latina, vols. 47–8. Turnhout: Brepols, 1955. Reproducing the text of the 4th edition of Bernardus Dombart and Alphonsus Kalb. Leipzig: Teubner, 1928–9.

——. *On the Good of Marriage*. Trans. Roy J. Deferrari. In *Saint Augustine: Treatises on Marriage and Other Subjects*. Fathers of the Church: A New Translation. New York: Fathers of the Church, 1955.

Bailey, Derrick Sherwin. *Homosexuality in the Western Christian Tradition*. London, New York, and Toronto: Longmans, Green, 1955.

Balthasar, Hans Urs von. *Theo-Drama: Theological Dramatic Theory*, vol. 1: *Prolegomena*. Trans. Graham Harrison. San Francisco: Ignatius Press, 1988.

Barth, Karl. *Church Dogmatics*. III/2. Trans. Harold Knight, G. W. Bromiley, J. K. S. Reid, and R. H. Fuller. Edinburgh: T. & T. Clark, 1960.

——. *Kirkliche Dogmatik*. III/2. Zurich: Evangelischer Verlag, 1948.

Bieler, Ludwig. *The Irish Penitentials*. Scriptores Latini Hiberniae vol. 5. Dublin: Dublin Institute for Advanced Studies, 1963.

Blenkinsopp, Joseph. "The Family in First Temple Israel." In *Families in Ancient Israel*, ed. Leo G. Perdue, Joseph Blenkinsopp, John J. Collins, and Carol Meyers Louisrille: Westminster/John Knox, 1997, pp. 48–103.

——. *Sexuality and the Christian Tradition*. Dayton, OH: Pflaum Press, 1969.

The Book of Common Prayer and Administration of the Sacraments and Other Rites and Ceremonies of the Church together with the Psalter of Psalms of David according to the Use of the Episcopal Church. New York: Oxford University Press, 1990.

Boswell, John. *Christianity, Social Tolerance, and Homosexuality: Gay People in Western Europe from the Beginning of the Christian Era to the Fourteenth Century*. Chicago and London: University of Chicago Press, 1980.

Bray, Alan. *Homosexuality in Renaissance England*. Expanded ed., New York: Columbia University Press, 1995.

Brooten, Bernadette J. *Love between Women: Early Christian Responses to Female Homoeroticism*. Chicago and London: University of Chicago Press, 1996.

Brown, Peter. *The Body and Society: Men, Women, and Sexual Renunciation in Early Christianity*. New York: Columbia University Press, 1988.

Brundage, James A. *Law, Sex, and Christian Society in Medieval Europe*. Chicago: University of Chicago Press, 1987.

——. "The Politics of Sodomy: Rex. V. Pons Hugh de Ampurias (1311)." In *Sex in the Middle Ages*, ed. Joyce Salisbury, pp. 239–46. New York: Garland, 1991.

Butler, Judith. *Gender Trouble: Feminism and the Subversion of Identity*. New York and London: Routledge, 1990.

Bynum, Caroline Walker. *Jesus as Mother: Studies in the Spirituality of the High Middle Ages*. Berkeley: University of California Press, 1988.

Calvin, Jean. *Institutes of Christian Religion*. Ed. John T. McNeill. Trans. Ford Lewis Battles. Library of Christian Classics, vols. 20–1. Philadelphia: Westminster Press, 1960.

——. *Institutio Christianae religionis 1559*. Ed. Petrus Barth and Guilelmus Niesel. *Joannis Calvini opera selecta*, vols. 3–5. 2nd ed. Munich: C. Kaiser, 1957–62.

——. *Sermons sur le Deutéronome*, vol. 2. His *Opera quae supersunt omnia*, ed. Guilielmus Baum, Eduardus Cunitz, and Eduardus Reuss, vol. 26. Corpus Reformatorum, vol. 54. Halle: C. A. Schwetschke, 1883.

Cappelli, Giovanni. *Autoerotismo: Un problema morale nei primi secoli cristiani?*, Nuovi saggi teologici, vol. 23. Bologna: Edizioni Dehoniane, 1986.

Clark, Elizabeth A. *Reading Renunciation: Asceticism and Scripture in Early Christianity*. Princeton, NJ: Princeton University Press, 1999.

Clement of Alexandria. *Pedagogue* 2 (*Le pédagogue*). Trans. Claude Mondésert. Ed. Henri-Irénée Marrou. *Sources chrétiennes*, vol. 108. Paris: Éditions du Cerf, 1965.

Collins, John J. "Marriage, Divorce, and Family in Second Temple Judaism." In *Families in Ancient Israel*, ed, Leo G. Perdue, Joseph Blenkinsopp, John J. Collins, and Carol Meyers. Louisuille, KY: Westminster/John Knox, 1997, pp. 104–62.

Countryman, L. William. *Dirt, Greed, and Sex: Sexual Ethics in the New Testament and Their Implications for Today*. Philadelphia: Fortress Press, 1988.

——. "Finding a Way to Talk: Dealing with Difficult Topics in the Episcopal Church." In *Our Selves, Our Souls and Bodies: Sexuality and the Household of God*, ed. Charles Hefling, Cambridge, MA and Boston: Cowley Publications, pp. 3–16.

Courcelle, Pierre P. *Recherches sur les Confessions de saint Augustin*. 2nd ed. Paris: Revue des Études Augustiniennes, 1968.

Curran, Charles E. *Catholic Moral Theology in Dialogue*. Notre Dame, IN: Fides, 1972.

——. "Homosexuality and Moral Theology: Methodological and Substantive Considerations." *The Thomist* 35 (1971): 447–81.

Cyril of Jerusalem. *Catecheses ad illuminandos*. In Migne *PG* 33:331–1128.

——. "Catechetical Lectures." Trans. Edwin Hamilton Gifford. In Cyril of Jerusalem, Gregory Nazianzen, Nicene and Post-Nicene Fathers, second series, vol 7. Reprint, Peabody, MA: Hendrickson, 1995.

Daly, Mary. *Beyond God the Father*. Boston: Beacon Press, 1973.

——. *The Church and the Second Sex*. New York: Harper & Row, 1968.

Dinshaw, Carolyn. *Getting Medieval: Sexualities and Communities: Pre- and Postmodern*. Chapel Hill, NC: Duke University Press, 1999.

Diogenes Laertius. *Vitae philosophorum* (*Lives of the Philosophers*). Trans. R. D. Hicks. Loeb Classical Library. Cambridge, MA: Harvard University Press, 1925.

Elliott, Dyan. *Fallen Bodies: Pollution, Sexuality, and Demonology in the Middle Ages*. Philadelphia: University of Pennsylvania Press, 1999.

Elliott, J. K. *The Apocryphal New Testament: A Collection of Apocryphal Christian Literature in an English Translation*. Oxford: Clarendon Press, 1993.

Epiphanius. *Panarion*. In *Epiphanius*, ed. Karl Holl, vols. 1–3. Griechischen Christlichen Schriftsteller der ersten drei Jahrhunderte, vols. 25, 31, 37. Leipzig: J. C. Hinrichs, 1915–33.

Fagley, Richard M. *The Population Explosion and Christian Responsibility*. New York: Oxford University Press, 1960.

Farley, Margaret. "An Ethic for Same-Sex Relations." In *A Challenge to Love: Gay and Lesbian Catholics in the Church*, ed. Robert Nugent, pp. 93–106. New York: Crossroad, 1983.

Fiorenza, Elizabeth Schüssler. *In Memory of Her: A Feminist Theological Reconstruction of Christian Origins*. New York: Crossroad, 1983.

Fletcher, Joseph. *Moral Responsibility: Situation Ethics at Work*. Philadelphia: Westminster Press, 1967.

——. *Situation Ethics: The New Morality*. Philadelphia: Westminster Press, 1966.

Foucault, Michel. *Histoire de la sexualité*, vol. 1: *La volonté de savoir*. Paris: NRF/ Gallimard, 1976.

——. *History of Sexuality*, vol. 1: *An Introduction*. Trans. Robert Hurley. New York: Vintage Books/Random House, 1980.

——. "Sexualité et pouvoir." In *Dits et écrits, 1954–1988*. Ed. Daniel Defert and François Ewald, pp. 552–70. Paris: NRF/Gallimard, 1994.

——. "Sexuality and Power." Trans. Richard A. Lynch. In *Religion and Culture: Michel Foucault*, ed. Jeremy R. Carrette, pp. 115–30. New York: Routledge, 1999.

Friedrich, Gerhard. *Theological Dictionary of the New Testament*. Trans. Geoffrey W. Bromiley. Grand Rapids: W. B. Eerdmans, 1968.

Funk, F. X., ed. *Patres apostolici*. 2nd ed. Tübingen: Laup, 1901.

Gearhart, Sally, and Bill Johnson, eds. *Loving Women/Loving Men*. San Francisco: Glide Publications, 1974.

Gilson, Anne Bathurst. *Eros Breaking Free: Interpreting Sexual Theo-Ethics*. Cleveland, OH: Pilgrim Press, 1995.

Gregory of Nyssa. *De virginitate (Traité de la virginité)*. Ed. and trans. Michael Aubineau. Sources Chrétiennes, vol. 119. Paris: Éditions du Cerf, 1966.

Gudorf, Christine E. *Body, Sex, and Pleasure: Reconstructing Christian Sexual Ethics*. Cleveland, OH: The Pilgrim Press, 1994.

Halperin, David M. "How to Do the History of Male Homosexuality." *GLQ: A Journal of Lesbian and Gay Studies* 6 (2000): 87–123.

Hamilton, Janet, and Bernard Hamilton. *Christian Dualist Heresies in the Byzantine World c. 650–c. 1450*. Manchester and New York: Manchester University Press, 1998.

Häring, Bernard. *The Law of Christ: Moral Theology for Priests and Laity*, vol. 3: *Special Moral Theology: Man's Assent to the All-embracing Majesty of God's Love*. Trans. Edwin R. Kaiser. Westminster, MD: New Press, 1966.

Harrison, Beverly Wildung. *Making the Connections: Essays in Feminist Social Ethics*. Ed. Carol S. Robb. Boston: Beacon Press, 1985.

Hauerwas, Stanley. "On Doctrine and Ethics." In *Sanctify Them in the Truth: Holiness Exemplified*, pp. 19–36. Nashville: Abingdon Press, 1998.

J. K. Huysmans. *À rebours*. Ed. Marc Fumaroli. 2nd ed. Paris: Gallimard, 1977.

Jerome. *Adversus Helvidium de Mariae virginitate perpetua*. In Migne *PL* 23:183–206.

——. *Against Helvidius on the Perpetual Virginity of Mary*. In *St. Jerome: Dogmatic and Polemical Works*, trans. John N. Hritzu. Fathers of the Church: A New Translation. Washington, DC: Catholic University of America Press, 1965.

——. *Hieronymus: Epistularum pars 1, Epistulae I–LXX*. Ed. Isidorus Hilberg. Corpus Scriptorum Ecclesiasticorum Latinorum, vol. 54. Editio altera supplementis aucta. Vienna: Österreichischen Akademie der Wissenschaften, 1996.

——. *Letters of St. Jerome*. Trans. Charles Christopher Mierow. Ancient Christian Writers, vol. 33. Westminster, MD: Newman Press, 1963.

John Chrysostom. *In epistulam I ad Thessalonicenses homiliae*. In Migne *PG* 62:391–468.

John Climachus. *The Ladder of Divine Ascent*. Trans. Colm Luibheid and Norman Russell. Ed. Richard J. Payne. Classics of Western Spirituality. Mahwah, NJ: Paulist Press, 1982.

Jordan, Mark D. *The Invention of Sodomy in Christian Theology*. Chicago and London: University of Chicago Press, 1997.

Justin Martyr. *Apologia*. In Migne *PG* 6:327–440.

Justinian. *Novellae. Corpus iuris civilis*, vol. 3. Ed. Rudolfus Schoell and Guilelmus Kroll. 8th ed., Berlin, 1963. Repr. Hildesheim: Weidmann, 1993.

Kosnick, Anthony, William Carroll, Agnes Cunningham, Ronald Modras, and James Schulte. *Human Sexuality: New Directions in American Catholic Thought, A Study Commissioned by the Catholic Theological Society of America*. New York: Paramus, and Toronto: Paulist Press, 1977.

Lambert, Malcolm. *Medieval Heresy: Popular Movements from the Gregorian Reform to the Reformation*. 2nd ed. Oxford: Blackwell, 1992.

Lambeth Conference (1930). *Lambeth Conference 1930: Encyclical Letter from the Bishops with Resolutions and Reports*. London: SPCK, and New York: Macmillan, 1930.

Lerner, Robert E. *The Heresy of the Free Spirit in the Later Middle Ages*. Berkeley: University of California Press, 1972.

Liguori, Alphonsus Maria de. *Theologia moralis*. Ed. Michael Haringer. In *Sämtliche Werke des heiligen Bischofes und Kirchenlehrers Alphons Maria von Liguori*. Abteilung 3: *Moraltheologische Werke*. 2nd ed. Regensburg: Georg Joseph Manz, 1879.

Lombard, Peter, *Sententiae in IV libris distinctae*. Ed. members of the Collegium S. Bonaventurae. Grottaferrata: Collegium S. Bonaventurae, 1981.

Lorde, Audre. "Poetry Is Not a Luxury." Reprinted in her *Sister Outsider: Essays and Speeches*, pp. 36–9. Freedom, CA: The Crossing Press, 1984.

Louw, Johannes P., and Eugene A. Nida. *Greek-English Lexicon of the New Testament Based on Semantic Domains*. 2 vols. 2nd ed. New York: United Bible Societies, 1989.

Luther, Martin. *A Sermon on the Estate of Marriage*. Trans. James Atkinson. In *Luther's Works*, 44:7–14.

——. *Deutsche Katechismus*. In Weimar *Werke*, Abt. 1, 30/1:123–238.

——. *De votis monasticis*. In Weimar *Werke*, Abt. 1., 8:573–669.

——. *Ein Sermon von dem ehelichen Stand*. In Weimar *Werke*, Abt. 1, 2:166–71.

——. *Judgment on Monastic Vows*. Trans. James Atkinson. In *Luther's Works*, 44:251–400.

——. *Large Catechism*. In *Book of Concord: Confessions of the Evangelical Lutheran Church*, ed. Robert Kolb and Timothy J. Wengert, pp. 379–480. Minneapolis: Fortress Press, 2000.

——. Letter of August 6, 1524. In Weimar *Werke*, Abt. 4, 3:327–8, no. 766.

——. *Luther's Works*. Ed. Jaroslav Pelikan and Helmut T. Lehman. St. Louis: Concordia, 1955–76, then Philadelphia: Fortress Press, 1955–76. Cited here as "*Luther's Works*."

——. *On Marriage Matters*. Trans. Frederick C. Ahrens. In *Luther's Works*, 46: 265–320. Philadelphia: Fortress Press, 1967.

———. *Von Ehesachen.* In Weimar *Werke,* Abt. 1, 30/3:205–49.

———. *Werke: Kritische Gesamtausgabe.* Weimar: Herman Böhlau, 1883–. Cited here as "Weimar *Werke.*"

Lutz, Cora E. "Musonius Rufus 'The Roman Socrates.' " In *Yale Classical Studies,* vol. 10, ed. Alfred R. Bellinger, pp. 3–150. New Haven, CT: Yale University Press, 1947.

McClory, Robert. *Turning Point: The Inside Story of the Papal Birth Control Commission, and How* Humanae Vitae *Changed the Life of Patty Crowley and the Future of the Church.* New York: Crossroad, 1995.

McFague, Sallie. *Metaphorical Theology: Models of God in Religious Language.* Philadelphia: Fortress Press, 1982.

McNeill, John J. *The Church and the Homosexual.* Kansas City, MO: Sheed, Andrews, & McMeel, 1976.

———. "The Male Christian Homosexual." *Homiletic and Pastoral Review* 70 (1970): 667–77, 747–58, 828–36.

Meeks, Wayne A. *The Origins of Christian Morality: The First Two Centuries.* New Haven, CT: Yale University Press, 1983.

Melanchthon, Philip. *Enarrationes aliquot liborum ethicorum Aristotelis.* In his *Opera quae supersunt omnia,* vol. 16, ed. K. G. Bretschneider and H. E. Bindseil, cols. 277–416. Corpus Reformatorum, vol. 16. Halle: C. A. Schwetschke, 1850. Rep., New York: Johnson Rep., and Frankfurt am Main: Minerva, 1963.

———. *Ethicae doctrinae elementa.* In his *Opera quae supersunt omnia,* vol. 16, ed. K. G. Bretschneider and H. E. Bindseil, cols. 165–276. Corpus Reformatorum, vol. 16. Halle: C. A. Schwetschke, 1850. Repr., New York: Johnson Repr, and Frankfurt am Main: Minerva, 1963.

Migne, Jacques-Paul, ed. *Patrologiae cursus completns . . . Series Graeca.* Paris: Migne, 1857–66. Cited here as "Migne *PG.*"

———. *Patrologiae cursus completus . . . Series Latina.* Paris: Garnier Fratres editores et J.-P. Migne successores, 1844–91. Cited here as "Migne *PL.*"

Milbank, John. "Can Morality Be Christian?" In *The Word Made Strange: Theology, Language, Culture,* pp. 219–32. Oxford: Blackwell, 1997.

Nelson, James B. *Body Theology.* Louisville, KY: Westminster/John Knox, 1992.

Nietzsche, Friedrich. *Jenseits von Gut und Böse.* In *Sämtliche Werke: Kritische Studienausgabe,* ed. Giorgio Colli and Mazzino Montinari, vol. 5. 2nd ed. Munich: DTV, and Berlin and New York: de Gruyter, 1988.

Nygren, Anders. *Agape and Eros.* Trans. Philip S. Watson. Philadelphia: Westminster Press, 1953.

Oberman, Heiko A. *Luther: Man between God and Devil.* Trans. Eileen Walliser-Schwarzbart. New York: Image Books, 1992.

O'Donnell, James J. *Augustine: Confessions.* 3 vols. Oxford: Clarendon Press, 1992.

Olyan, Saul. " 'And with a Male You shall Not Lie the Lying Down of a Woman': Meaning and Significance of Leviticus 18:22 and 20:13." *Journal of the History of Sexuality* 5 (1994): 179–206.

Origen. *Commentaria in Matthaeum*. In *Origenes Werke*, vol. 10, ed. Erich Klostermann and Ernst Benz. Griechischen Christlichen Schriftsteller der ersten drei Jahrhunderte, vol. 40. Leipzig: J. C. Hinrichs, 1935–7.

Pagels, Elaine H. *The Gnostic Gospels*. New York: Random House, 1979.

Paul VI. *Humanae vitae: Encyclical letter of His Holiness Pope Paul VI on the Regulation of Births*. Trans. Marc Calegari. San Francisco: Ignatius Press, 1998.

Payer, Pierre J. *Sex and the Penitentials: The Development of a Sexual Code, 550–1150*. Toronto: University of Toronto Press, 1984.

Peter Damian. *Letters*, vol. 2. Trans. by Owen J. Blum. The Fathers of the Church: Mediaeval Continuation. Washington, DC: Catholic University of America Press, 1990.

——. *Liber Gomorrhianus (Epistola 31)*. In *Die Briefe des Petrus Damiani*, vol. 1, ed. Kurt Reindel. Monumenta Germaniae Historica: Die Briefe der deutschen Kaiserzeit vol. 4. Munich: MGH, 1983.

Peter of Poitiers. *Compilatio praesens*. Ed. Jean Longère. Corpus Christianorum Continuatio Mediaevalis, vol. 51. Turnhout: Brepols, 1980.

Philo of Alexandria. *Works*. Trans. F. H. Colson and G. H. Whitaker. Loeb Classical Library. Cambridge, MA: Harvard University Press, 1929–62.

Plutarch. *Moralia*. Trans. Frank Cole Babbitt. Loeb Classical Library. Cambridge, MA: Harvard University Press, 1927–.

Porter, Roy. "Forbidden Pleasures: Enlightenment Literature of Sexual Advice." In *Solitary Pleasures: The Historical, Literary, and Artistic Discourses of Autoeroticism*, ed. Paula Bennett and Vernon A. Rosario II, pp. 75–98. New York and London: Routledge, 1995.

Prudentius. *Peristephanon*. In *Prudentius*, vol. 2, trans. H. J. Thomson. Loeb Classical Library. Cambridge, MA: Harvard University Press, 1953.

Reynolds, Philip Lyndon. *Marriage in the Western Church: The Christianization of Marriage during the Patristic and Early Medieval Periods*. Supplements to Vigiliae Christianae, vol. 24. Leiden and New York: E. J. Brill, 1994.

Rocke, Michael. *Forbidden Friendships: Homosexuality and Male Culture in Renaissance Florence*. New York: Oxford University Press, 1996.

Rogers, Eugene F, Jr. *Sexuality and the Christian Body: Their Way into the Triune God*. Oxford: Blackwell, 1999.

Roper, Lyndal. *The Holy Household: Women and Morals in Reformation Augsburg*. Oxford: Clarendon Press, 1989.

——. "Sexual Utopianism in the German Reformation." *Journal of Ecclesiastical History* 42 (1991): 394–418.

Rubin, Gayle. "Thinking Sex." In *The Lesbian and Gay Studies Reader*, ed. Henry Abelove, Michèle Aina Barale, and David M. Halperin, pp. 3–44. New York and London: Routledge, 1993.

Ruether, Rosemary Radford. *New Woman, New Earth: Sexist Ideologies and Human Liberation*. New York: Harper & Row, 1975.

——. *Sexism and God-Talk: Toward a Feminist Theology*. Boston: Beacon Press, 1983.

"Salmanticenses." *Collegii Salmanticensis Fratres Discalceatorum Cursus theologiae moralis.* Venice: Nicolaus Pezzana, 1724.

Schleiner, Winfried. "'That Matter Which Ought Not To Be Heard Of': Homophobic Slurs in Renaissance Cultural Politics." *Journal of Homosexuality* 26:4 (1994): 41–75.

Scroggs, Robin. *The New Testament and Homosexuality: Contextual Background for Contemporary Debate.* Philadelphia: Fortress Press, 1983.

Smith, Harmon L. "Contraception and Natural Law: A Half-Century of Anglican Moral Reflection." In *The Anglican Moral Choice,* ed. Paul Elmen, pp. 181–200. Wilton, CT: Morehouse-Barlow, 1983.

Smith, Morton. *Clement of Alexandria and the Secret Gospel of Mark.* Cambridge, MA: Harvard University Press, 1973.

Stout, Jeffrey. *Ethics after Babel: The Languages of Morals and their Discontents.* Boston: Beacon Press, 1988.

Strachey, Lytton. *Eminent Victorians.* London: Penguin Books, 1986.

Summa virtutum de remediis anime. Ed. Siegfried Wenzel. Chaucer Library. Athens: University of Georgia Press, 1984.

Taylor, Jeremy. *Whole Works of the Right Rev. Jeremy Taylor, D.D.* 3 vols. London: Henry G. Bohn, 1850.

Tertullian. *De baptismo.* In his *Opera Catholica.* Ed. J. G. P. Borleffs. Corpus Christianorum Series Latina, vol. 1/2. Turnhout: Brepols, 1954.

Thayer, Henry Joseph. *A Greek-English Lexicon of the New Testament.* corr. ed. New York and London: Harper & Brothers, 1899.

Thomas Aquinas. *Opera omnia iussu impensaque Leonis XIII. P. M. edita.* Ed. members of the Order of Preachers. Rome, 1882–. Imprint varies.

——. *Summa theologiae.* Ed. Institutum Studiorum Medievalium Ottaviensis. Ottawa: Studium Generalis Ordinis Praedicatorum, 1941–5.

——. *Summa theologiae: Latin Text and English Translation, Introductions, Notes, Appendices, and Glossaries.* London: Eyre & Spottiswoode, and New York: McGraw-Hill, 1964–73.

Trible, Phyllis. *God and the Rhetoric of Sexuality.* Philadelphia: Fortress Press, 1978.

Van der Meer, Theo. *Sodoms zaad in Nederland: Het onstaan van homoseksualiteit in de vroegmoderne tijd.* Nijmegen: SUN, 1995.

Wasserschleben, F. W. Hermann. *Die Bußordnungen der abendländischen Kirche.* Halle: Graeger, 1851. Repr., Graz: Akademische Druck- und Verlagsanstalt, 1958.

Wesley, John. *Thoughts on a Single Life* [1765]. In *Works of John Wesley,* vol. 11, pp. 456–63. London: Wesleyan Methodist Reading Room, 1872. Reprint, Peabody, MA: Hendrickson, 1894.

Wilde, Oscar. *The Picture of Dorian Gray.* In *The Complete Works of Oscar Wilde.* New York: Barnes & Noble, 1994.

William of Auvergne. *Guilielmi Alverni . . . opera omnia.* 2 vols. Paris: A. Pallard, 1674. Rep., Frankfurt am Main: Minerva, 1962.

Witte, John, Jr. *From Sacrament to Contract: Marriage, Religion, and Law in the Western Tradition.* Louisville, KY: Westminster/John Knox, 1997.

Subject Index

and marriage 109–13
and monasticism 59, 60
and oral sex 105
and sodomy 80
authority
   biblical 19, 20–46, 80
   familial 42
   institutional 8, 17, 19, 84, 86, 124,
      135, 138, 139
   and speech about sex 134, 142–4,
      146, 148–9
   and women 73

baptism, and sexual abstinence 56
Barth, Karl, *Church Dogmatics* 142
Basil of Caesarea 52
Bede, *Ecclesiastical History* 81 n.5
Bernard of Clairvaux 164
   Letter 322 56 n.26
bestiality 33, 86
   and masturbation 99–100
Bible
   as authority 19, 20–46, 80
   and denomination 20–2, 31, 44
   and interpretation 20–1, 23–37, 43,
      44–6
   and scholarship 22–44, 45
   and textual norms 38–44
   and textual purposes 31–6
   and textual terms 24–31
   and textual topics 36–8, 124–5, 164
"bio-power" 133–5, 136–8, 144,
      148–9, 151, 172
   and contraception 138–9
Blenkinsopp, Joseph 159 n.2
Bogomils, and alternative ideals 73
Boswell, John 28–9
bureaucracy, secular 77–8, 94, 103,
      133–4, 136–7, 146, 171–2

Cajetan, Thomas de Vio 102
Calvin, John
   and adultery 120–1, 122, 125, 127
   and celibacy 60–1, 91–2

Institutes 59–61, 91–2, 120–3, 127
   and marriage 60–1, 120–3, 125
   Sermons on Deuteronomy 121–2, 123
Carmelites, Discalced 93
castration, and celibacy 48–9
Catharism, and alternative ideals 73
Catholic Theological Society of
      America 146–8
celibacy
   and Augustine 54–6, 109, 110, 113
   and Calvin 60–1, 91–2
   as early Christian ideal 47–9, 51,
      72, 74–5, 117
   and Luther 57–8, 91
   in medieval writings 57
   and Protestant Reformation 57–60,
      91–2
   and sodomy 91–2
   and Wesley 61–2
change, social 132–3, 141, 146, 174
chastity
   and Augustine 56
   and Foucault 95, 136
   and Luther 57–9, 91
   monastic 97–9
   and Paul 64
   and Taylor 68–9
Chaucer, Geoffrey, *Canterbury Tales*
      57
child abuse, accusations of 73
children
   and monogamy 127
   and procreation 110–11, 117, 120,
      130, 139, 159
Christ, betrothal to 65–8, 69, 83, 114
Christendom, and Christian ethics 18,
      131, 134, 137–8, 141, 148, 152,
      154, 171
Chrysostom, John 30
Clement of Alexandria 24–5
   Pedagogue 114–17
clergy
   and control over sex 95, 124, 136
   married 124

Index of Biblical References